T0197437

Emissaries
of the
Order of Melchizedek

Book I

Antera and Omaran

BALBOA.
PRESS
A DIVISION OF HAY HOUSE

Balboa Press books may be ordered through booksellers or by contacting:

Balboa Press
A Division of Hay House
1663 Liberty Drive
Bloomington, IN 47403
www.balboapress.com
1 (877) 407-4847

Print information available on the last page.

ISBN: 978-1-5043-5537-7 (sc)
ISBN: 978-1-5043-5538-4 (hc)
ISBN: 978-1-5043-5536-0 (e)

Library of Congress Control Number: 2016906176

Balboa Press rev. date: 05/05/2016

Contents

Acknowledgments

First and foremost, we are grateful for the Beings of Light who continue to patiently guide us—as well as challenge us—on our journey. We also thank the many friends and spiritual family who encouraged us to write this story. Special appreciation goes to those who read and edited the manuscript, making big improvements: Deborah Cardenas, Amy Schoenhofen, Michael Wopat, Terrie Burns, and Juliette Looye.

Thank you!

Preface

This book is the first of a series relating our true adventures, as well as a continuation of Antera's book, *Twin Flames: A True Story of Soul Reunion*, which chronicled the start of our relationship, the realization that we are twin flames, our subsequent deep healing, and the beginning of our spiritual work.

Through our journey together, we have worked directly with Beings of Light in the Order of Melchizedek, including many Ascended Masters and angels such as St. Germain, Jeshua (Jesus), Mother Mary, Isis, White Buffalo Calf Woman, Gaia, Melchizedek, Metatron, and many others. This has been possible because of Antera's unique ability, since childhood, to speak directly with these Light Beings.

The Order of Melchizedek is a cosmic organization, not a human one. This group has been instrumental in developing and encouraging the evolution of consciousness in our universe, especially in humanity and our planet because of the big shifts and changes that are happening here. We are all "in the spotlight" as we collectively move forward in the smoothest way possible, each of us doing our part to bring more spiritual awareness.

The spiritual service the two of us have been given through the years is our contribution to this evolution of consciousness, and we continue to carry it out to the best of our abilities, while living in the physical world with all its other demands. Almost all of this service has been given in our spare time as volunteers. It has provided us with many golden opportunities to learn personal lessons and evolve, and we consider that to be the biggest reward, along with seeing the growth of Light and awareness in the people we have taught and helped along the way.

During 20 years of land healing, we have met and worked with ancestral spirits, devas, elementals, inner Earth devas, mountain and valley spirits, and other interesting beings. Our profound communications with Divine Mother led to the discovery of the Order of the Blue Snake, which continues to bring healing to the planet through the Divine Feminine. Creating the Earth Healing Grid, on the request of the Masters, has required us to travel extensively in the service of balancing and uplifting this beautiful planet. We witnessed the birth, for the first time in ages, of a new Ascended Master retreat. But let's slow down a bit . . . we're getting ahead of ourselves.

This first book of the series starts with events in 1998 and continues through the year 2005, where the second book begins. Many words of the Masters we received during this time period are included in these pages because the lessons they contain are appropriate for all people on a spiritual path. We hope others can benefit from this wisdom and not have to learn some things the hard way, like we did! When reading their words, the reader will receive energy from the particular Master talking, so the greatest blessings can be gained by focusing on the Master while reading. These lessons are timeless and very appropriate for whenever they are read, even long after we are gone from this world.

A glossary at the end is included for terms the reader may not know, and the first occurrence of these words in the text are marked in boldface type.

We are very grateful for having this opportunity to serve. We hope you enjoy reading about our journey as much as we are enjoying living it!

Antera and Omaran, 2016

1

The Mountain Calls

Antera and Omaran loved Mount Shasta, there was no doubt about it. A majestic volcano in northern California that rises to over 14,000 feet elevation, it is a spiritual **vortex** of massive proportions, and draws spiritual seekers to it like a magnet. Mount Shasta City, a small alpine town of 3500 people, is nestled into the southwest side, where the energies are the highest and most pure.

Ever since their spiritual marriage on its slopes in the spring of 1994, they had known it was a special place that resonated with them and their life together. It was only a five-hour drive from their home in Mill Valley, north of San Francisco, and they went there as often as they could. Now, in 1998, the day after their legal marriage, which was also held on the mountain, they were already thinking about looking at property so they could move there.

On this trip, just to see what was available, they went to a realtor in town, who gave them a list of houses for sale. They drove by several but none really drew them in. As they drove around, they noticed that some areas were much more desirable than others, and they learned more about the area.

That afternoon they were in Berryvale, the popular natural foods store in town, picking up some food for dinner. Omaran saw a friend and went over to chat. He seemed to make friends anywhere he went and already knew quite a few in the small town. He talked about their wedding the day before, and how they were now interested in finding a house so they could move to Mount Shasta. A woman nearby happened to overhear the conversation and came up, introduced herself, and said that she had a property she wanted to sell, but it only had a yurt and a small cottage on it now. Omaran got her address and made an appointment for the next day.

When they arrived there, they immediately loved it. The property was beautiful! Tall oak trees towered above, there were walkways lined with irises, gardens, and even a special area dedicated to **Mother Mary**. It was 1.5 acres, and looked like a park. The owner lived in the small cottage on the property while she worked on it, because she had torn down the main house. They left with visions of the lot dancing in their heads.

"What do you think? Will she sell? She seemed unsure, like she didn't really want to," Antera said as they started their drive back home.

"We'll see. I love it. And much of the work is already done to the building site—the trenching, electrical, water. We'd have to use the existing foundation." He was already thinking like the builder he was.

"The only thing is, the **nature spirits** seemed unhappy that she is thinking about leaving. Some of them came to me when we were in the garden near the big oak tree, and they seemed very disturbed. I wonder what that is about."

Since she was a small child, Antera had been able to communicate with non-physical beings, and throughout her life she had benefitted from the profound teachings she received from Beings of **Light**. They had been her biggest supporters, mentors, and personal teachers through this lifetime. Over the last five years, since she and Omaran had been together, he had also reaped the rewards from her unseen connections in "high places," learning the most important lessons directly from the many great Masters who talked to and through her. Antera considered it normal, though she knew that others didn't have that ability and must be living in a reality that is extremely limited, like being blind.

Throughout her previous career as a seismologist, and all the scientific training she'd had, it had been best to not talk about her mystical side, though she knew that most big scientific discoveries came through intuition. She had learned how to turn the connection off and on as needed so it did not distract her in everyday life. It was ideal that Omaran was on the same **spiritual path**.

He said, "Hmmm. Well, let's ask the Masters about the property when we get home. I have a feeling they like it. Nature spirits will cope." He quickly amended, "That sounded pretty harsh—I didn't mean it like that. We'll talk to them, of course."

"Yes, I suppose they will cope." She sighed. "You know, I really don't want to go back to the Bay Area. I want to stay here. Maybe we can make the move sooner."

"I love it here too. As soon as we find a place, we can make it happen," he said.

"Would you really want to build a house? It seems like such a big project! I know you have done it before, but wow . . . ."

"The building site is already prepared there, so that makes it easier. In fact, I've never built a house for myself. This would be the first. Imagine designing and building a house that is perfect for us!"

They arrived home after being gone for a week, and now here they were, actually married! What a journey it had all been to this point in time. From meeting in 1993 and discovering they were **twin flames**, to working through and overcoming many obstacles to their reunion, and finally to now, getting married, five years later.

Before they met, Antera had already worked for two decades on healing her **four bodies**, physical, emotional, mental and spiritual. But though Omaran had been very advanced in three, it became obvious that he had neglected his emotional body, an imbalance that had caused many challenges to the couple. Though they were happy to have most of the difficult times behind them, they both agreed it had all been worth it. Their progress along their path of spiritual evolution had required they go through that intense deep healing, prompted by those five years of trials.

The next day, the two of them sat on the couch in their living room and prepared to meditate together, which they did often. The old house they rented in Mill Valley was surrounded by tall redwoods, which gave them the feeling that they were isolated from neighbors. One of the trees had grown onto the house up near the roof line, which Omaran had discovered when up on the roof. The redwood had actually fused with the outside rafter, making the tree a part of the house . . . or maybe the house was now a part of the tree. This made the house creak like a tree house when the wind blew. They had grown accustomed to the movement and noises of the house, as well as the sloping floor of the living room. But others who came over to their meditation classes often were very thrown by it as they walked to the front door to leave, thinking their balance was affected by the meditation. It was quite funny to watch.

They got comfortable as the house swayed with the wind and the front door suddenly opened after a strong gust struck. This had happened many times before, so with a chuckle Omaran got up and closed it again, locking it so they would be undisturbed, then went back to the couch. Antera tuned her awareness to the energy level of the Masters to see if anyone wanted to talk to them.

After a moment, **St. Germain** addressed them. An **Ascended Master** who is well known in spiritual circles for his tireless work on behalf of humans and raising consciousness, he had been one of Antera's personal guides for decades.

St. Germain said, "The true work always comes together when the two of you come together. And up until now, you have not been completely together. There has always been a separation of sorts in your intent and in your abilities to move forward into the service. Now that your intent has crystallized, you can see clearly a path that lies ahead, at least for a short distance ahead. It is very difficult to see far ahead at this time. Now the flow opens!"

Omaran said, "Yes, we can feel that shift after getting married. And thank you so much for your support and for presiding at our marriage ceremony."

They had set up a place for St. Germain in the center of the wedding circle, marked by a small circle of rocks, and they had stood in front of him as if the Master had been physically present. All the unseen Masters had been given special places in the ceremony, even though only a few of the people could sense them. It had been a truly magical wedding.

"My pleasure," said St. Germain. "I see that you have put quite a beam of energy into the property that you saw. It is a beautiful piece of property. One of my favorites in the area, and I have had my eye on it for a long time. This is one opportunity for you, if you can find a way to make it happen. It is not the only path, but it is one of my most cherished areas, especially the gardens."

"I thought you would like it. We will really try to make it happen," Omaran said.

"It is much more difficult to connect with you here than it is up at Shasta. When you move, we will have much better communication, to facilitate your growth and the work you are taking on. Not only the part of the work that I am interested in, but also the part that you are working on with the other Masters who guide you.

"Lord **Metatron** is waiting for you to have the space and opportunity to share the geometrical devices and build the pyramid. Mary is serving as a spiritual counselor. You have many friends, since you have many interests and many skills."

"Yes, we are so grateful to you and all the Masters." Omaran thought about all the wonderful guidance they had received since he and Antera had reunited. Archangel Metatron, a vast Being of Light, had taught them about sacred geometry and shapes and encouraged them to build a large pyramid. The guardian of the future pyramid had even come to Antera two years before and introduced himself. They had also been blessed with some magical copper and crystal forms large enough to sit inside. These had been given to them from the previous caretaker, who said Metatron had told him to do so. According to Metatron, these were simpler representations of similar devices that were on **Atlantis** long ago, but they held the same powerful energy for spiritual growth today. Omaran could hardly wait to have more land to have room for these devices and to actually build a pyramid.

St. Germain said, "And you are ready! The agreement that your **I Am Presences** made, through your marriage, is well along the way of being complete. When you are in solidarity with each other, there is nothing that will get in your way. There is nothing more powerful than this union with intention. But remember to remain open. Remember to look at your fears and doubts, to release them before they become blocks.

"You can help other couples coalesce their service together to the world. I would like to remind you that now is the time for couples to serve together. And now that you have anchored in the **Twin Flame Archetype**, more and more couples will be serving together in some way. This has not been very common in the past. In most relationships, each person has a separate job, and even those who are connected at a soul level might not have the opportunities that are required to work together in service. You can teach them what they need to do.

"We are in great need of couples to serve! There is no better way. The new paradigm of soul-based relationships is emerging. The old paradigm of shallow relationships has broken down. This is the new way. The old forms have been breaking down. This is what you are helping with."

They knew they would learn more about how they would be helping other couples be in spiritual relationships, ever since St. Germain had arranged for them to be given the job of holding the Twin Flame Archetype. Over a year ago, the couple had experienced an unexpected visit from the Master, who had taken them to meet the previous holders. This other couple had held the special flames of this archetype as a focus for many years, and they had decided it was time for another twin flame couple to take the job. Plus, it had turned out that the previous holders were a couple they knew from the distant past, making it a reunion as well. It had been a very moving experience, and the energy had been anchored in during their marriage ceremony.

So they listened with interest each time more of this was revealed. When St. Germain finished teaching them, they sat in quiet meditation for a few minutes. When they opened their eyes, they hugged.

"We are so blessed!" Omaran said.

"Yes, we are . . . and maybe moving to Mount Shasta!"

Over the next few weeks, Omaran was in touch with the owner of the property they liked. The owner was noncommittal yet continued the discussions. Antera and Omaran started feeling like she was resistant. The Masters continued to say that she was being put to the test, and her time on the property was finished, but apparently she didn't have the tools she needed to ease whatever she was afraid of.

The couple continued to send good energy to the owner, the resident nature spirits, and the property. Phone talks were not productive, so they eagerly returned to Mount Shasta a month later to continue talks with the owner in person, and because they just had to get back to the mountain. If they couldn't make a deal with this property, they would start looking elsewhere.

On this trip, they decided to camp at their old campsite, where they had stayed for six weeks several years ago. That had been an amazingly transformative period of time for them. They had gotten very familiar with all parts of the mountain while hiking every day, in the process finding **power spots** as they were guided to particular areas to meditate and sense the energies.

The journey to their special campsite required a drive up an old dirt road that was not maintained, and as they drove, it became obvious that no one else used the road. The manzanita branches on both sides were very overgrown. Tan Man, their old Toyota truck, was beat up enough that a few more scratches didn't matter, and they plowed through as far as they could, finally stopped by a large tree trunk across the road.

"This one's too big to move. Looks like we'll walk from here!" Omaran declared. "We'll need to make several trips."

"It's just around the corner and up the hill, right? I hope you can carry the water."

The camping equipment and food were bulky, but the six-gallon container of water was quite heavy as well as unwieldy. It was worth it, Omaran kept telling himself as they trudged up the rest of the road and up a steep bank of loose, dry dirt. They had left their campsite as invisible as possible last time they had visited, erasing all traces and footprints, and it seemed the effort had paid off. No one had been there. Setting up the tent and living areas was easy, between large white firs. The rock circle for the fire was uncovered and they gathered wood for a small fire.

"Feels like we never left." Omaran sighed as they sat next to the fire.

"Yes." Antera thought about all they had been through the last few years.

She looked around at the campsite, which looked like it hadn't changed at all, except for some baby firs that were taller. There had been so many changes in their lives, and they had been through so much healing since the time they had camped here. The six weeks they had spent here had been a time of major healing, both individually and in their early relationship.

She thought about both the good and difficult aspects of the time they had camped here. Omaran at his worst, bringing through the darkest energies and attacking her verbally, balanced by the beautiful, profound, spiritually-uplifting experiences they had gone through together. It was amazing they had made it through, and well worth it. Now they were actually thinking of moving to the mountain.

This was where they had discovered that they had been Earth healers, or **land healers**, together in the ancient land of **Lemuria**. Antera had brought up memories of going through intense training to become one of the group who kept the harmony of the land. Back in Lemuria, they had worked from a temple, and they would sense where difficulties were located then send the energies needed to heal and balance. And when reports of conflicts between people or communities would come in, their job was to soothe and heal the disturbance energetically from a distance.

This mountain seemed to have a direct energetic connection with Lemuria, so it was no wonder they had been drawn to this mystical land.

"I sure do love it here," Omaran said, stating the obvious.

She nodded as she stared at the fire. "It will be interesting to see how it all works out so we can live here."

Antera had always had strong faith and knew things would work out smoothly unless one of them got in the way. Omaran, on the other hand, had faith sometimes, but at other times his fears or doubts came up to block the flow. The Masters had told him this move to the mountain would be a faith builder as long as he controlled his mind and kept his thoughts positive. The couple had no idea how they would support themselves when they moved, much less find the money to buy a house, and this was a part of the process . . . trusting that all would fall into place smoothly.

When he actually thought about the unknowns, Omaran did get a little fearful. How would they support themselves financially? He pushed those thoughts aside.

He said, "I just want to get a place first, then think about other things. I wonder if the owner of that lot will really sell. It seems weird how she keeps talking to us but never says okay let's make a deal. Like she's stringing us along."

"She is very afraid of letting it go. I'm not sure why."

"I'm glad Michael and Jeen will be here tomorrow to look at it with us. It will be interesting to get their feedback."

Michael, Antera's ex-husband, still felt like family to both of them. The three of them had been through so much together, from the time Antera had announced she met Omaran and wanted to be with him instead of Michael, through all the meditating and healing the three of them had done to make it a smooth transition.

Michael and his lovely wife Jeen were now involved with the spiritual work they were doing, as well as the formation of a nonprofit spiritual center. They had agreed to come up and look at the property, since if it worked out, it would be both a home and a place for events of the center.

"Me, too," Antera said as she stared into the fire. "We've done so much **lightwork** on the property—purification, blessing, and charging it up. It's almost like the more we want it, the more the owner retreats energetically. Do you think she feels the energy we've been sending?"

"Yes, maybe that is the problem. We have powered it up so much that now she wants to stay because it feels so good there."

Antera chuckled. "Wouldn't that be ironic?"

Michael and Jeen met them the next day, and the four of them went to talk to the owner. She served them some tea, then told many stories about the property and other properties, but seemed to avoid negotiations.

When the owner excused herself for a few minutes, Jeen said, "Well, there's absolutely no doubt in my mind that she has no intention of selling this property, at least not now."

Jeen had a knack for stating what was what, and they all realized that she was right. It had taken Jeen's fresh eyes and frank manner to see the truth. Perhaps the owner had wanted to sell at first, but most likely had become aware that it was indeed a very special place, and she honestly just could not part with it at this time.

After the meeting, the four of them had lunch, caught up with each other, and Michael and Jeen left for home. So that was that. Antera and Omaran decided to give up on that property and look for a house instead.

When they discussed the experience that night by the fire, they concluded that it was a good lesson in manifestation . . . when to push and when to surrender to **Divine Will**. They had worked energetically on the property, enhancing it, thinking that would be enough to make it theirs. But the owner had changed her mind about selling, perhaps even because of this energy work. Knowing that trying to change the will of another is unethical, they had only sent love to her. So it was a balance between creating what they wanted without being attached to the specific form it took.

Though the property had seemed perfect, they knew something even better would come up. They didn't express it to each other, but they were both a bit relieved that maybe they wouldn't have to build a house after all. They enjoyed the rest of their camping stay, taking some favorite hikes, and drove back home.

Moving to the mountain, where the **veils** were thinner and **Spirit** more present, seemed like a necessary part of both of their growth, so Antera and Omaran hoped it would work out. The dense energy of the city felt like it was closing in on them, even though they lived in a beautiful area that was across the bay from the big city of San Francisco, and next to wild areas of Mount Tamalpais. The city was still close enough to impact them psychically. Sometimes Antera, who was more sensitive to it, felt that the **psychic energy** of so many people caused her to have to work a lot harder in her meditations and energy work, just to shield some of it out. She wondered how people could live right in the middle of cities.

Apparently Archangel Metatron was also concerned about it. One day, while the couple was sitting together in meditation, he connected with Antera and this was one of the things he commented on.

The Archangel said, "I also want you to know that the energy of where you live now is becoming less and less supportive of your healthy living and ability to serve in an efficient way. We see you struggling with this, and doing the best you can with the energy that is at hand. We are also very glad that you have plans to leave. It is an essential part of your path.

"You will find that more and more people who are sensitive to energy will be leaving also, because the energy here no longer supports the spiritual path. It is no longer easy to break through these dense energies, and it is not going to get any easier. You have done very well in staying grounded and tuned in to Mother Earth. You have done very well in maintaining your connection and surrounding yourself with the **lightbody**.

"But the fact is, there are so many people around your area who are reacting emotionally to these turbulent energies, projecting their fears and anger around them into the atmosphere, that if you could see the energy on the **etheric** plane, you would know that even though you do not have physical smog, you have what you might call 'etheric smog' or '**astral** smog.'

"It is growing denser and denser. As these astral energies grow denser it makes it much more difficult to maintain the spiritual focus, stay grounded, and reach your **Higher Presence**. This is, of course, why you feel drawn to travel out of the astral smog as often as you do.

"And we, in our way, are working with you energetically to make sure that it does not affect you too adversely. You have created a field around your house, but once you leave the house and go out into other areas, you are not nearly as protected. You are subjected to more of those subtle influences, which are becoming less and less subtle, and more oppressive. When you feel this, just remember that it is oppressive energies from other people.

"It is very important that you stay grounded and tuned into the planet, to draw most of your spiritual energy up though your **grounding**

cord, so you are not tempted to draw energy from around you. Draw energy from above, from your Higher Presence, and bring it from below. But in no case should you be drawing in energies from around you! In this atmosphere it will only clog your **chakras**. I would also suggest that you don't leave your chakras open when you leave the house."

Metatron's words were validating to hear, and Antera was pretty much ready to leave the area as soon as they could arrange it. Although she loved living in the circle of redwood giants, her favorite trees, and next to Mount Tamalpais, she didn't have a strong attachment to the area.

Omaran, however, was very attached to this land, and felt pulled in both directions. He had raised two of his children in Marin County, and his oldest son was settled in the southern Bay Area. Mount Tam, as it was affectionately called by the locals, had been his dear friend for almost two decades, and he had hiked or run most of the nearly 200 miles of fire roads and trails. He felt the mountain had greatly healed him through a lot of his emotional turmoil, and he would miss that part the most. It had been an integral part of his life for so long. He had never had this kind of relationship with a mountain or any land before, so thinking about leaving it was quite a challenge for him.

It was clear, however, that his time here was over and the benefits of this land had by now been outweighed by the aspects that weren't so good for them. In fact, living here seemed to be holding them back, and he did understand that. So he pushed his attachment out of his mind and thought about what a short drive it was from Mount Shasta to Mount Tamalpais—only five hours.

2

Moving Forward

Once the decision to move to Mount Shasta was made for sure, Antera and Omaran became excited and anxious to make their getaway, but they also knew they had much to wrap up in the Bay Area. They both had jobs, Antera working for a small publisher of spiritual books, and Omaran with his own construction business, a career he had wanted to leave for many years. If he built a house for them, he hoped it would be his last one. He had a lot of energy and a strong body, but as he got older, his body complained more and didn't have the stamina of his youth.

He wanted so much to make a living with their spiritual work, but so far teaching spiritual classes had not paid the bills. Moving north to a small town meant even fewer people available to attend. Everyone they had talked with in the alpine town had said people bring their own businesses when they move there, or they work by Internet. So he wondered how they would make a living there.

"I hope I won't have to keep doing construction after we move," he said one day as they were eating dinner at their small oak table in the dining room. He was especially tired after a long day.

Antera gazed out the window at the circle of redwood trees. "You know, you could probably delegate the harder jobs more. Your workers are younger." She almost said "and stronger," but stopped herself. Men tended to have pride about those kinds of things, and Omaran was quite a bit older than she was.

"I don't want to ask others to do a job I'm not willing to do myself."

"Willing is one thing, doing is another."

"Hmm." He didn't want to talk about that, and concentrated on his large salad.

"Okay, well, I'd just like to see you come home less tired so you have more energy for our spiritual work." She knew this was a safe approach.

"I always have energy for that!" he affirmed, knowing it wasn't always true. Some days he just felt like he wanted to go to bed after dinner, though he didn't allow himself that luxury.

She looked again out the window to their back yard, with the redwoods she loved, and the small creek flowing past at the back of the property . . . so green and lush. She could see the remnants of their mostly unsuccessful garden, which needed more sun than the trees allowed. The wildflowers were wonderful in the spring, she thought. She would miss some aspects of this place.

She turned back to her dinner, finishing the salad and serving herself some baked acorn squash. "You may still need to do construction part time when we move."

"I know. But part time would be a great relief. In a small town, the cost of living should be less."

"Well, I'm hoping I will be able to continue working for the publisher, at least for a while. Maybe I could work from a distance. I'll ask Byron when the time comes, but not yet."

Antera knew that Byron, the owner of the small publishing company, would be flexible, because it would be hard to replace her. Plus, he had become good friends with both of them. She had faith that it would work out.

She continued, "The Masters really want us to create the **mystery school**. At least I got the nonprofit corporation finished, and the website up, that should help. Maybe there is more we can do online."

The Internet and websites were still very new to the world, but she had taught herself to program HTML to make a website for the publishing job. This skill came in handy for the center they were creating. Since they had been together, they had felt the calling to create the center with its mystery school, to fulfill part of their spiritual mission. It was slow progress, though, because they both had to work to make a living in the expensive Bay Area and they didn't have a lot of extra time.

"I just wish we could get a lot of money from somewhere," Omaran said. "That would free us up to do our real work. Wouldn't it be wonderful if the Masters could arrange that, and support us financially somehow? Think of what we could accomplish!" He was thinking out loud and didn't expect an answer. He knew the Masters didn't work that way, and it was up to the humans to make the physical part of the agreement come together.

Antera said, "Yes, that would be nice. I know! What if we could precipitate gold into our hands! Maybe that is possible!"

"Yes, I wonder if that is possible . . . ." Omaran considered it. "Surely St. Germain would know how. I'm sure we would need to work directly with the **elements**, and nature spirits."

"I guess gold would be a combination of earth and fire elements, right? Get on it, Omaran!" Antera laughed. "One more thing to put into your busy day!"

"Well, maybe I just will."

The slow progress they were making on creating the spiritual center and other spiritual projects, a result of working full time, was still on their minds that evening, when Antera brought St. Germain through. As usual, the Ascended Master asked if there were questions, and Omaran was prepared. He asked first, "How can we speed up our mission? It seems to be going so slowly."

St. Germain replied, "Your growth is the most important service that you do! It is important that you not get too caught up in other service that takes you away from your primary service, which is to evolve yourselves and become the **Christed Beings**!

"That is your most important service despite the fact that you have a mission to accomplish. Any mission you have and any service you provide is always secondary to your bringing in the mighty I Am Presence! Bring it in fully and in its most glorious Light. If you do this, then your other work goes so much more smoothly. You become the beacon of Light that draws to you, magnetically, everything you need.

"Is this clear?"

"Yes, I think so," Omaran replied. He decided not to ask about precipitation of gold. "We just want to move forward and have more time to do everything we can to make this planet better."

St. Germain explained further, "You become masters of the human existence so that you can manipulate matter at will, from a position of Light and power—manipulate energy flows around you, between you and others, and between you and all objects—so that you can have control over the matter in your area of contact! There is no more important work than that! This is your service, your primary service, and your primary task! All else is an outgrowth from your evolution into Christed Beings.

"Since you have been working on developing this sense of power in the Light, you have seen its effects already. Look at how it affects your attitudes toward everything you do. If you are firmly positioned in the Light of your I Am Presence, then everything you do takes on the power of that Presence. All of your activities go so much more smoothly from that perspective."

"I have experienced that," Omaran said. "When I am in the flow, and do the energy work, everything is definitely smoother."

"There is no room anymore for beings who cannot take their power through the God Source, who remain powerless and think that is spiritual. Because humans have had so many issues about power, and they have used power from the personality perspective, there is much fear of the abuse of power. It is a major human lesson! Only when you are fully God Realized can you use power completely for the Light. Only when you are firmly attached to your I Am Presence can you receive your full power.

"Then there is absolutely no way it can be abused. If you are coming from the pure Light of your Christed Self, if your heart is fully open to **Divine Love**, there is nothing else that can come through it. If you always keep that in mind, and think about it during the day as many times as you can, then it will be yours! Forever! We need some powerful beings on the planet today!

"As I help you acquire this power, and learn to use the Light from the God Self, you will be able to have an effect on the course this planet is taking, more effectively healing others and creating acts of Light. And this I am teaching you!

"I want to make it very clear that seeking power is never a pure activity. Power comes as a result of seeking God, not of seeking power. Power comes to you naturally when you merge with your Christed Self. As you come from that place of Divinity, of purity, and of Light, then you may use the God-Power as it is given.

"No Master goes long periods of time without thinking of the Source of all of his or her creative energy. In everything you do, you can acknowledge and give thanks to the Source of all your energy. And this brings you closer to that Source. It brings you more of that energy. It speeds your evolution.

"Even when you are working and your mind is occupied with your work, there are ways to keep part of your mind on the Source. You can do repetitions of phrases, like mantras, or you can simply remember every few minutes to acknowledge your connection. There are many ways to remind yourself and to bring that God-Force into your work through your hands, through your heart, or through your words.

"Maintain a constant attitude, a constant focus, so that when you wake up in the morning your very first thought is on Divine Love and Light. Bring it into you to start your day, and make it your very last thought before you go to sleep.

"This is what is required! Is it all understood?"

Omaran felt the strong impact of St. Germain's words and the power behind them. "Yes, absolutely. I will try to keep my mind focused while I'm working. I haven't been doing that."

"Try?"

"Okay, I will do it."

St. Germain laughed. "That is the conviction I want to hear. The *try* word is usually used when people don't think they can do something."

"I know that. I will stop using that word."

"Very well, my brother. I leave you now with my blessing."

They sat for a while as the Master put his hand on each of their crowns and raised their energy to an even more expanded state of bliss. It was wonderful.

3

Red Butte

Antera was sitting quietly at home in Mill Valley when she was given an image of building a "**Light Field**" around Mount Shasta. This would be a giant energy form that would balance and uplift the volcano's energy, and the project would need to start before they moved there. It was September of 1998 and they had planned to visit the mountain in a few weeks. As the Masters described it, creating the field would require Antera and Omaran to be physically at the mountain, but it wasn't clear whether they would have to climb to the top, a feat they had accomplished a few years earlier. Antera did not want to climb again, but with some hesitation, she casually told Omaran about the guidance.

"But don't get any ideas about making that 7000-foot climb again. Once was quite enough for me!" she firmly told him. "There are plenty of places they want us to visit around the mountain first, anyway."

As she knew he would, Omaran jumped on it excitedly. "Maybe we won't need to make the climb. Did they say where to start?" But he was thinking, of course they would climb.

"They said we can choose where to start. And they will guide us as we go, as always."

He said nothing, and turned away. But she could literally see and hear his mind working as he embraced this new project. Omaran started planning immediately, something he was very good at, and she could easily sense what was going through his mind. He was excited about hiking on the mountain, and really hoping they would be able to climb the peak again. Now they had a good reason! Next he would no doubt start telling friends they were hoping to climb the next summer.

Looking at her husband, and blocking out the mental planning he was doing, she noticed that his thinning hair was getting quite long and ragged-looking in the back. Several times she had suggested a haircut, but he was holding onto the little hair he had left. There was a bit of denial about the grey color and balding, which had progressed in the five years they had been together. Ah, but it was a part of his charm. However, a trim would certainly make for a cleaner look. She made a mental note to ask him again, later.

They took the planned weekend camping trip to the volcano, and decided to hike to an upper meadow, a place they had never been. New places were always exciting. They had started a cleansing fast, and didn't have their usual energy, and this looked like an easy hike—not too steep but high in elevation. They drove up the main highway to where the road ended, and took off on a trail above the tree line, hiking over a pass. The spectacular views down into the valley below, as well as up to surrounding peaks, kept their attention as they walked in silence. Mental perspective always seemed so very clear when up at high elevations.

"I understand how we can do the Light Field now," Antera suddenly said. "We can prepare the main Light structure in sections, creating several smaller ones around the mountain then tie them all together."

Omaran nodded. "Okay, where would we do those?"

"I'm not sure yet, but we will know when we need to know."

They dropped into a valley and stopped at a very small spring to drink straight out of the ground. It was some of the best tasting water they had ever had, as if it were the exact chemical composition their bodies needed. The intense life force of the water vibrated their bodies.

Red Butte, a small volcano, loomed ahead, too steep to climb without ropes and serious climbing gear. It was quite impressive, and aptly named because the rocks had a reddish color to them. As they hiked on past the butte, their attention was caught by some birds on the top, who started making a lot of noise. The couple stopped to look, and could barely see the birds flitting around up there.

"I can't tell what kind of birds those are," Antera said, shading her eyes with her hand.

"Me neither."

They listened and watched for a moment more, then Antera said, "Sounds like they are calling us up there!" She didn't really think they would follow, given the steepness of the climb, but it was an interesting thought.

"I don't think there's any doubt. Let's go!" was Omaran's retort.

"What, now??"

"Sure, see that swale there? Looks like we could get up there. It's steep but I bet we could make it."

Sure enough, the birds were pointing out probably the only place along the rock wall that could possibly be climbed without ropes. How could they ignore such an invitation? The planned hike was abandoned as they left the trail to make their way up the volcanic rocks. Even without food, they both had plenty of strength. It was very steep and the ground was composed of loose rubble, slowing their upward progress as they slid back with each step, but it wasn't far.

The top of the climb was in the central valley of the small volcano, and they both were immediately enthralled. It looked like another planet.

Omaran said, "I've never been in any place that is as unique as this!"

"Me neither. I can't imagine that many people make it up here."

The lay of the land, with its piles of rocks and flat sandy areas in between, drew them into exploring. As they hiked around the whole top, they watched the birds eat pine cones and marveled at the many old, twisted whitebark pines, reportedly hundreds if not thousands of years old. The whole place was absolutely magical.

By the time they had made a circle around the top, exploring as much as they could while allowing time to get back before dark, they knew that this was the place to create the first of the Light structures around the base of Mount Shasta.

"Let's climb up to the highest point." Omaran pointed to the peak, which was only about 200 feet higher.

Antera followed him up and over volcanic boulders, until they were at the very top of Red Butte.

"Well," Omaran observed, "We're obviously not the only ones to climb up here. Look, there's one of those double cans."

They had seen these on many peaks they had climbed. The cans were rusty and weathered from the extreme temperatures and weather, the two cans nesting to protect the small notebook and wooden pencil inside. He opened the faded notebook and they noticed that not many people had signed in. They added their signatures and a few words, using the small, blunt pencil, and replaced the can.

"We better get started with the energy work," stated Antera.

They got as comfortable as possible on the sharp boulders. Accustomed by now to doing meditation and lightwork in the most uncomfortable of positions, they didn't hesitate. They visualized the size of Red Butte and the biggest Light Field they had ever created, encompassing the entire hill and surrounding areas, and extending up the flank of the main mountain.

They asked for their bodies to be used together as conduits for Light as they went through the process. Antera felt a huge current of energy, like a bolt of lightning, released upward out of the peak, through her system and out the top of her head. Then another bolt struck from above and was anchored through her grounding cord into the rocks. She knew that they would never take on more than they could easily handle, though it was mighty intense. Omaran also felt the power of the experience.

"The Spirit of Red Butte is thanking us," Antera said afterwards. "Do you feel her?"

Omaran opened his senses. They had learned that most major peaks had a **deva**, or **mountain spirit**, associated with them. "Yes, I do. Did you get her name?"

"Purity is what I'm hearing. She literally keeps this area pure, so wants to be called that."

"Nice. Having her name makes it easier to connect with her later. Anything else she wants to say now?"

"She is excited that we came here and chose this place for the Light Field."

"Tell her we are excited to meet her and grateful. We love it up here. It's different than any place we have ever been."

"You can tell her yourself, you know," Antera said. "She hears you."

"Of course," Omaran said. He thought, but I can't hear her back so it's not the same.

They had finished the first part of the Light Field. They climbed down and hiked the long way back to the truck.

Back at the camp at dusk, they were sitting on logs and talking by the campfire when it started to lightly sprinkle. They got up to cover some things, and when they turned around, they gasped. There was a striking rainbow, dominantly pink in color, right where they had created the Light Field, and about the same size! It was like seeing the Light Field itself, from a distance. They gave thanks that the Masters had acknowledged their success in such a dramatic way.

Later that evening, St. Germain came through Antera to confirm what they had accomplished, and just after he said his closing words, the good-sized campfire went out, as if he had blown it out in another dramatic gesture. It was suddenly very dark, and they both opened their eyes in surprise. More special effects! They burst out laughing, feeling very lucky that the Masters had given them such a fun project.

Over the next few weeks, Antera noticed that the current from that blast of energy on Red Butte had opened something in her head, allowing a greater flow of Light, and she walked around in bliss much of the time. Though Omaran felt more connected, he wasn't quite as affected as Antera was, and he felt just a little disappointed. Little did he know that the next site in the Light Field, which had already started calling them, was destined to be a profound adventure for him.

4

Black Butte

Black Butte is a striking feature. It looks very much like a giant pyramid, rising up just north of the town of Mount Shasta, and west of the main mountain. Its energetic, sacred presence is strong to those sensitive to such things, but to others it is merely a backdrop. This would be the next site of the Light Field.

It was five weeks before Antera and Omaran could make the drive up to Mount Shasta again. During the week before their trip, Omaran was having a lot of telepathic interaction with Black Butte, thinking about it quite a lot while he worked on his current remodeling project. He was also emotionally on edge all week, for no apparent reason, and it wasn't until after their next adventure that they understood why. Antera stayed away from him as much as possible, hoping he would work it through on his own.

St. Germain told them that there were beings living inside the butte, in another dimension, and they were preparing for the couple to come there and create the Light Field. This was exciting for Antera, who looked forward to meeting them, but for Omaran, who was already on edge, it felt like the pressure was on.

Part of Omaran really knew that he would be guided to the right place as each new adventure or activity presented itself. But at the same time, another part was full of anxiety because this time might be the exception and he wouldn't be able to find the places the Masters wanted them to visit. Fortunately, he had spent a lot of his youth in woods and undeveloped areas, and he seemed to have an innate sense of both direction and memory of where he had been and how he had gotten there. But this seemed quite different.

Antera sensed the sudden contraction of Omaran's energy when he thought about meeting the beings inside Black Butte. "Omaran, you're amazing in the woods and everywhere we hike, so why do you doubt yourself in this?"

Omaran shrugged and said, "Yeah, it's true. I do feel comfortable on Mount Tamalpais, or Mount Shasta. But to get to one specific place on those mountains that I've never been to, or to find one particular tree on the entire mountain that's holding special frequencies, has been a bit challenging. I don't want to let the Masters down."

"Well, we succeeded in finding those blessed trees, didn't we?" They had been asked by Metatron a few years before to find trees he had blessed and make flower essences from them.

"Yes, but it wasn't always easy."

"What I see is that you always do well unless you let your doubts get in the way," Antera said. "That is what makes it hard. Otherwise, you are in the flow."

"Well, thank you. Usually I know that, but I'm still working on it."

And with such great timing that only the universe can provide, he was about to receive an opportunity to confront his doubts head-on.

Because they considered this a spiritual journey, they decided to fast for this trip, to heighten their spiritual connections. This meant reduced physical stamina, and though the hike to the top of Black Butte is a vertical climb of almost 2000 feet, there is good trail, and they had climbed it once years before. They thought they should be able to make it if they took their time.

Then the obstacles began.

Tan Man broke down right when they arrived at the campsite. The clutch stopped working. It was Friday, and Monday was the soonest a mechanic could look at it. Luckily, they had planned to meet up with Antera's son Tycho, so he offered to give them a ride to the trailhead on

Sunday. It was October, and Antera and Omaran had never camped on the mountain so late in the year. Nighttime temperatures were quite cold—down into the teens—and they used all their blankets. When they awoke in the morning, they were very surprised to find that their six-gallon water jug was completely frozen.

On the morning of the hike, the indications were positive. The chilly air prompted Omaran to start a campfire as soon as he got up, and it was blazing warmly when Antera came out of the tent. They sat next to the small fire pit, and closed their eyes to meditate. Immediately, a log started making a loud hissing sound, such as they had never heard, as it degassed blue smoke. They opened their eyes and observed the show, thinking it was a good sign.

Just before leaving, two large, black ravens flew into the camp and sat on a big branch of a fir tree only 15 feet away. Seeing ravens this close was amazing enough, but then the birds proceeded to serenade with the most unbelievable rhythm and clucking noises, the two of them working together to create a symphony of percussion that left Antera and Omaran in awe. It was taken as another encouraging sign for the mission, and it prompted them that it was time to go, as the October days were not very long.

So they piled in Tycho's truck and bounced along the bumpy roads toward Black Butte. Unfortunately, his truck happened to be low on gas, which would have been all right if they could have found the way to the trailhead, but for some reason it eluded them! There were many dirt roads, with no signs, and though it all looked familiar, the roads kept ending in dead ends. When they came to a large pile of gravel blocking one road, Omaran impatiently decided that he'd had enough. He wanted to strike out on foot from there, rather than running out of gas in the middle of nowhere. It was 12:30, so they arranged to meet back at the same place at 6:30. Omaran said he had a good internal clock, which Antera hoped was true since they did not have a watch. Tycho left, with some hesitation, and the couple started hiking down the road.

Omaran had an excellent sense of direction, and Antera's had never been very good, so if she didn't have a map she totally relied on his lead. He had never failed her in this regard, surprising her many times with his ability to find his way back when she hadn't a clue. Their hiking routine was for Antera to lead, and Omaran to gently correct her direction, often telling her the trail goes the opposite way than she would have turned.

This time, however, she started to think something was wrong . . . something was affecting his judgment. When the road they were following started going in the wrong direction and away from Black Butte, he decided to go cross country toward where he thought the trailhead should be. She realized for sure that he had lost it when he started practically running down a steep slope into a canyon, and it was very doubtful that even he could find his way back. He was out of the flow, of that she was sure.

"I'm not going down there!" She yelled after him.

"Come on! We must be getting closer!"

"No. You come back here. I won't go another step until you stop and get yourself back in the flow." She sat down on the ground. "You need to get centered. This isn't right."

"We can't stop. We have to make it all the way to the trailhead, then climb to the top, and make it all the way back before dark! We have to keep going! Time is precious."

"We have to stop. Sit." She insisted. "This is a sacred journey, and we need to be in the flow for it. If that means we don't make it today, it's all right. I'm sure there is a good reason."

Exasperated and frustrated but left with no choice, he reluctantly climbed back up the steep slope and sat next to her. They closed their eyes and were silent for a few minutes. Turning his attention inward, Omaran asked what was going on and quickly got an answer.

He shared, "It's kind of the same thing I've always done, using my will and male energy to force my way through. And I think the bigger part is, again, fear of letting the Masters down."

"The Masters never want us to be afraid. If you have fear, there is something for you to learn here, and if you can find what that is, we may be able to make it. But being driven by fear is no way to go."

He was able to relax then and think more clearly, so they decided to go back to the main road and hope to see someone who could give directions—or better yet, a ride. They dusted the dirt off and slowly made their way back. Antera was feeling very tired already, maybe because of not eating, and she had serious doubts that she could make the climb up the butte even if they found the trail.

Back on the bigger road, after hiking a few minutes, a small side road appeared and someone had etched a big arrow out in the dirt pointing down it. It was going toward Black Butte, even though it was an old logging road that hadn't been used for years, so they followed it. After about a quarter of a mile and a few meanders, it ended, so they backtracked. Another dead end!

They kept going, and followed a road along a string of telephone poles that looked like it was likely to go somewhere. A couple of miles later, they came to a major-looking intersection of dirt roads, and there were three people walking toward them. Directions at last?

Antera said, "Wouldn't it be funny if they wanted to ask us the same question?"

When they got close, the other group asked, "Do you know how to get to the Black Butte trailhead?"

It wasn't really that funny. The people had also driven down many roads in failed attempts to find the right one. The five of them decided to hike together down one of the roads that came into the intersection. It had a red gate closed across it. Though it didn't seem likely that the rangers would close access to the butte, the consensus was that it was reasonable to close it this time of year before winter. As they all hiked down this road, they found it leading farther and farther away from the butte. After about a mile, Antera and Omaran turned around. The others kept going.

When they got back to the intersection, two trucks with hunters in them, as evidenced by guns in racks, were parked next to each other as the drivers talked. When asked, they said that the trailhead was only a mile up the other road, the only other option. Antera was exhausted, and the thought of one more mile uphill hardly seemed worth it, or possible. Even if she could make it, that was just the start of the real climb! Omaran was better off physically, but still emotionally stressed, and he was very determined.

So they went, Antera forcing her body to keep taking steps. At the trailhead, Omaran tried to convince her that there was enough time to make it to the top and back. She could only say she would try.

He gave her a hug and said, "Take some of my energy. I have plenty." They started on the trail.

Then something magical happened. As soon as Antera stepped onto the trail, it was as if she'd crossed a barrier, like a **portal**, and all the heaviness lifted. She mentally connected with the beings inside the hill and asked them for wings to help her get to the top. A flood of physical energy came in. Suddenly she felt very light, and found that she could hike the grade without even getting winded. In fact, as she hiked she got more and more energy, and she thought she could almost run up the hill!

But then she looked back. Omaran was far behind. This was unlike him; he was a strong hiker. He looked like he was carrying the load of the ages up that hill. It seemed his was the opposite effect, and he got more and more tired.

Antera waited for him. "Just connect with the beings in the mountain, they will give you energy!"

"I'm trying. I just feel so heavy."

"I'll take the pack then. Will that help?" She knew she could carry the pack and still fly up the mountain.

"No, I need to carry it."

"Why? Don't be ridiculous."

"I don't know why, I just know I need to carry this load to the top. I feel very, very heavy."

Perhaps it was the male force again clouding his judgment, or pride, or something deeper. At last she convinced him to stash some of the stuff by the side of the trail, and they continued up, Antera dashing ahead in spurts then waiting for him to catch up.

It got colder and colder as the wind picked up. Antera was perfectly warm because of the exertion, but Omaran was obviously hurting. With some effort, she convinced him to stop, and she tied her extra shirt around his neck and got his gloves out of the pack. He looked so pathetic that it was almost comical, and she had to try hard not to laugh. It was so unlike him, and she was feeling so exuberant! It was almost as if deep inside he wanted to suffer, as a necessary part of the journey. She was having a great time, loving every minute of the climb, and he was dragging with each step, using his willpower to continue. He had never felt like that before.

They did reach the top and belted a few hallelujahs for making it and overcoming such obstacles. Against the odds, they had made it. It was so cold that they didn't stay long. They sat for a few minutes inside the old foundation at the peak, a small square area with three-foot-high walls, partially protected from the wind. They took off their gloves just long enough to create the Light Field while standing back-to-back. The field was even bigger than the one they had made on Red Butte, extending across the valley for miles.

During the process, the heavy energy Omaran had carried was completely released. "I feel much better now!" he declared with a sigh. "We did it!"

His face certainly looked better and on the way down his steps were lighter. Antera thought about running down but knew it was not a good idea because volcanic rocks are so abrasive if you fall on them. Anyway, Omaran wasn't quite up to that!

They hiked like mad and got back to the meeting spot 15 minutes early, and Tycho was there waiting. They went out to a restaurant and broke their fast with gusto.

The next day, they were able to drive the truck, without a clutch, to the shop for repair. They found a nice area in some woods to sit, and Antera channeled St. Germain, hoping for feedback on their hike and difficulties of the previous day. St. Germain always preferred that she contact him outside, and he came through loud and clear.

"I would like to tell you that your mission yesterday was a success!" the Master said. "You moved past the obstacles, came upon your target, and created a lovely focus of Light around the mountain. Your intent was pure, and your hearts full of love for the land and the mountain, so it was successful. And we thank you for this effort.

"As you move away from this area and go back to the city, you will slowly notice what this trip has done for you. It will be more apparent. While you are here, the energy is much more rarified and it is much easier to lift veils, so the effect it has had on you may not be quite so obvious.

"I am open to questions of any kind."

Omaran said, "I have a couple of questions about yesterday's journey. As you know, at the beginning we were not where we wanted to be, and I just started walking headlong through the forest. Was it my resistance, or was there another kind of resistance that we were up against?"

"All resistance is of the same source. Picking up that energy of obstacles was only possible because you had some of that within yourself. Therefore, it is posed as a lesson, a means for you to prove that you can master such a situation . . . that you can maintain your calm and your connectedness without giving in to it. Because you surmounted and made your way there, it is that much sweeter and more powerful.

"You see, if it had been a very easy journey, it would not have been as powerful. Because you had to go through resistance, and overcome obstacles, the challenge was much greater and the focus of energy there was much greater as well.

"The focus of this particular mountain is quite different than that of Red Butte. The journey you took was symbolic, in many ways, of what this mountain stands for. You might have noticed that you, Omaran, had a much harder time of it than Antera. She was able to break through and connect with the beings in the mountain, asking for their help. They lifted her up, literally. You had to break through resistance each step of the way. Partly this is because of your energetic makeup and some of the weight that you carry in your energy field. And some of it is because you are a man, and you carry the male energy.

"The particular challenge of this mountain was through the male vehicle. Therefore you broke through most of that energy on your way up."

"Well," Omaran said, "right at the trailhead, it was as if the two of us had a shift in energy. And that's the most tired I can remember being on any hike or trek ever."

"Yes, you carried much more than your own weight up that mountain."

"Is there something that I could do in future journeys like this that would help make them go smoother?"

St. Germain said, "Any journey has its own reasons and its own energy patterns. And every one will be different. Your challenge will always be to follow the flow . . . to give up expectation, and to go toward your goal. If there are major obstacles and you find you cannot get to your goal at that time, then you release it. A major lesson for you was to accept that it may not happen and to go with that flow. As soon as you did that, the opening appeared. That took a little while."

"Yes."

"If you can remember what you went through and not allow that to happen again, your journeys will be easier. It is always easier to go with the flow than to go against it. Trying to force something that is not meant to be is a very difficult path. The flow is always the path where the energy is going. Follow it, even though there may be obstacles to go around, and you will be able to do it. And make sure that your heart and your mind are pure and clean and ready . . . important in any journey."

The primary mission of creating the Light Field on Black Butte had been accomplished, but the effects of doing this continued as Omaran analyzed his reactions and practiced the right use of male energy. He found himself in situations the following week where previously he would have gotten upset and charged through an obstacle using force, but now he was able to stop himself and turn within to his **Divine Presence** for guidance, to see where the flow was. It was a lesson well learned.

5

Ordination

The winter solstice of 1998 was coming up, and since they thought it might be their last in the Bay Area, Antera and Omaran wanted to do something special. For years, they had held ceremonies on each equinox and solstice to mark these important alignments between Earth and sun, and to use these powerful times of year to amplify intent. Each ceremony they did had a theme, proposed by the Masters. This one seemed even more important.

Energetically, something seemed to be brewing. Energy was ramping up as they approached the millennium. Antera had known since she was a small child that she was here to help with the transition of humanity into higher consciousness, and she had looked forward to this time as one of possible big changes, both in the land and in consciousness.

The **Y2K** (Year 2000) computer issue had recently been discovered, and many were concerned about it because it could possibly shut down computers worldwide unless it was fixed. This brought up fear for many, but at the same time, it caused renewed interests in self-sufficiency, rural living, and a return to simpler ways of life, which were generally positive. Antera and Omaran were hoping to move the next year anyway, and get out of the city, so the timing was good in case Y2K did hit hard.

As they meditated on the theme for the solstice, the words ***Christ Light*** and *ordination* kept coming into their consciousness. They decided to ask the Masters if that was supposed to be the theme—or something related to that. And if they were being ordained, what were they ordaining into? Antera channeled Mother Mary one evening in November, to see if they could get some clarity.

Mary said, "Good evening. I bring you my tidings and joy. I bring you my love and everlasting peace. How may I be of service this evening?"

Omaran answered, "I have a question. Considering all that we've been through in the past, it might sound a little silly, but . . . what exactly is the **Christ energy** or Christ Light?"

She answered, "That is a very good question. And one which I would very much like to answer. I define it as the energy that descends upon you as you are 'Christed,' or anointed with total awareness or enlightenment. This is the energy that you become one with when you fully become merged with your Higher Presence.

"This process has happened to many on the planet. You are only aware of a few, those who have publicly proclaimed that they have been anointed with the Christ energy. Others have done so quietly and have completed their service and their work on the planet.

"So that is the Christ energy by my definition, and of those with whom I associate, including Jesus and many of the Ascended Masters who have incorporated the Christ energy. There are those on your planet, however, who consider the Christ energy to be a particular Master, who comes through an individual when they are ready for teaching. This is simply a different definition. Generally a Christed one is one who has learned to bring the energy of the Higher Presence fully and completely into all four bodies."

Omaran asked, "So then only a few people have brought in the Christ Light?"

Mary clarified, "I have been through the process. It may seem simple by my definition, but it is a very unique process to this planet. The enlightenment that is available on this planet now is not available anywhere else! It has its own unique characteristics and energy signatures. So you could say that the Christ Light is only available on this planet, although the energy itself is everywhere.

"The way I have defined the Christ Light, it requires only to become one with your Higher Presence. However, at different times on this planet, different energies have been available. It is true that each being who becomes one with his or her Higher Presence, takes on slightly different energies depending on when and where it happens.

"There are many variations in the frequencies available at each time. Every Master who has been on the planet and achieved mastery has brought in what I would call the Christ Light or **Christ Consciousness**. But each one was in different times, and therefore brought in different frequencies.

"The frequencies that Jesus was able to bring through were uniquely suited to him and his energetic makeup. His purpose for coming was to bring in energies of Divine Love and forgiveness. Therefore, he carried a tremendous amount of those energies with him when he became the Master. But, it is still Christ Consciousness no matter who does it or what their purpose for being here is.

"When Buddha came he had a different agenda and things to teach because he appeared among people who had different lessons to learn. But they were both Masters, and others have been Masters on the planet and have come for whatever reason they were here.

"So it is well not to confuse the reason for coming, the purpose of the lifetime, with the Christ Light and the merging with the Higher Presence. Remember also, that these tales get more and more exaggerated with time, and any Master who has walked the planet has been doubted many times by those around him or her. Jesus was no exception. He was a man who achieved his own quota of Light, and was able to hold more Light than those around him, despite the society and the conditions. If it had been so apparent that he held the Christ Light, there would have been no doubt. But many doubted him.

"You live in a time when you also doubt your mastery because you think you have to be perfect. You do not have to be one hundred percent perfect to bring the Christ Light in and be a Master. It is a matter of degree, and once you carry enough Light, then you attract more like a magnet, and it goes very quickly. It would be impossible to be perfect while in a human body. Even the greatest Masters were not perfect."

Omaran said, "Thank you so much, that really makes sense. We have another question. What kind of ordination will we be going through?"

"The ordination is an initiation into the higher service, and this is very special. It is for those who have had many, many lifetimes and have dedicated themselves to the service of the higher **realms**, the **Great White Brotherhood**, and the spiritual hierarchy of this planet. It is actually an initiation into the **Melchizedek Order**, with which you have both been involved in the past, though you don't have conscious memories of it.

"We will be speaking to you more about that later. I can tell you that I'm very, very happy that you are going to go through with this, and I think you will find it to be quite enlightening. It will fill you with an incredible surge of Light. By taking the vows for the order, you will receive a special transmission, frequencies that tie you to the Brotherhood.

"It is a dedication of yourselves to the higher purpose in a formal way. For even though you have dedicated yourselves as much as you can while you are working jobs and living in the world, by formally announcing it at this initiation, you will be completing a cycle that started many, many thousands of years ago for each of you. There will be a general feeling of relief, a letting go of some lesser energies that you no longer need to hold onto."

"Thank you, Mary," Omaran said. "And what should we do to prepare for this ceremony?"

"To prepare for this event, of course I suggest fasting. A good week of cleansing and fasting would be appropriate. This may mean that you continue to eat fruit and juice, and perhaps green vegetables during this time. But a general cleansing of the body leading up to this time would be very appropriate.

"There is also an emotional purification that would be appropriate as well. As you cleanse the physical, the emotional body will call for its own cleansing. We suggest that you take a day to purge yourself of all that you sense to be in resistance to this initiation, between now and then. Simply think about it in your meditations, call in the energy of this initiation, and then ask yourself if there is any resistance. If there is, allow it to come up to express itself and release. Use your breath to release, and dig very deep within all of your chakra systems to let go of all that resists.

"Also, in looking at your mental body, find any beliefs or little tapes you have running that may be contrary to the purpose of bringing the Christ Consciousness energies into your system.

"Spiritually, you are already working very diligently. We simply ask you to add the thought of the Melchizedek Order to your meditations to spiritually prepare. You are dedicating your lives to the service of God-Goddess, the I Am Presence. This ceremony is a culmination, not a beginning. This means that the time spent in preparation before the ceremony is far more important than the ceremony itself. It only marks the ending of a cycle. So it is the purification up to the ceremony and in the ceremony that is most important."

"Thank you! That sounds perfect. I think we are ready, and I am excited," declared Omaran.

"Good! We are looking forward to it."

After Mary withdrew her energy, Antera opened her eyes and waited for Omaran, who was enjoying the energy space. They both always received very expanding energies when Antera channeled, and it was nice to sit in them for a while afterwards.

"We are going to be ordained into the **Order of Melchizedek**!" she said, when Omaran opened his eyes.

"I've heard the name," Omaran said, "but I don't really remember much about them. It must be an honor, though."

"Yes, this must be the big shift I've been feeling coming up."

"I'll fast for a week," he declared.

"Ha! I'll fast for two weeks!"

"Heck, I'll start tomorrow! Four weeks!"

They laughed.

"A lot to get ready," Antera said. "Where can we do the ceremony? It will need to be indoors in winter."

"I know just the place! Larkspur Theater. I did a lot of work for their remodel and they never paid me fully, so they said I could use the space any time I wanted. I'll call them tomorrow."

"That sounds great. It is big, so we can have a good-sized group."

The Order of Melchizedek, they later learned, is a cosmic order, concerned with the entire universe and not only this planet. However, because of the big and exciting changes to humanity currently taking place on Earth, a large percentage of the order's resources and beings are focused on Earth life. All Ascended Masters and angels are a part of it, aiding its purpose of guiding the consciousness and evolution of human beings.

It was something Antera and Omaran took very seriously, even reverently, as they prepared for their formal ordination in their spare time. More information was given by the Masters about how to do the initiation, and they sent out invitations to some people they thought may want to participate. As the date of the solstice approached, they did their personal preparations and advised those who also wanted to be initiated to do the same.

Unfortunately, the closer they got to the date of the initiation, the more stressed and upset Omaran became. It was very hard for Antera to be around him when he was like that because when he got upset he tended to blame her for everything, only to apologize afterwards when he calmed down again. This pattern had been a problem since they had first gotten together, and she had learned not to engage him while he was under the dark influences, which caused him to overreact to every little thing and make problems where there really weren't any.

He was much better now than he had been years ago. She had even separated from him for a while back then, which was one of the hardest things she had ever done, and that had forced him to do some serious healing. But his pain still surfaced occasionally, and when it did, he acted like she was his enemy. So when this happened, she stopped talking to him except for the most important communications, waiting until he could get himself together and figure out why he was really upset. He was never upset at what he thought, and afterwards he could sometimes get to the real issue, which never had anything to do with her. And usually, when he was being extremely contrary, he was partially aware that he was behaving like a jerk, but at this point in his life he wasn't able to identify in the moment whether it was something from his past or some energy he had allowed to attach to him from someone else. Either way, his pattern was to not deal with it.

Even though she knew this behavior of his well, it was especially disturbing that he was spewing out harmful thoughts and emotional energy during this very important time of preparing for their initiation into the Order of Melchizedek!

"Omaran, you need to control your thoughts!" Antera told him the day before the ceremony. "Don't you know how important this is? Why can't you be nice? Do you want to spoil the whole thing?"

"I'm not the one spoiling it! It's you!"

"Oh, for heaven's sake. Don't go into those old mental tapes. We are leading up to a very important ceremony, and it is a time for peace, not stress. If you are upset, look within to what is coming up for you to heal. I'm not the cause of your pain."

"Oh, no, it is never your fault, it is always me." Omaran said sarcastically.

Antera sighed and went back to ignoring him, rather than engage this **entity**. Sometimes she wondered if he would ever heal all the dark side of his personality and the thoughts that called in these entities. But she decided she would not let this distract her or prevent her from fully taking in the important energy that was building up for the next day. She would get her ordination whether he did or not.

Omaran was not thinking clearly, and he knew it. Why was he acting like this? Was it his doubts about his abilities creeping in again? He felt like every time he had what he thought was pressure, he forgot all the tools he had been taught and tended to fester on thoughts he didn't really want, and then he would get upset. Maybe he didn't deserve to be ordained in the Order of Melchizedek! Maybe he was a fraud and was not worthy at all. He couldn't get guidance like Antera could. Why did the Masters want to work with him, anyway, if he couldn't even stay focused on the Light at an important time like this?

And now he had the Black Butte experience to reflect upon. It had had a big impact on him. St. Germain had helped Omaran learn that he would only be affected by something if a part of him resonated with it. So now, with the upcoming ceremony, he knew that his upset meant there was a part of him that resonated with crummy energy. This was great to understand, but it didn't ease the feelings. It was a downward spiral that he thought he was powerless to get out of. Releasing these thoughts and feelings when he was in them was about as easy as reversing the spin of the Earth and making the sun rise in the west!

The day of the ceremony, they loaded up Tan Man with all the ceremonial equipment and energy devices, and they headed toward the theater. As they were driving, it snowed! Little flakes floated down. This was a very rare occurrence in the Bay Area, and though it didn't stick, they all felt joyfully blessed and took it as a very positive sign.

The theater was warm, though dark, and the group of about 30 people formed two circles, an inner circle of those who were being initiated and an outer circle of those who were supporting and receiving other benefits. As the Masters were called in, those unseen beings also took places in a larger circle around the people, and the energy ramped up quickly.

The perfect blessings were received for each individual, and when it was time for the personal initiations, Antera went into the center to receive the transmission from the Order of Melchizedek first, through her direct connection. It was a profound input of energy that connected her in an even stronger way to this cosmic group. She was then able to call the energy through for the other initiates, as instructed by the Masters.

Omaran was feeling guilty, thinking about how awful he had been the last few days, and that he hadn't been strong enough to stop his harmful behavior. It was like it just took him over and he couldn't control his thoughts. He had many doubts about his worthiness to receive this initiation. Before his turn came to go into the center, he was contemplating whether he should back out and say he wasn't ready.

The days leading up to this initiation had been so difficult for Omaran. He knew he really wanted to be calm, loving and accepting, but he hadn't been. Now it was probably too late to make amends for all the negative thoughts and emotions he had spewed about, which made him feel even worse.

Here in the sacred space of the ceremony, or when Antera was bringing forth words from the Masters, everything seemed so easy and understandable. So much love! Why couldn't he get here on his own? He took a deep breath as the ceremony continued. He was feeling better and better but still not sure if he deserved to be ordained. Perhaps at the last minute something would happen to make sure he wouldn't go through with it.

But after watching Antera look so blissful as she received her transmission from the order, and then seeing her turn to him and nod, he knew he would go through with it. He went to the center of the circle and felt the transmission go into his crown chakra, which started spinning faster. Then the energy flowed down through his whole body. Much of the heavy energy he had been carrying was instantly lifted by the Masters. Wow! He was very glad he had gone through with it.

6

Aftermath

It was a few days before they checked in again with the Masters. Something amazingly profound and deep had happened during the initiation, and they could both sense changes occurring at levels previously inaccessible. During these few days, it felt best not to talk much with each other so that they could integrate the energy shifts essential for their own individual paths.

Omaran was still thinking about how he had been so irritable the days leading up to the ceremony, as if there was a part of him that wasn't ready. Now he felt better than ever, but he secretly hoped his transgressions had not prevented him from receiving the full impact of the transmission. Feeling unworthy had been a long-time pattern, and it had kicked in big time. In fact, he wanted to put off hearing from the Masters because he was still a bit ashamed about his behavior leading up to the solstice.

When they finally sat down to contact the Masters and get some feedback from them, Mother Mary spoke through Antera.

She said, "Blessed be, my Holy Children! You are now of the Order. Please do not doubt for a moment that the sacred ceremony was complete and that your ordinations have been duly filed, recognized by the Order of Melchizedek, and by the Great White Brother-Sisterhood, as you call it."

Antera chuckled, knowing Mary was referring to her own dislike of the "brotherhood" name, which implied male members only. Though she knew the name came from a time in the past when many male nouns were used to imply both genders, in this day and age it was no longer appropriate to exclude females. So she had asked if it could be called brother-sisterhood, and the Masters had agreed.

Mary went on, "We honor you for taking this step, we honor you for doing your very best to follow the Light on a planet where it is difficult to follow the Light. We give you our highest blessing and regards. Let there be no doubt about this manifestation of your energies and the recording of this ordination.

"You are now aligned with the highest forces of the planet, officially and formally, and in your hearts. We know you recognize that this means service to the Light, to the best of your abilities. It does not mean you have to be perfect. It does mean that your intentions are always perfect, that your intentions are to align with the Light, and to carry out the service that is given to you through your Higher Presence as a carrier of the Light, and coming directly from the Order of the Universal Melchizedek.

"Omaran, the resistance that you felt prior to the ceremony, may I speak of this?"

Omaran had been afraid she would bring that up. "Yes, of course."

"Do not fault yourself for this. Though you might have reacted differently or handled it differently, the resistance you felt was a very powerful dark force, which comes up to impede these kinds of ceremonies of the Light. It settles with you because a small part of you still resonates with it. But, since you did go ahead with the ceremony, you did receive your ordination, and that small part can be dispelled.

"You want to be perfectly clear emotionally during ceremony, because whatever isn't, will be magnified during such a powerful channeling of energy. Because these things are magnified and brought to your attention, they bring about a healing or spiritual crisis that forces you to find a way to heal. When you put yourselves around the sacred circle, it may seem very symbolic and simple, but you are calling in and generating incredible forces. You are calling together massive energy to work a purpose.

"It is very important that you are not only very clear on that purpose, but that your emotional makeup is cleansed, which is, of course, why you go through all the purifications and blessings before starting the major body of work in the ritual. We are very pleased with the amount of Light that all of you brought through."

Relieved, Omaran said, "So Mary, does this mean we need to act differently now? How will this affect us in daily life?"

"You are now Holy Ones! It does not mean you have to act differently, but it does mean that you are aligned with a Holy Order and that you are representatives of this order. So keep in mind that your actions, your deeds, your thoughts, and your words all reflect back to the order. Anytime you are not clear in your communications, it is best not to speak. Anytime you need to speak instead of letting deceptions go by unacknowledged, it is beneficial to the order that you do speak and bring attention to all that is not honest, all that is not of the Light. But do it in a gentle, compassionate, and loving way.

"Being aligned with the Light does not mean that you allow others to take advantage of you, or that you allow yourself to be in the company of those who do not serve the Light, unless you are there to help them heal and are acting in the capacity of a minister. You are ministers of the Light, ministers of the Holy Order, this is your primary function on the planet now.

"We hope that you take it as seriously as it is offered, and that in time, as you work into your full capacity as representatives of the White Brother-Sisterhood and the order, that you will begin to receive even clearer directions, so that you may accept service in the opportunities that are given to you. Keep in mind always that you are a Man and Woman of God, and that this is your primary function.

"Do you have questions?"

Omaran, feeling better but still not great about his behavior, really wanted to change the subject. "I guess we're both thinking March will be the month we'll move, so we can be settled in Mount Shasta by April. Is that good for timing?"

"Yes, I would not change that. I see no way for you to get out of here sooner. I do suggest that you continue to work on manifesting what you want energetically, so you can pull this together quickly and easily. Focus on it in your meditations and prayers, twice a day. And since you are not yet clear on exactly what it is you want, visualize what you do know you want, and allow the higher forces to take care of the rest.

"The plan is fully in place and even though you are putting your energies into a new home there, remember you still have to follow the flow. So leave a slight possibility of something better to come along, just in case. It is an important part of the process.

"We can hardly wait for you to be up there, because the energy here is so dense, and becoming denser by the day. You will be amazed at how clear your meditations are when you finally get out of this area, how easy it is to focus and do your spiritual work, and how much easier it is to communicate with us. The chaotic energies are making it very difficult for any energy sensitive people to be comfortable and focused."

"Thank you so much for everything, Mary," Omaran said. "We are really looking forward to the move."

Omaran became more resolved than ever to stay centered. He felt that he was given a great gift through the initiation, but one he wasn't sure he deserved, despite what Mary had said. Inside, he struggled with the thought that the Masters wouldn't give him anything he wasn't ready for. And he certainly wasn't sure about being called a Holy One. The concept was nice, but here he was, a building contractor in the real world, not someone living the spiritual life of a monk.

He really tried to live up to what the Masters expected of him, and there were times that he felt truly masterful and other times he knew he blew it completely. Fortunately, the bad times were fewer and fewer, and he knew that by far most of the time he was generating very good energies, so hopefully those counteracted the times he fell into the negativity.

Antera and Omaran were very busy with their jobs and moving preparations, so it wasn't until a few weeks later that they heard from St. Germain. They didn't have any questions but liked to hear from the Masters for feedback and information.

"I greet you!" St. Germain said through Antera. "Congratulations on your ordination!"

"Thank you very much. I hope we can live up to what is expected of us now," Omaran said.

"I want to tell you something, and it is important. You have both been on this planet, achieving your destinies and missions for a long time, as you know. And now you are ripe! Now you are birthing into the higher realms of Light, back to where you came from. As you go back, you go back with much more than you came here with.

"'Tis a joyous thing to see two twin rays rejoined and brought back together to achieve the ultimate of union! It is your destiny and an important part of your mission! And the highest expression you can bring forth to the planet.

"Though there are many aspects of your world that are changing, this focus must be held throughout all of these times! It is so important that you not lose your focus on that which is sacred, that which brings you into your God Selves. This is always the primary focus. The secondary focus is the union of two God Selves into One! The merging of the twin rays!

"I tell you this because it is so easy to get caught up in the material existence when there is such rapid change and so much happening in the outer world, so you are pulled in many directions. There are many asking for help, many suffering, and the Earth itself cries out in pain! Yet, you must hold your focus!

"You can do only so much. As you hold your focus on the Light, you will recognize all of the drama for what it is. You will recognize the temptation. You will recognize that others are merely playing out their patterns and tapping into those **thoughtforms** that have not been healed. But do not let it sway you from your purpose and your mission!

"You are now a priest and priestess of the Order of Melchizedek. When you restated your vows to the order, you gave up life as you knew it. You dedicated yourselves to the service that is not of this world yet affects this world in a greater way than anything else can. What does this mean? This means you serve the Light! This means every decision comes from the Light.

"I do not want you to think you are under pressure to perform. My only desire here tonight is to raise your perceptions in the highest way possible, so that you know what is expected. We placed our bets on you, and we are very glad that we did. It was a gamble to elevate you to the holders of the Twin Flame Archetype last year. But I bent some rules because I saw that you could fulfill the station. And now it seems you are up to it, at last!

"I do not want you to misunderstand what I say. I say this so that you know I have great faith in you, and this means you can have great faith in yourselves. I do not take gambles that I am not very sure that I can win. So tonight I am acknowledging that you are in full service of this office, of the twin flame holders, and your probation is over.

"This is cause for celebration! Perhaps you did not know you were on probation, and that is well and good. But tonight, we celebrate as I bring you this news! It is not, of course, my decision alone. There has been much watching and waiting, and you have been before the Karmic Board, and now you are accepted. Please accept my congratulations."

Omaran was surprised. "Thank you. We didn't know we were on probation. But we are glad we passed. We do take the twin flame office and the initiation seriously, and thank you for having faith in us."

"You are welcome. Thank you for your dedication."

After St. Germain withdrew his energy, Antera and Omaran talked some more about their plans, the move, the mystery school, and their own evolution. Being ordained certainly was more important than they had thought. So much had already shifted in their lives, and it was certainly exciting. They wondered what was next.

Two weeks later, as they sat together in the living room meditating, Antera was suddenly filled with an intense Light that was intelligent but different from any of the Masters with whom she usually talked. In fact, it wasn't a particular being; it was more like a pure undifferentiated energy from the Divine.

She said, "There is an energy here that calls itself the Blue-White Light from Source."

"I feel it, wow, so intense!" Omaran said. He felt like he was being lifted right out of his chair.

"It is forming words to go along with the energy transmission."

The Blue-White Light said, "The greatest Light, the greatest Spirit must come directly from the Source of all Light, the Source of All That Is, in this universe. You are being opened to receive more direct transmissions from this Spirit of All Spirits, to be expressed in your daily lives. You are being elevated to the highest station you can be elevated to, while living on the planet at this time! You are being opened to the highest frequencies that the human body can process!

"Ground this Light down into the planet through the souls of your feet, through the palms of your hands. Since you have become a part of the order and ordained once again, by your own free choice, into the Order of Melchizedek, you are given access to these energies that are the creative energies of pure manifestation! The energies allow you to connect directly to the **Universal Mind**, using the most creative and universal forces, to create whatever it is that your mission and your service requires!

"When you are creating the work of God, you may use these energies. When you are creating with the full force of the universe behind you and creating the forms that most reflect that which is being created on the highest levels, you will have a full portion of this energy given to you. You may call it to you by holding the thought of the Universal Creator. All forms are not only possible—all forms are already created!

"As you call in the highest energies of manifestation in the universe, you create the largest bridge possible, from the densest matter to the finest matter of God—the pure creative essence. That is the largest bridge that can be built! You have merely now to call the Universal Creative Force to be with you in your creative process. You will create that which is ordained, that which is reflective of the highest forms in the universe. Any form you build shall be built according to the laws of the most sacred forms, the most sacred geometries, the most sacred thoughtforms, the most sacred thought processes, and completely aligned with this energy. This is ordained through the order for those in service on the planet!

"You may use this energy for creating anything that is sacred, that reflects the most pure forms, and contains the highest energies . . .

building this bridge to its firmest support. This builds the strongest bridge and makes heaven on Earth. With these creative energies pouring through you, all that is God-like is possible. This is how you can fully recognize which is the proper path, which is the path that builds the greatest bridge. Because with this creative force pouring through you it will only flow when the bridge is being built. If you stray and create that which is not fully aligned with the God-Force, then this creative energy will no longer flow through you. You will be able to tell right away if you are tuned and paying attention to this flow.

"Remember what it feels like! You will always have an indicator within you, built in, which helps you make decisions, which helps you follow the path of greatest service to the Universal Order, and the path of greatest growth for you . . . creating the forms on the planet, both physical forms and thoughtforms. Constructs in the mental area are fully as important as those that are built with the materials of the planet.

"We ask that you keep in mind the God-Force moving through you . . . and that each of your actions reflects the greatest and highest energies. You are being given the highest service that you can achieve. If you take it to its highest form, there will be much energy shifted on the planet! You have been designated as carriers of the God-Force! Of the most High Creative Force. This comes with responsibility. It comes with your mission."

The transmission ended as quickly as it had begun. Antera and Omaran looked at each other with wide eyes.

"I don't even know what to say!" Omaran said. "I feel like I'm totally filled with Light and just completely buzzing!"

Antera nodded. "Yes. I feel different. That was a direct transmission from Divine Presence. I could hardly contain the energy enough to translate into words as it came through."

"I have no idea how you managed to do it. I feel purged. We certainly have received many gifts since our initiation, and I have no intention of ranking them, but right now, I just feel like I'm somewhere else. Like I'm floating in a sea of Light, somewhere up in clouds . . . I can't explain it, I'm still more *there* than *here*."

7

The Big Move

It was in late February when Antera and Omaran went to Shasta again for more house hunting. It was unseasonably warm for a couple of weeks, so they decided it was a good time to go, hoping the roads would be clear of snow and safe to drive on.

Omaran had decided that, given the cold mountain winters, he wanted to have a passive-solar house that would be heated directly by the sun. This design required a large mass of some kind to soak up the sun's heat and then store it, radiating it into the house after the sun went down. After looking at a few homes and trying to imagine how to remodel them to create this kind of system, he decided there was no way. He would have to bite the bullet and build from scratch. So with some reluctance, they started looking at undeveloped land.

Since the last time they had looked at properties, they had started discussing various other options. They had looked at types of alternative building, but after checking with the county, Omaran had found that most of these choices weren't accepted—not even straw-bale construction, which was accepted as a good ecologically sound method elsewhere. Siskiyou County was not as progressive as some others, unfortunately. So most of Omaran's building research focused on passive-solar building.

He had found that there were quite a few different ways of bringing passive solar into a building design. One way was to construct a cement block wall on the south side that would retain the sun's heat of the day and then radiate it into the house at night. Only a few small windows were allowed on that side, which didn't appeal to either of them.

Another way used water heated by the sun as it moved through tubes on the south wall during the day, which would then radiate the collected heat from holding tanks into the house at night. That didn't sound great, but one water system had actually aroused Omaran's interest. It was definitely elaborate but much simpler in design, which meant there was less that could go wrong. It involved placing several hundred five-gallon plastic bottles in the attic with a clear plastic roofing system, so the sun would warm the water during the day.

When Omaran had expressed his interest in this system to Antera, she had burst out laughing. Then she had said in no uncertain terms that she hoped he was kidding, and there was no way she would live in a house that had 18,000 pounds of water above their heads! They were moving to a volcano, after all! Antera's previous career had been as a seismologist, and though they were moving out of a seismically active area, the part of her that was tuned to earthquake hazards was not giving in to that risk. So Omaran had continued his research.

The seventh book he had read on passive-solar design proved to be the lodestone. It was by an engineer from Vermont, and there were many homes that had already been successfully built with his design. It used a big heat sink below ground level, like a shallow basement. It was filled by many tons of tamped base rock, insulated, and covered by rows of large cement blocks aligned north to south, with vents at each end to permit heat circulation. All this was then topped by a concrete slab. The more windows on the east, south, and west sides the better, to collect the radiant heat and send it down. Bingo!

Now all they had to do was get the land, find the money, and begin!

One important criterion for any property they bought was being able to see the mountain, so they quickly ruled out certain areas where it wasn't visible. On their last day there, the realtor gave them directions to a 2.5-acre lot, higher in elevation than the town, and at the edge of the national forest. They followed her directions, turning on a rough dirt road that had no road sign, and making their way slowly until they saw a "For Sale" sign stuck in some bushes. They got out and faced a very thick forest of manzanita bushes. They found they couldn't walk even a few feet onto the land! Omaran gave it a good try from several places, but it was very difficult to make headway through the thicket.

Antera dismissed it immediately, even though the views all around were magnificent, because one thing she really wanted was trees, and these were definitely bushes—and extremely thick ones at that. Maybe there were a couple of oak trees on the lot, but it was hard to tell where the property lines were for sure.

"Since we're here, I want to go into the middle of the property, just to see what the views look like from there," Omaran said.

"Ha, ha! Good luck."

"I think I can do it. I'll walk around and see if it is any easier somewhere else. You will be able to hear me."

He did make his way in, crawling his way through the thicket very slowly. Along the way, he discovered a small mound that, after he sat on it for a couple of minutes, felt very sacred to him, and he knew instinctively that if they ended up with this place, there would be no building on the mound area.

It took 40 minutes to make it to what he thought was the center. The view was outrageous! Mount Shasta to the northeast, Black Butte to the northwest, Castle Crags to the southwest, Spring Hill to the west, and the foothills of the mountain to the east. Because of the lack of trees, the entire sky was open. Omaran was transfixed, especially after living in Mill Valley, where the beautiful redwoods that surrounded their house only allowed about four hours of direct sunlight on the longest summer days.

"I love this!" he proclaimed to Antera, the mountain, the forest, the land, and anyone else who might be passing by.

He found a slightly quicker way out. Antera surveyed him as he emerged. His jeans were torn, as was his shirt, but surprisingly, he only had a few scratches on his arms even though he had literally been crawling in the thicket.

"I know there are good views, but I really do want trees!" Antera wasn't interested in the property and wanted to move on.

"And it certainly would be a lot of work to clear the manzanita," Omaran realized. He wasn't too keen on that. It would be starting from scratch. No, it would be way beyond scratch. It would be starting in the hole. They left the mountain and went back home.

The next day at dinner Omaran said, "You know, I've been thinking about that manzanita property we saw. I know it isn't ideal, but for some reason I can't get it out of my mind."

"Really?" Antera still felt resistance to it but had to confess. "Well, actually I did have a dream about it last night. It was like it called me. So I've been thinking about it, too."

"I know it doesn't have trees, but of course we could plant them."

"They take so long to grow."

"There is a forest of firs, pines, and oaks right across the road."

"It just isn't the same," she said. "But I'll try to be open, since it has been calling both of us."

The calling didn't cease; in fact, it got stronger. After a couple days, they had both decided it was their property beyond any doubt. Neither of them could get the property out of their minds. So Omaran started planning how they could purchase it. They didn't have any savings to pull from for the down payment, so he knew they would need to be creative with financing. First they needed to buy the lot, then get a construction loan. There was much to plan quickly if they were going to make it happen this year. Omaran knew that in this climate, he would need to start building as soon as possible. To make it through the winter, the house would need to be closed in by November. He loved to plan, and this was exciting.

Considering that they had no resources to speak of, it was amazing how quickly everything fell into place. Omaran gathered letters of recommendation from clients, subcontractors, suppliers, and the bank where he had been getting his construction loans. He also asked one of his brothers and two friends for small short-term loans. These phone calls were very difficult for Omaran to make, but their desire for the land was a powerful motivator, and he knew that once they got the construction loan, they could immediately pay back these personal loans. After scrounging together the down payment for the lot in this way, they took one more trip up to Mount Shasta to make an offer on it. While there, they found a small three-bedroom house in town to rent while they built. The purchase went through within a week, and a loan was secured shortly after that.

It all happened so fast that it seemed like a miracle.

Antera gave three weeks' notice to Byron, who promptly said, "You can't leave! We have to think of something else."

She had been thinking of a way to keep working for him after the move. It would be nice to have some income, and good for the company if she could wean from it slowly. "How about if I take the company computer with me, so I can work from there by phone, email, and mail? I may be able to drive down here once in a while."

"How about once a week?"

"I don't think so, it's too far. And we are going to build a house! Surely there will be plenty I can do from a distance."

"Perhaps so. Will you at least come down to train a new person when I find someone? Or several people to take your place?"

"I won't be able to come back for long. But I'll do what I can," she said.

"Okay, take the computer and all your files for now," he agreed.

As moving day approached, they rented the largest U-Haul truck available—26 feet long. The plan was to load it first, then Tan Man. Antera's small Toyota, Zippy, would be towed behind the big truck. Their street in Marin was narrow, winding through the forest, and their driveway had a steep downhill grade. The only way to get the enormous truck in was to back it all the way from the corner and then down the driveway. Antera stood in the street to hold traffic and guide Omaran in, a harrowing process that took about 15 minutes and many adjustments. He finally got the truck in their driveway with almost no room to spare from the street to the porch.

Now all they had to do was fill it. And fill it they did. Michael came over to help, and to lend his packing expertise. As Jeen had often put it, Michael had five planets in Virgo, and that made him super good at organization. They knew he would do a good job, and as Omaran watched him, he decided Virgos really do make the very best packers.

By the time they were done, they might have been able to squeeze in one more pillow, but that would have been all.

Tan Man looked like something the Okies of the 1930s would have been proud of, packed way over the top of the lumber rack, with everything tied down and ready to wobble down the road. Antera would be driving Tan Man while Omaran drove the U-Haul.

When the time came to leave, Omaran gunned the huge truck and started to pull out of the driveway. He went about ten feet . . . and came to an abrupt stop. He kept trying, but then he finally opened the door and got out, wondering what the trouble was. The truck was hitting bottom. The steep driveway had not been a problem going in, but now, with the truck fully loaded, it sat a lot lower and was stuck on the chassis where the driveway met the road. For a fleeting moment, he thought they would have to unpack, drive the truck out, park it somewhere far away, and carry things to it little by little. No! There had to be a way. They both silently called for help.

Suddenly, Omaran got an idea. He ran around the garage to where he had left some 4x4 and 6x6 planks of lumber. He hauled them up to the truck and put them just in front of the tires on the left side. After driving up onto the boards, he was able to slowly inch forward. It was working! The truck was halfway into the road, but so far, no one had tried to drive by. After progressing about six feet it dragged bottom again. Omaran hopped out and repositioned the stringers under the same two tires, driving up on them. It went another six feet and stopped again. He gave thanks for no traffic, knowing that he and Antera were getting much help from their guides and angels. Finally, on the fourth attempt, he was able to force the truck forward enough that it was completely in the road.

Whew! They both breathed a sigh of relief. Omaran put the wood back, they attached Zippy to the back of the U-Haul, and they were finally on their way!

It was the 30th of March and the temperatures were in the 70s, so as they made their way up Highway 5 they were dressed in T-shirts and shorts. As they were approaching Redding they could see some dark clouds further north, and then a big sign appeared on the highway with a flashing message that said, "Road closed up ahead due to snow—chains required."

These were the days before cell phones, so Antera and Omaran had no way to communicate with each other except by flashing their lights or pulling off the freeway. They stopped in Redding to discuss the situation. The mountain was still an hour away and a few thousand feet higher in elevation. Should they chance it and hope they could make it through the storm, or give up and find a place to stay the night in Redding?

After eating a quick dinner, they filled both trucks with gas and managed to find some warmer clothes. As they were heading out of the gas station, Omaran spotted a highway patrolman parked on the side of the road. He pulled right over and parked next to the patrol car, got out and asked the officer if he thought they could make it to Mount Shasta with both trucks. The cop hardly glanced at the Toyota, but he took a long look at the U-Haul, then at Omaran, then back at the U-Haul, then back at Omaran. He finally said, "I think so." It was not quite a ringing endorsement, but it was enough. Antera and Omaran decided to go for it. They agreed to drive slowly, and headed north.

Twenty miles up the road, the snow started . . . and they still had 40 miles to go . . . in the dark. It was light snow, but Antera had never driven in snow before, so she stuck to the tracks of the U-Haul and followed closely. Fortunately, Tan Man had good all-weather tires. Commercial trucks whizzed scarily by, passing them as if the drivers didn't care about the road conditions. On one sharp curve, they had to quickly dodge an overturned U-Haul trailer that was lying on its side, blocking the lane. The driver was outside frantically waving traffic around. There was no place to stop and help, so Omaran and Antera kept going.

Omaran was breathing heavily. He ignored the big rigs as they passed, concentrating on keeping his truck following the tracks of other cars through the snow, and trying to see as the snowflakes came straight at him. At the same time, he kept glancing in the side-view mirror to make sure Tan Man was close behind. As the snow got heavier, there was only one lane so the big rigs had to slow down. It was a relief that those large trucks could no longer pass.

On the last uphill grade, they were stopped by a traffic control station. Omaran explained that they were moving to Mount Shasta, their final destination. To their surprise, they were waved through, though neither of their trucks had chains or four-wheel drive.

The snow was about four inches deep on the highway, coming down quicker than it could be plowed, so they continued very slowly to the crest of the hill and got off at their exit. Omaran didn't dare try to stop. He went right through a stoplight, then around several corners without braking, so the truck would not slide. Finally, the 26-foot truck slid, spinning a bit, to a stop right in front of the rental house. Antera pulled into the driveway and got out, noticing that her legs were shaky. She hoped she would never need to drive in snow after dark again.

Omaran sat for a moment, giving thanks that they made it. That had been one stressful drive! Antera knocked on the driver's door of the U-Haul, wondering why Omaran wasn't getting out. He slowly opened it and all he had to say was, "Thank heavens I learned to drive in Michigan!"

Since they didn't know how to work the heater, Antera and Omaran unpacked their sleeping bags, curled up on the cold living room floor, and tried to sleep. They were home!

8

Walking Stick

"Isn't this exciting? We actually moved to Mount Shasta! Sometimes I can't quite believe it." Omaran was radiant, though tired from sorting and unpacking. Boxes in various states of emptiness were scattered here and there among piles of things yet to find a place.

"I know," agreed Antera. "Sometimes I wonder how we pulled this off. And we got some land!"

"I don't want to get so busy that we don't go hiking often—every day, if we can. The snow isn't too deep in most places."

Antera nodded. "I don't mind hiking in a few inches of snow. It's like marching, and it's good exercise."

She had never lived in a place where it snowed before, and this was a particularly long winter, still snowing in April, so they were getting a good taste of it. A California native, Antera had grown up near San Diego, then lived in the San Francisco Bay Area. The first week they were in Mount Shasta, she saw more snow in more forms than she had in her entire life before that. Who knew snow had so many different forms? She was delighted by it. When they asked their neighbor when it usually stops snowing in the spring, they were told, "It snows until one day it just stops."

Omaran knew that once the building started he may not have as much time to hike, so he wanted to get out on the mountain as much as possible while they waited for the construction loan. They were working on the house design together when they took breaks from settling into their rental house.

He said, "Want to go around 3:00?"

"Okay, I just want to finish getting the computer set up." Antera was the tech person of the house, for which Omaran was grateful. He had little use for computers.

That afternoon, they drove on a dirt road that someone had told Omaran about at the local laundromat. After parking, they followed their inner urgings and soon found themselves on a bear trail winding up a creek bed. The snow was only a few inches deep, but as they went higher, it got deeper. One unique thing they had discovered about hiking in snow is that animal tracks are very clearly seen. They had fun identifying the tracks they came across, and the fact that neither of them was very good at it didn't stop them. The only ones they were sure about were bear tracks.

Whenever they hiked, they also practiced sensing the energy of the places they went, and they listened to their guidance as they were lead to new places. So when they came to a fork in the creek bed, they paused, looked at each other, and agreed they were both strongly drawn to follow the right-hand fork, where a huge boulder almost seemed to be beckoning them.

Omaran commented, "I sure would like to see St. Germain in the flesh someday. I wonder if he ever appears to people physically anymore."

Suddenly, Antera felt pulled up to the ridge on their left, and pointed. "I want to go up there."

They climbed the steep bank, then stopped and stood there for a few moments. A tremendous surge of energy poured through them both. St. Germain was indeed there, but not in the flesh. His energy was very palpable, and this place they had been led to was amazingly powerful. They sat on a rock for a while to absorb the spinning energy. They had found a local vortex, or power spot.

Back at home that evening, St. Germain talked to them about it, saying that there were good reasons they were hiking in the area, besides for exercise and exploration. It was part of their service to the Order of Melchizedek to heal the land by clearing out adverse energies from certain spots, including vortexes and **ley lines** where energy was stuck and not flowing as well as needed. This work was in addition to the Light Field they had started building. St. Germain ended by saying he would guide them to the right places, and just to follow their inner directions like they did that day.

For some reason, even though they had always been good at this, just knowing it was expected of them put the pressure on! Nevertheless, a couple of days later they set out, determined to find another power spot. They parked the truck and headed north toward Black Butte on a dirt road. Their plan was to continually try to sense St. Germain as they hiked because he had said he would be ahead of them leading the way. So each time they came to a decision point, they stopped, closed their eyes, and attempted to sense which way he had gone. This turned out to be more difficult than it sounded.

"Which way are you getting?" Omaran would ask.

"No, first you tell me which way you get."

They were trying to feel with their hands as well as all their inner senses, but it just wasn't that easy. They felt that if they didn't get it right, they might miss a power spot or something important!

At one point, Omaran stopped and said, "What do you feel from that tree over there?"

Antera's hands were buzzing, so she knew that healing energy was flowing out of them. "Just that we need to do some healing in this area. Why, what are you feeling?"

"Oh, I guess nothing."

"No, tell me. Why are you doubting suddenly?"

"I don't want to make a mistake, and I think that is blocking me," he realized.

Suddenly she burst out laughing. "This is ridiculous! We've always been good at this."

He laughed also. They were so determined to get it right that they had lost their natural abilities to follow the right path. They decided to relax about it and go ahead as they always did, trusting that they would end up where they needed to be. That's when it got easier, and instead of stopping to check at each junction, they just went ahead, the two of them always choosing the same way.

At one point, the road bent sharply to the right and Antera had a strong feeling that they were not to go in that direction. The only other option was straight through thick manzanita, which was never a good option. She stopped.

Omaran said, "I feel we are close to something important. Follow me."

He found a way through the thick brush, and they didn't go far before emerging into a grove of old pines.

He stopped, and said, "This place has strong energy."

They sat down to experience it. Antera didn't feel anything. She couldn't even contact St. Germain, and she started to get frustrated. There was some kind of block keeping her from her normal connections! It didn't feel good at all.

Omaran said, "Let's sing a little song I wrote about balance and harmony."

He began singing, hoping she would join in, but she just didn't feel like singing. She didn't feel very harmonious! She wondered what was happening, as it was highly unusual that she couldn't make her connections. Also, she was feeling heavier and heavier, like a weight was descending over her. The strange thing was that Omaran felt fine and even liked the place.

Since Antera couldn't sense, she thought maybe they could get information using a pendulum instead. Omaran had one with him, so she asked a few questions:

"Is St. Germain here?" (Yes.)
"Will you answer some questions?" (Yes.)
"I can't feel you. Is that all right?" (No.)

That's when Antera knew she had to get away from there. There was something about that place that really disturbed her, and even as they walked away she felt very tired and heavy.

"Are you feeling like you did the day we climbed Black Butte before we found the trail?" Omaran asked.

"Yeah, I guess I am. Maybe it is the energy here. There is something very unsettling about it, but I don't know what yet."

"I'm actually not feeling one hundred percent either."

A short distance away, they rounded a bend and unexpectedly found themselves in the exact spot where the whole Black Butte adventure had begun. This was where Omaran had gotten very upset and acted irrationally, and Antera had gotten very tired! So they suspected that this was an area in need of big-time healing. Omaran led them back to the spot where they had been on that day last year. As they got closer, Antera started to feel nauseous, while Omaran felt more and more dizzy. They sat on two tree stumps and looked at each other.

"You get the feeling that something very bad happened here, like a murder or something?" Antera asked him.

"Yes, that thought crossed my mind, but I wasn't going to say it. Let's just bring in the Christ Light."

"Okay."

They closed their eyes. Two Native American spirits immediately appeared to Antera, a male and a female. She brushed them aside and concentrated on bringing in healing energy, but they kept coming back. So she looked at them more closely. They were a couple, dressed in buckskins, which made her think they were from the past, and they seemed very sad. Antera asked them if they wanted to say something.

The woman didn't say a word. The man identified himself as Walking Stick. He showed Antera pictures of a violent scene that had occurred in the past on that very spot. The place had been a sacred area to them and their tribe, but the others came and destroyed it deliberately, torturing them as they were tied to two trees. But that wasn't the worst of it. He knew the ways of the elements, and in his anger he had put a powerful curse on the area. That curse had trapped them there all this time. He still seemed angry but also tired, as if he was ready to relinquish, and maybe even forgive and move on.

Antera related all this to Omaran, and he immediately started sobbing. This was not something he did very often—in fact it was almost shocking to Antera. She stood up and realized suddenly that they had quite possibly been sitting on the offshoots of the very two trees that the couple had been tortured on!

She couldn't help herself and started laughing hysterically out loud. Out-of-control laughter, even though she could see that Omaran was very sad. It just seemed so funny that they would be drawn to that very spot. Through both laughter and tears, they released the emotional tension that had been stuck in the area.

When the laughter subsided, Antera told Walking Stick and his lady that she and Omaran would come back later and do a ceremony to cleanse the area. Antera and Omaran left, feeling a lot better than when they had arrived.

A few days later, equipped with sage, rattle, corn meal and crystals, Antera and Omaran made good on their promise. After hiking in a very wide circle around the place, they centered in and without any planning, Omaran walked around the perimeter of the area, rattling and chanting, while Antera saged the center around the trees and sang a song she made up on the spot.

Release the anger, release the fear,
Let go of sadness, it's all now clear.
Bring in the joy, bring in the love,
Holy Spirit shining from above.

When they had finished, they sat on the stumps again. Antera contacted Walking Stick, describing to Omaran what she was perceiving. Walking Stick and his lady were different, much clearer, and their faces were now visible. They looked very beautiful, much better than before.

"I am deeply touched by what you have done for us. Now we can let go of our chains. We are so grateful," Walking Stick said while they both bowed.

"You are very welcome." Antera replied.

"There is one greater than us here," Walking Stick then said, and he gestured.

Antera followed with her inner eyes. There was St. Germain, standing there in glorious bright light, wearing purple and white robes. The Native American pair got down on their knees in front of him, waiting for him to appraise the situation. He told them that all was forgiven, the karma had been dissolved and it was time to move on. They had served their sentence and could now put it all behind them.

The Master was very gracious, enveloping them in his Light, and as Antera watched, they shed their old garments, as if they were taking off cocoons, to emerge as bright Light-filled beings. It was quite a metamorphosis, and they became very beautiful.

St. Germain said, "The Light will now spread out over the surrounding area, and this will become a sacred place again, as it was before."

He then turned to Antera and Omaran and said, "Thank you, my blessed brother and sister of the order. You do a great service, a much-needed service that benefits many, not just these two souls. There are many more who have also been drawn in to this trap. You have released them. They'll now go to the Light. They turn to the Light.

"The most holy and blessed ones can now reach into this area. Even I could not penetrate into this place fully before, and now I can. Now the Light can shine, and all the Masters have access along this line of energy. We are very grateful for this service. We see your intent and your strong dedication, and we give you our most sincere gratitude. We honor you.

"Now that this spot is cleared and we can bring the Light in, it makes it that much easier for the Light to go to other areas. For clearing out this particular point makes other minor points in the area accessible, where the energy is slightly clogged. Now there will be a large flow of energy going through here, and the other areas might start to have difficulty with the increased flow. So there will be some adjustments to the energy and some clearing in adjacent places. This line goes directly into Black Butte and connects to the major channel there. This node point, or vortex, is now healed. It now allows the energy to flow back and forth through the butte and along this line of energy into the other areas.

"We hope you have enjoyed this assignment and will cooperate further in other service of this type of **land healing**. It seems to be a strong point with both of you, as I suggested before, and this has been your initial assignment. Of course, I did not know it would be quite so difficult the first time you came here. Perhaps it was a lot to take on. But you did what you could, and now it is complete."

Omaran was sobbing again. St. Germain asked gently, "Are you quite all right?"

"Yes, I'm getting better. Perhaps there is some stuff here that I resonate with also, and I've been releasing it myself, I guess. I'm not sure."

"You do tend to take it on at times. It is good to see it released from your system and your heart opened. Walking Stick and his mate are giving you a beam of energy to open your heart further, and this may be what you are feeling. It is their gratitude and their joy. They honor you. They see you as great beings."

Omaran was still crying. "We send them our love and our thanks. And wish them well."

St. Germain continued, speaking to everyone, "I thank you once again and ask that all of you give your gratitude to your I Am Presence. All of your undying love and gratitude. That is where it belongs, with the source of your being, with your God Self and with God. Let us turn to this now. Let us not forget who we are. Let us not turn to worship others. True worship is only for the greatest Master of them all. Let us give our thanks to the Source, the Mighty I Am, for arranging all of this that has happened, for calling in all the beings necessary to make this transformation happen, for providing us with this opportunity to serve, for giving us all of these blessings, all of this Light, all of this Divine Love, for each other and the Source.

"And let us call all of the other beings involved into this Light and invite them to call on their Higher Presence—all of the animal beings, devas and **elemental** beings, all of the tree spirits. We invite them all to be blessed, fully and completely blessed and purified, with the undying Light and love from Source. It is a magical spot, and we are so blessed to be here, we are so happy and joyful for this opportunity to see the effects of the most **Holy Spirit** at work."

St. Germain turned to Antera and Omaran and said, "I now leave you to get home before it is dark. Take with you this wonderful blessing."

Antera and Omaran opened their eyes and felt truly elevated beyond words. It had been a tremendous emotional release for Omaran, and he felt much lighter, though drained. As they walked back to the truck, they noticed a very unusual cloud formation. The cloud was bright pink and extended out from the mountain like a huge wing—long and straight with a pointed tip. It was not like any cloud they'd ever seen before. It looked like a huge bird sitting on the mountain, with its winds stretched out to them. They decided that such a beautiful display had to be the artwork of the Master St. Germain.

9

The Ancients

"This is a great workout!" Antera exclaimed. "I love walking uphill in the snow."

"Yes, it is, and even more so because of the elevation." Omaran was carrying the daypack, which he always insisted on, so the extra weight gave him even more exercise. He was glad his body was so strong.

It was a sunny day in late April, and though there was still snow on the ground, winter seemed to be winding down on the mountain. They had started out that day for their wedding site on the western slope, and had driven in on dirt roads as far as they could before parking and walking. It was the highest elevation they had hiked so far that year. However, along the way, they had been drawn off in another direction on a different road, so they abandoned their plans and went that way. They had grown accustomed to being flexible with where they went, so they could follow their guidance and find places they needed to be.

"Listen," Omaran said as he suddenly stopped.

"Did you hear something?"

"It's so quiet!" They both stood for a couple of minutes and took in the silence.

They were in a plantation, planted after a great fire decades ago, and the pines were about 15 feet tall, looking more and more like a natural forest. The whole area felt very magical. A lot of love and caring had gone into the planting of all those trees, and the successful result rivaled nature's forests in beauty and energy.

As they resumed climbing, the snow patches got thicker and more frequent until there was more snow than dirt. The road was very overgrown with bushes. Suddenly Antera heard a voice.

"Lords Rock."

She stopped and turned to her left to see who was talking, but there was no one there.

"Did you hear that?" she asked Omaran.

"What?"

She focused on where the voice had come from, and her attention went to a big boulder on the side of a hill across a drainage. "That rock outcrop just told me its name! Lloyd's Rock or something . . . no, Lords Rock!"

They changed direction and walked toward it. It seemed to be beckoning them very strongly. The bushes were much too thick to climb up to it, but they made their way through some deep snow to a spot as close as they could easily get. They sat on a pile of branches and gazed at the large, lumpy boulders. One big rock looked like a head and face.

Antera listened some more to see if it was going to say anything else or explain why they had been called there.

The same voice said, "The Ancient Ones want to connect with you."

"Who are they?" she asked.

"They are the ones who have been here holding the energy of this place for many millennia, since Lemurian times."

Antera relayed what she was hearing to Omaran, and they were both very interested. They hoped to meet these Ancient Ones.

The voice continued, "This is a portal, an entry point into the caverns where the Ancients live. Few enter these days. They wanted to make contact with the two of you."

Antera then was shown the etheric form of the portal, which was a crystalline pyramid surrounding the physical rock, with one side red, one green, and the other two yellow. It was dazzlingly bright.

"This is what the portal looks like. They want you to be able to recognize it."

Antera described the portal to Omaran. "I'm getting a sense that they are a little tired of their post and are hoping to get some help. They sensed us coming and were hoping we could help them—perhaps by bringing fresh energy into the project and their work."

Slowly, some beings began to emerge out of the pyramid-rock. They weren't physical but were in their etheric bodies, vibrating just slightly faster than the physical. Hesitantly, they showed themselves to Antera. They were quite tall and stately. Antera said nothing to the beings, but she described what was happening to Omaran. He was able to sense them too. It seemed the Ancient Ones were checking Antera and Omaran out.

"They are starting to trust us now, seeing that we are listening and we are open. They live inside the ridge," said Antera.

The Ancients said, "This is our place. This is our home. We invited you here. We see the work that you do, we sense your purity of heart, we sense your connections with the Order of Melchizedek and with the Christ energy, and we also want to have a connection with you. We are also part of the ancient mystical Melchizedek Order but we have our own area, and we are connected to you by the ancient continent of Lemuria. That is why we have the connection now. The work that we do, you used to do on that ancient land. Whereas you departed, we stayed and continued the work as best we could throughout all the changes, throughout all the turbulence.

"We had to go into the **higher dimensions** and into the land, the caverns, because it was not suitable for us on the surface any more, in the physical dimension. But we do have physical aspects, we are not entirely in the fourth dimension. There are parts of us that show up in the physical, just as this rock shows up as a rock and in the etheric plane it has the other pyramidal shape. So we have a presence in the physical as well as in the etheric form."

Antera said, "Thank you for showing yourselves to us. I don't think we can make it up there to the rock. It is too steep and thick with manzanita."

"One day you will. There is an easier way." The being pointed toward the east. "But it is enough for now to make this connection and know that we have invited you."

Omaran said, "I'd like to thank you for honoring us with this invitation. I was just looking right now to see if I could figure a way up. I don't know if we can make it, but we will. We both know we were land healers in Lemuria. It is so absolutely wonderful to be back and making these ties and connections. We are open and ready to do anything we can to help. Thank you so much for making your presence known to us. We look forward to our association."

Antera commented, "They are saying we aren't supposed to tell anyone where this is. Lords Rock is a fortress, entirely protected because it is so hard to get to. In fact, there is something special about the shape of this whole hill. Maybe we'll have to look at it on a map. We can't see all of it from here.

"They are feeling our energy and thanking us for our attention and our infusion of energy to them. This doesn't happen very often . . . . Now St. Germain is appearing. He says that they've said all they want to say, and they are waiting for us to release them . . . or dismiss them, or something."

Omaran made a formal gesture. "Thank you for coming and making your presence known to us. We send you Divine blessings."

"They are going back in," said Antera. "They don't like to be out for long. Germain is saying that he likes to stand up on that rock! Ha ha! It is one of our power points."

St. Germain said, "Pay attention to where you are sitting right now. Ground this energy straight down. You are sitting on a line of energy. This line of energy extends all the way down to your property. So simply note the feeling of this, so you may more easily find it when you get there."

He left, and the adventure was over. But Antera and Omaran both secretly hoped that when they did make it to the rock, they would find a real cave entrance there.

As they started to leave, a red-tailed hawk appeared and flew in circles around Lords Rock as if to accentuate the importance of it. As always, they suspected St. Germain's influence in this display and gave thanks before leaving.

10

Wesak

The **Wesak** Festival, a yearly gathering near the mountain that in 1999 was drawing thousands of spiritual seekers, was coming up. Antera and Omaran knew they wouldn't be attending this event, but they weren't sure exactly what they would do that weekend. Given that the energetic impact on the area was very large, they knew there would be work to do in helping the area integrate the generated energy, but how they would do that had not yet been given. They accepted that often they got very little lead time in their service requests, and that kept them interested and totally in the flow of the moment.

It turned out that on Friday, the first day of the event, they were drawn to a smaller, higher-elevation part of the ridge where Lords Rock was located. They headed in that direction. They had been to this ridge before, and as they hiked, they talked about the little adventure they had last time. On that walk, they had seen some huge bear tracks. They had seen many bear tracks on their hikes, but this bear had the largest feet, and presumably the largest body, they had ever seen. Still, they had continued on until all of a sudden, both had gotten the message to stop and turn around fast. It was as if the bear had been warning them to get out of his territory, or else. They had both stopped and looked at each other wide-eyed, then turned around quickly, heeding the warning. Checking over their shoulders many times, they had walked very fast, expecting the giant bear to be following them, but they had made it away safely. Though the bear was probably long gone, this time they avoided that place just in case, taking a longer route. The small ridge was a fairly easy climb to a long, thin pile of rocks on the top. The energy felt good up there, and they sat for a while.

Antera told Omaran, "I think this place is named Crescent. It keeps telling me that, but I don't know why it would be called that."

From where they were, it looked like a linear feature, not shaped in any way like a crescent or arc, but they accepted it and started calling it Crescent Ridge. After looking at it from other angles later, they saw that it actually did have a curve.

The place was special to Antera because it was there, years before, that she had learned about the power of sunsets—the real power. On that trip, they had arrived there just before sunset and were sitting facing west. The plants and trees all around them were focused on the human newcomers, as usual, and she could feel the life-force energy unselfishly being given to the two of them. As the sun got lower toward the distant ridge, she literally felt all the plants and trees around her suddenly withdraw their energy from her and turn their attention to the sun to watch it set. It was as if it was a magical and meditative time for them, and not to be missed. One moment the plants were completely focused on the people, and the next they were all facing the sun, taking a time-out and ignoring everything else. It was a profound experience for Antera, and one she never forgot. Since then, whenever she was out at that special time when the sun goes down, she stopped with the plants to say goodbye to the sun and give thanks for the day.

On this visit, it was too early to see the sunset. They sat for a while, and that was when she got the message of what else they were being asked to do that weekend. As she often did with service requests that sounded difficult, at first she tried to ignore it as if she hadn't heard. It was persistent, however, so then she toyed with the idea of not telling Omaran, thereby avoiding it because she couldn't do it alone. But as usual, she eventually gave in.

"Well," she sighed, "I know what we are supposed to do, but it's not easy."

"Okay, what?"

"Today Crescent Ridge, tomorrow Lords Rock, and Sunday . . . Black Butte. We are supposed to anchor in and stabilize the energy being generated by the Wesak event into these three power spots."

"It's a little early for the butte. Still lots of snow up there. I was hoping to wait another month at least before that hike." He scrutinized the butte from the ridge's vantage point for a few minutes, looking at the north side, which was covered with large snow banks that were probably obscuring the trail. "I think we can do it! And if that is what has to be done, we will!"

Ever the dedicated spirits, they thus accepted the mission from the order.

After gathering the energy from the Wesak group, which was very powerful and charged, and anchoring it satisfactorily through their systems deep into the rocks of Crescent Ridge, they hiked over to a place where they knew of a **medicine wheel**, a stone circle where local people did ceremonies. They had been there many times and knew where it was even though it was under snow. Finding a bare rock to sit on, they closed their eyes and immediately felt a big rush of energy.

"Did you feel that?" Antera asked.

"It felt like the lights just turned on."

They didn't know what it was but assumed it was associated with what the Wesak group was doing. It felt good, so they sent it out to the surrounding area. Their hands were buzzing with projected energy. Before leaving, they walked around the circle and stood in the middle, singing and chanting.

As they were driving down the highway back to town, they suddenly had the urge to stop at the entrance road to the property they were in the process of purchasing. The very moment they stopped and faced east, the moon came up over the mountain. It was mesmerizing. This was the Wesak moon, and the most powerful transmission either of them had ever experienced through Luna. Its presence was overwhelming, and it moved so quickly that in what seemed like only a couple of minutes, it had risen completely and was distancing itself from the horizon. They looked at each other in awe and concluded that this had been a special blessing for the work they were doing.

The energy was way too charged up for sleep that night. Their bodies were restless and buzzing as they lay awake and tried to integrate the energy. Short on sleep, they started for Lords Rock the next day, which for some reason they thought would be a short hike. Rather than go up the steep face of the hill, they decided to go around the back and contour in. The walk around the back was easy, and they stopped to refresh themselves at a power point they had found earlier. Then they searched for a place to go through the manzanita that covered the hill.

They had to guess where the rock would be on the other side of the hill because they couldn't see it. The progress was extremely slow. Anyone who has not tried to go through thick manzanita on a rocky slope would not understand the difficulty. It was very hard for Antera and Omaran to find a place to put their boots with each step. Plus, among the live plants were dead branches that did not give at all. One wrong step or lost balance on the slope, and those sharp branches were deadly . . . but they did not think about that. They asked for protection and had faith that they got it. Omaran led the way, breaking down branches and trying to make it easier for Antera, whose legs were shorter than his. They trudged toward where they thought Lords Rock would be.

More than an hour and many bruises and scrapes later, Antera mentioned that she thought they were contouring in too high on the hill because she felt the rock calling from lower down the slope. A bit farther, and Omaran said, "Uh-oh!"

"What?"

"You were right. I think that is it way down there!" He pointed to an outcrop a few hundred feet further down. That may not sound like a great distance, but right then it represented an arduous and painful trek and was very disappointing news after they had come so far.

Turning back without reaching the goal was not an option, so a course change was made toward the outcrop below them . . . in hopes that it was Lords Rock. They wished they had paid more attention to its position on the hill when they had viewed it from the other side. Now they had to go on intuition, as they continued the arduous trek. At last they arrived and, to their relief, it was the rock outcrop they had been seeking. However, it had taken so long to get there that the sun was very low in the west and they knew they couldn't stay long.

First was a climb to the top of the boulders to take in the view. The energy was so strong that they both felt dizzy and had to use their hands to steady themselves instead of walking upright. They sat and worked on calling in the Wesak energy to anchor it. The energy of this place, combined with the event energy, was so powerful that it took all of Antera's attention just to experience and balance it, so she had to trust that they were doing what was needed. It was like being in a giant vortex of swirling energy, trying to maintain the balance and stability in the very center without being swept off in the currents.

When they had reached their limits, they climbed down and explored a bit around the rocks. There was a small cave, perfect for sitting in, and it felt like they were inside a womb. They had to give up on the slim hope of finding a physical entrance into the caverns of the Ancient Ones, for that was not to be on this trip. But they were not disappointed with the huge energy of the place.

They remained in an altered state when they decided to take a different way back, slowly making their way down the hill instead of climbing back up. It felt as if they were not of this world entirely. Antera could see energy moving through everything, and the world did not seem as solid. That made the descent even more challenging because the branches didn't seem as solid, but they still hurt as if they were! However, she also found that navigating the flow of energy as she was going, rather than navigating the physical branches, actually made it go easier. Halfway down, she looked up at Lords Rock, silhouetted against the sky. There was a gorgeous pink glow shooting out of its top, which matched the color of the sunset in the west.

After another restless night, as their bodies were challenged to integrate all the energy they were taking in, on Sunday they started out early for Black Butte. It was cloudy and cold, and the butte wasn't even visible as they approached. Omaran had gotten strong guidance to bring a small shovel and pick in case there were steep snow banks to cross, since they didn't have ice axes. Antera resisted carrying either because their wooden handles made them very heavy.

"You need to carry this. I heard a voice say, 'Antera will carry the pick,'" Omaran said.

She couldn't argue with that and held the pick in one hand while he carried the shovel.

The roads to the trailhead had been marked a bit better since their fateful climb the previous fall, and they found the small parking area easily. It rained off and on as they made their way up the steady gradient of the trail. The rain turned to snow and the trail turned to snow at about the same place. In fact, the trail disappeared. Fortunately, a man had hiked it a day or two earlier, and his large prints in the snow led the way. He obviously knew where the trail went, and they blessed him for that, and for giving them confidence that it was doable.

As they got to higher elevations, the snow banks got steeper and steeper, and Omaran used the shovel to dig out each step as they traversed them. If they slipped, it would not be a pleasant landing on the rocks below. But as long as they were focused upward in the climb, and not looking down, they felt safe.

They were being very careful, but on the last traverse Antera felt one of her feet start sliding. Then it got faster and the other one gave way. She shouted, "Whoa!" and rammed the pick into the snow as hard as she could, expecting it to stop her slide immediately, but it didn't. It took another six feet before it took hold and she stopped sliding . . . right before the slope got much steeper and she may have been a goner. As she hung there holding onto the pick, Antera was able to kick a foot-hold into the snow. Omaran used his shovel to quickly dig out steps down to her, grabbing onto her firmly when he reached her and not letting her go until they had made it up to the trail.

Even though the sliding incident was frightening for Antera, she recovered quickly. She had learned what the pick was for, and it actually gave her confidence that if it happened again, she'd do the right thing. Wow, was she glad Omaran had received that message about her carrying the pick! However, it affected Omaran more deeply. He was truly shaken, and after that became more protective of her whenever they hiked on steep slopes.

There was no place to stop, so they continued to the top, reinforced the Light Field they had created up there, and channeled in the Wesak energies. It was very cold, and even though they had come well prepared with lots of clothes, they couldn't stay long. There was no view to look at, only thick clouds.

It turned out that going down those same snow banks was much scarier because they were looking down instead of up and could easily see what was below. Antera shoved the pick in with each step, and Omaran used the shovel as a stabilizer. When they crossed the bank where she had slipped, Omaran had to stop for a moment. He wondered whether he could go on. He had to heal the energy of fright he had left in that spot. Slower this time, they crossed, breathed a sigh of relief, and the rest of the way down was easier.

As they hiked they diffused the tension by making light of the experience. Antera said, "I don't think anyone else would do this kind of land-healing service, do you?"

"No wonder we were asked. Maybe we are the only ones who would."

"Think about all those other people, sitting comfortable and warm, meditating together at the event. Sounds kind of inviting right now, doesn't it?" she asked.

"Well, we've been there, done that. Now is the time for us to do active service and that's what we are getting."

"I wouldn't want it any other way."

It took about a week to fully recover from the Black Butte climb and the whole weekend. It had taken a lot more out of them than they realized because of the intensity of the focus needed and the stress in their bodies. Plus, they had very little sleep all weekend.

They did get feedback from St. Germain after they had rested.

He said, "I would like to speak in particular about the work that you did and the three core power spots that you visited. As you know, there are many power spots all around the mountain. This is because

Mount Shasta is one huge vortex, one huge power spot, and all around are these eddies and currents and streams of energy flowing out and interacting with each other. You have been working specifically with one very large flow of energy from the main mountain to Black Butte, and through a number of power spots along the way. There is a very large column of energy flowing this way. You can determine how far out it goes, its breadth and frequencies, for it contains many different frequencies, or colors.

"Crescent Ridge is not a vortex. It is a place where there is, however, entry into and out of this main energy line. And you will find that there are these kinds of energy power points at various places along the line, and each one has specific frequencies. Some of them are the spiraling energies of vortexes, in or out or oscillating between the two, and some are simply places where the power is so balanced that it is stable. It does not go in or out, it simply is a place of great power of particular frequencies. Such is Crescent Ridge.

"Lords Rock, you met and now experienced physically. By the way, the top of that hill is also very powerful, but Lords Rock is an entry point of the Ancient Ones. The cosmic energy flows in there and feeds the energy flow along the ridge. And you happened to sit right on the spot, as usual! You may find that by this exposure you will be having some openings in the head energy centers because this is the area that is affected by that spot.

"Then, of course, there is the butte, on which you persevered in your very dedicated way, to reach the top. You know how powerful that spot is and the significance of it. Inside is a base for the Order of Melchizedek, and they are very grateful for your work. You have cleared a tremendous amount of energy all around the base and up toward the top, and you have anchored in new frequencies for the planet. These frequencies of the intention and dedication for the transformation of the planet have given the order new life and hope.

"By acting as a conduit for the energies in these spots, you have really done your job! You anchored in that energy so it can now go out to the other power spots on the planet! You anchored it in where it counts the most.

"Are there questions about this?"

"Thank you," Omaran said. "This is very interesting, and makes us feel good. Is it important for us to know the difference between whether a spot is more a vortex or a power spot?"

"You will be able to feel if there is spiraling energy, and if you cannot directly feel it, you can sense it with your pendulum. Or you can ask. The importance is in their function. They are all important spots, but they each have a different function, a different frequency and a different use. This is what you are mapping out. You will find that some spiral in and some spiral out, and some are merely tremendous generators of energy that tend to open up your energy centers when you sit there. Some act to take out of your energy field that which is no longer needed, and some you will need to stabilize.

"The very nature of these kinds of energy points is that they are not stable over long periods of time. They shift and they change, depending on the energy surrounding them, depending on if there are any people around, depending on how the energy is shifting on the entire planet. Sometimes they change course just like a river or stream. You can go and stabilize them by being there and having that as your intention. The mere fact that you are there, even if you have no intention at all, helps to stabilize the energy because you are grounding rods. You ground the cosmic energies into the planet. This is a major gift that you two offer."

Omaran said, "Sometimes we just go into an area and hike but don't find any power spots. Is this still good for the land and stabilizing it in some way?"

"Oh, yes indeed! You know that. Wherever you walk, you help to stabilize things. You are very masterful at this. Surely you know that by now!"

"I'm getting closer to believing it."

"You are both very good at bridging these energies, and you are very well grounded, which is not usual among humans. So yes, wherever you go, you tend to stabilize the land, and if you are conscious of what you are doing, it makes it even more powerful."

St. Germain went on to discuss more details about finishing up the Light Field they had started the previous fall, adding two more points when they could during the coming summer. But he cautioned them not to rush. The house project was very important.

"You are creating a house dedicated to the I Am Presence! It will be a sacred project, filled with Light, and consciously built so you can live there in harmony as a dedication to the God-Force. This is the image that is envisioned.

"Know that if you hold this vision, everything will fall completely into place. It is only if you waver in your faith or in your vision that difficulties come up, or delays, or inefficiencies. We are fully aware that you need to complete this in a record time, and at the same time do things in a conscious and loving manner, and that requires complete attunement and being in the present moment with the God-Force. This may seem to take longer, but you will find that your work is much more efficient and goes much quicker than you thought possible when you remain conscious and when you require that anyone who works on it also does the same. Do not be afraid to ask this of anyone who works on it, about the prayerful way of working, with pure intent. If they respond positively, they will learn tremendous lessons through this work. If they cannot respond in a positive way, then they will not work on the house. Is this agreeable?"

"Yes, yes certainly."

"Know that it is so, and it will be so."

Omaran truly wanted to work this way, in theory. But actually putting it into daily practice in construction was another matter. He did have some doubts.

11

Manzanita

It was fun to design their own house, incorporating both the passive-solar design and sacred geometry. They had decided on a golden-mean rectangle as the basic shape, and it felt very harmonious. Antera drew the layout and Omaran drew the detailed plans from that, submitting them to the county to get all the needed permits and complete the construction loan.

Now for clearing the land. What a job that would be! Omaran found a local man named John who had a backhoe, and hired him to clear the manzanita. He was a burly man who lived close by, so he could drive the machine right to their house. The snow had stopped for the season.

The plan was to do all the work while staying tuned to Divine guidance and the spirit of the land. It sounded so easy. Antera and Omaran agreed that if anyone who was working there ever got out of sorts or started polluting the area with impure thoughts and emotions (including themselves), that person would have to leave until they were better. This would be a very different process than Omaran was used to in his long career as a builder, working with guys who definitely weren't in a spiritual frame of mind. He wasn't sure it was even possible.

Before they cleared the land, Antera talked with the Manzanita Deva, the nature spirit in charge of the manzanita bushes. They knew that if they worked with the nature spirits, instead of ignoring them or working against them, the nature spirits would help make it go more smoothly. It paid to keep them happy on the property, especially when they were about to do some destruction such as was necessary here. Humans had been very inconsiderate of nature spirits over the last few thousand years, at least, and there was a general mistrust that took effort to overcome. Most people didn't even think they were real!

Antera had spoken with many of them and knew they were real, just vibrating at a slightly higher rate than humans. She found the Manzanita Deva to be very accessible for advice, and she and Omaran tried to do as the deva suggested. They made a formal announcement to all the local animals and plants about what they were going to do and gave them a mental picture of the vision. The deva asked that they assign some areas to be wild and uncut, a perimeter around the property plus one special spot in the interior. They were not to be touched.

Not everyone Omaran talked with or hired understood why he was doing things the way he was . . . trying to minimize the intrusiveness of the construction process. Omaran explained to John, "We want you to carefully pull up the manzanita bushes one by one, and shake the dirt off the roots before piling them up."

John had done plenty of manzanita clearing. He frowned. "Now let me get this straight. You want me to pull each plant up and shake it? Why? Do you know that will take twice as long?"

Omaran didn't dare say the Manzanita Deva had requested it. They were new to this town, after all. "Yes, I know it will take longer. We just want to preserve what little soil there is." The brute force method of digging and scraping forward was out of the question.

John shrugged and replied, "All right then, it's your dime. I charge hourly."

It took over two weeks to get the clearing done, but it went very smoothly. John thought Omaran was a bit eccentric in his methods, but they joked about it, and John did a good job, piling the manzanita neatly in rows after shaking the dirt off. Antera and Omaran had measured in from the edges and tied rags so John would know where to stop. He only worked a few hours a day, at a comfortable pace. John was the perfect person for the job. Definitely slower than Omaran was used to, but it was all right, because now he could see that it would take a while to cut up and sort the huge piles of brush.

As areas became exposed and walkable, Antera and Omaran were able to dowse for ley lines and other energy features on the property, and lay out the exact position of the house as well as the pyramid they planned to build when the house was done.

Years ago, when the guardian of the future pyramid had come to Antera, it had been exciting to think about it, but at that time they hadn't the funds or space to build a significant structure. Omaran had done some research and bought plans from some pyramid builders in Michigan, however, so they wanted to include space for it in the overall plan of their new property.

As they walked around, they were excited to find and map out two big ley lines—pathways of energy flow just under the surface of the land. Antera had learned to dowse for these when she was a teenager, and Omaran found he was good at it also. They knew that different ley lines have different frequencies, which could be described as colors, and the two they found were blue and violet. St. Germain had taught them more about these flows of energy, and warned them to be careful with the location of the house so it avoided crossing them. When structures were built across these energy flows, it could slow or block them, thereby disturbing the energy of the entire area.

While all this was going on, Antera was working part-time in their home office for the publisher, managing to get done a large percentage of the work she had been doing before the move. Omaran was putting out his feelers for some part-time work, so he could continue on the house. He had added enough onto the construction loan to pay himself some, and that would help, but he needed to work, also.

Spirit brought that to him easily. He was at the headwaters of the Sacramento River filling his six-gallon water bottles at the gushing spring. It was such great drinking water, that people came from other places to fill their bottles, just as Antera and Omaran had done before moving there. A car pulled up with Virginia license plates. A man and a woman got out with their bottles.

Omaran joked, "I know it's good, but that seems like a really long way to go for water."

They all laughed and introduced themselves. The couple were a brother and sister, called Vince and Mariah, who had just recently moved to Mount Shasta. Mariah was very much into the spiritual life and was here because she was so drawn to the energy of the mountain. Vince admitted that he was a newly-awakened beginner in spiritual matters, but he had such trust in his sister that he had opened up very quickly with her help and established a strong connection with his own higher guidance. Omaran liked them both immediately and wanted them to meet Antera. He felt a special connection to Vince, who had just left his job as lighting director at a theater in Minneapolis.

It turned out that Vince and Mariah had just bought a large house that needed remodeling, and they were delighted when they asked Omaran to take the job and he accepted. Antera and Omaran marveled once again at how Spirit provided for them, and how it worked out well for everyone!

12

Surrender

One evening in early May, Metatron spoke to them for the first time since they had moved. Often when Antera sat to talk with the Masters she let them decide who would speak, depending on what questions she and Omaran wanted to ask or on what the Masters wanted to tell them, rather than trying to call in a particular someone.

This time, Archangel Metatron was present, and apparently also interested in the building project. He had been one of their main teachers about sacred geometry and especially the importance of the pyramid shape.

Metatron said, "This is my first contact with you for quite a while. And I find it so much easier to contact you here compared to other places you have been. I come in regard to the sacred geometry and the pyramid questions that have arisen, as well as your project with the sacred land and building.

"I am also being called to help power up and add my energies to this project and to the pyramid that you will be building. The pyramid is the most sacred shape . . . a building block of this universe. It is to be treated with utmost care and sacredness. The intent must be pure. For each pyramid carries a life force of its own and should be treated as such!

"I have seen the plans for the pyramid that you shall be building, and I am very excited about it. Before you actually do the building it is proper sacred practice to place a corner stone that anchors the energy and grounds it at one of the corners before the building begins. The proper placement of this corner stone will be of great importance."

Omaran said, "Do we need the corner stone for our house as well as the pyramid?"

"Yes. Indeed I am already selecting a stone for you and you will be coming across it in your travels. It is about the size of . . . a soccer ball. I'm trying to think of something that you can relate to. It will call out to you.

"It is proper practice to do a special ceremony around the corner stone in the process of placing it, to put the intent into it. It is an ancient practice to ground and place the first stone of the building in ceremony before beginning the rest of it, to completely align the building and its position physically and in other realms. Since it is already being built in the other realms, it is up to you to find that exact position that aligns it with what is already being built. That will be done with the corner stone because it will be very charged up, centering it in such a way that it is aligned fully. If it is not aligned fully, it will take much longer to build and there will be problems."

"I have a sense now that the stones will be in the northeast corner of each structure," said Omaran thoughtfully.

"That is correct."

When they talked about this after the immense presence of the archangel had receded, it was intriguing to think that the house was already being built in the etheric realm, and their job was to duplicate it in the physical. This was a new concept.

"I'm trying not to feel pressure about finding the exact spot for the corner stone, not to mention finding the actual stone Metatron has chosen," Omaran confessed.

"Stones always call out to us. And I don't think it will be hard, if we do it together," Antera said. "We know where the ley lines are, and generally where to place the house."

"Yes, but the exact place . . . ."

"Let's go one step at a time. All those piles of manzanita need cutting up. Is burning still allowed by the fire department this month?"

"Yes, I'll start that as soon as I have a good pile of brush."

He was handling huge piles of manzanita, saving and cutting the parts that were burnable in their woodstove, sorting out and piling up the burls that were too large for the stove, and making burn piles for the small branches. These would have to be burned before the dry heat of summer, when a burn ban would be in effect. It was almost overwhelming, and a much bigger job than he had imagined, but they wanted to use as much of the wood from their manzanita as possible, rather than just burning everything, as most people did. That seemed very disrespectful, as well as wasteful. However, he could now see that it may be years before it all got sorted, so he only concentrated on the immediate area where the house would be built.

Fortunately, by talking to people in town, he found a hard-working man to hire, and it went faster with the two of them. Antera also helped when she could. The weather in May was very pleasant, but as they worked through June and it warmed up, they both noticed that they didn't have quite the stamina as usual, though they were both energetic.

"Have you noticed the intense yang energy on the land?" Antera asked him as they were cutting wood. She was holding the branches as he cut them with a chain saw. "I think it is the most I've ever felt. We need more yin here—more gentle, nurturing energies."

"Maybe after we get water and plants going, it will help," Omaran said.

"I hope so. This energy seems so raw and difficult to take in my body."

"You think that is why we get tired more easily? I certainly feel the rawness you are talking about," Omaran replied. "In fact, I've never felt this kind of raw energy anywhere. I wonder how long it's going to take to integrate this. As I look up at the mountain it's almost like I can feel the energy just sliding down the slopes, heading right for here." He looked up, then added, "I think the intense sun is also part of it. It seems like it is so much more radiation because of the elevation and thinner atmosphere."

He didn't say it, but he wondered if the intense energy of the land was part of the reason he was having trouble with his mind going into what Antera had years ago called tape loops. It was hard to concentrate sometimes and keep his mind in the present moment with positive thoughts. And it seemed to happen the quickest when he was doing mundane tasks that really didn't require any thinking. When he finally caught his mind going places he didn't want it to, which often lead to anger at some situation, he would then start chanting or doing affirmations to bring it around. He sure wished he could get control sooner, though, before he got angry. But, he thought, at least he was better than a few years ago.

Antera dragged over the next long branch of manzanita, placing it on the cutting stand. "Yes. I can't imagine how intense it will be later in the summer!"

Omaran cut the branch up, and as she removed and stacked the pieces he said, "The well dowser is coming tomorrow, let's hope he is good so we can get a good well in."

"Water would be so good!"

They were both good dowsers, but had never actually dowsed for water, so when the well driller had said his father was a water dowser, they had decided to get another opinion. They had both dowsed a map of the property, and had an idea of where they preferred the well to be, but lack of confidence in their skills and the large cost of drilling made a professional assessment more desirable.

When the older man came with his forked stick the next day, he seemed very sure of himself, walking along the very roughly-cleared ground until he felt his stick dip. "Yep, this looks like a good place to drill. But I'll continue checking," he said.

After more walking in the soft, dry dirt made from volcanic ash, the water dowser came to his best recommendation and they marked the spot. It would be a couple of weeks before drilling could happen.

Though the well site was not exactly where they had both assessed, it was close enough to give them more confidence in dowsing for the exact house position. They went ahead with that and marked the northeast corner of the house.

Power and phone lines came next. To avoid more unsightly wires in the air, they decided to bury them. The trench was 300 feet along one edge of the property, and 3-4 feet deep. John came over with a backhoe and dug it quickly, and Antera helped Omaran lay out the pipes. She had an uneasy feeling when John then replaced the dirt and filled in the hole. It seemed that, since they still needed to pull the power and phone lines through the pipes, it would be safer to do that before they were buried, just in case there were problems.

But John assured them, saying, "I've done this almost 100 times. It is really easy, you'll see."

The next day they followed John's instructions and attached an industrial vacuum to one end of the pipe, and put a string tied to a plastic bag on the other end, in hopes that the vacuum would pull it through. But this is when obstacles started. First, the suction wasn't very good and the bag went through very slowly. Then the vacuum died completely. They had to call it a day. The next evening they went out again, with a better vacuum Omaran had borrowed. At last, the first string was pulled through the phone conduit, and they were able to tie a rope to it and pull that through also.

But the bag and string would not go through the other pipe, for electricity. After trying twice, each time unsuccessful and requiring them to wind up 500 feet of string onto a spool again, they stopped and decided to really concentrate their will and visualize the bag going through. When this didn't work either, they were surprised.

"There must be a really good reason that this isn't working, if we can't change it using the force of both our wills!" Antera declared to Omaran.

"Do you think that maybe we aren't supposed to be on the grid at all?" Omaran said as he sat on the soft dirt, tired and defeated.

They had planned to make most of their own power with wind and sun, but thought it best to still be hooked up to the utility grid in case more was needed now and then. "That thought occurred to me, but we've already come this far and spent so much."

He shrugged. "Well, at least I'm not letting it get me down, which is a big step for me. Normally I would be very upset, but this time I am seeing that there must be a bigger picture, a higher reason we don't know about."

"I'll see if the Angel of the Land has anything to say when we get home." This beautiful deva had been assigned to oversee the property, shortly after they had started the project.

Clearly, she did have something to say. Later that evening after dinner, Antera contacted her.

"I wasn't told!" the deva immediately said.

"You weren't told what?" Antera asked.

"About the digging! I must be warned before any digging! This is sacred ground and it must not be broken in any way without my knowing. I must prepare, and you need to do a blessing."

"Is that why we are having problems?"

"Yes. Not only did you cut into the Earth, but you went right through what you assured us was a wild area that would remain untouched."

She was talking about the part of the trench that had been cut through a manzanita area, which they had designated as wild so the nature spirits knew they wouldn't be disturbed there.

"We are sorry," said Antera. "What can we do now to change the energy of the project?"

"You can bless and heal where you have dug just like you heal other areas that are scarred. Walk over it and let healing forces come out your hands. Do a blessing to soothe the nature spirits. And from now on, be sure I am told!"

When Antera told Omaran what the deva had said, he confirmed that he had not warned the land about the trenching. "I just totally forgot to tell her," he said. They were tired, and decided to do some healing the next day.

After planning a new approach, they came back the following day to try again. They burned sage, said a blessing, reassured the nature spirits, and walked the length of the covered trench. But alas, again and again, they were still unsuccessful at getting the string through. That was when Omaran lost it. His anger started coming out in the way he was acting and talking to Antera. She understood his frustration, but he was handling it very poorly. She asked him to take a few minutes to sit and center himself, but he refused.

"You are violating our agreement to not desecrate the land by negative energy, so get ahold of yourself or leave as we agreed!" she demanded.

"No, I won't leave. There is too much to do and we've wasted days on this stupid power line!"

"Okay then, I'm leaving. I won't have any part of this." And she left, walking the two miles back to their house in town.

As she walked along the highway, she thought about Omaran, and how he could take an agreement like this so lightly. Didn't he understand what it meant to keep an area sacred? If he could not control his anger this early in the building process, or at least leave when he couldn't control it, what kind of energy would he put into their house? Did he not believe in what they were doing here? Why didn't he have faith, after all they had been through?

She got home and sat alone to meditate and settle herself. Asking her guidance for help, she hoped they would tell her how to best deal with Omaran's anger.

They said, "This is an important test for him, and he needs to go through it. He will build more faith in the process. In the meantime, we advise you to refrain from channeling any messages for him, until he has built his faith to a deeper level."

When he got home, much later, he didn't want to talk. But she insisted.

"We are doing this project together, and we have to be on the same page with this," she said.

"I know that. I'm just so frustrated with the power line. We can't build without power."

"So, are you going to get angry and out of control over every little problem that comes up? Surely you realize that this poisons the project! There are always going to be challenges in building, you should know that!"

She told him what the Masters had said, and the possibility of not having communications from them hit hard. Apologizing, he said he felt awful, and vowed to do better from now on, so they dropped it.

As it turned out, he would soon have more lessons in faith. They were getting ready for a road trip to Los Angeles. The first night on the road, they stayed in a motel, and in the morning as they were packing up to go, he said his money was missing. He had put it on the dresser under his wallet, a wad of 20-dollar bills for gas. They looked everywhere, then decided it wasn't there and left. He was very upset, and swore that he had put it there and it disappeared.

Antera gave the money a blessing and asked that it go to someone who needed it more than they did, and suggested that he do the same. He said he'd try. Later, while he was driving, he brought in his Higher Presence and was able to completely let go of it. Finally all right with the money disappearing, whether someone took it or he had lost it, he found peace. Reaching down to scratch his lower leg, he felt a bulge in his sock. He reached in and pulled out the wad of money! Astounded, he absolutely knew that if it had been there before, he would have felt it. It had magically appeared as soon as he had let it go!

It was a good lesson in letting go and allowing the God-Force to work, and just to make sure he really got it, the same wad of money disappeared again the next night! This time he didn't get upset, and was able to have faith that all was in order. Sure enough, it appeared again later, in his pants pocket, though he swore he had checked all pockets. It seemed that his money was dematerializing and rematerializing, so he could develop his faith. He accepted this, and it worked. It was all about surrender, and he had to "Let go and let God."

When they returned home they did get the power line fixed, by shoving a plumber's snake in from each end, then digging up the middle. There was no obstruction in the pipe, and it remained a mystery. When it was all done, they stood looking at the long trench and gave thanks.

"Well, the lessons just keep coming, don't they?" mused Omaran.

"Yep, but only as long as we or you need them."

"I have to admit, I'm not excited about going through them, but I'm very grateful and appreciative once I'm on the other side."

It was a good lesson for him! After that he had renewed faith, and was much more careful about his anger. He talked to and thanked the nature spirits daily, informing them whenever he was going to do anything that may disturb them. If he did get frustrated, he caught it much more quickly and cleared the energy as soon as possible.

13

Who Needs Food?

Six weeks prior to the Summer Solstice, Antera had received guidance saying that if they wanted, they could give up food entirely and live on energy and Light. The process of learning how to do this would speed up their evolution into higher consciousness. The very idea broke into strong beliefs about the needs of the physical body. They had heard of breatharians, people who had lived long periods of time without food, but was it really possible in this day and age?

Since moving up to Mount Shasta, they had been so full of the God-Force that it did indeed make sense to let that same force nourish and sustain the body. Perhaps this was a way to really bring the Divine Presence fully into every cell of the body, which they had been working on for years. As far-fetched as this idea was, that people could live without food, it was intriguing enough that they talked about it and decided to give it a go. The worst that could happen is they couldn't do it, and they would have to go back to food.

"What do you think?" Antera had asked Omaran, while she was making dinner. He was getting out the plates, and setting them on the counter.

"Well, if you're up for it, then, yeah, I'll do it. In a way it would sure make life easier. Think about it. We wouldn't have to shop, cook, take time for meals, cleanup . . . maybe we wouldn't even need a kitchen in our new home."

"Oh, I think we'll still want one, we'll have company over sometimes."

"I think I'd miss pesto the most."

"Really? Of all the foods, pesto? I'm thinking I'll miss chocolate. But I'm sure we could have a little bit now and then if we wanted."

So they had started a cleansing program in preparation, eating only green vegetables for a week then only fruit for two weeks. They had been doing cleanses several times a year for a long time, and thought that their bodies were in pretty good shape for it. The plan was to finish with food by the Summer Solstice ceremony. Because the timing happened to coincide with university graduation of one of their sons, and several social occasions, it was a challenge to be around a lot of people eating!

When asked, they had told people they were fasting, to which some replied that it was pretty weird on such a party occasion. Several people had asked how long they were fasting, and Antera had answered, "We generally go three days before a ceremony," which satisfied them. Once she had said in a joking manner, "Indefinitely," which brought laughter and no more questions.

During the solstice ceremony in Los Angeles, Antera and Omaran had received a transmission from the Divine Presence that would bring the Light into every cell. The transmission had been so powerful that Antera hooted and laughed, full of joy. Omaran hadn't felt that kind of joy, and his doubts had crept in about whether he had really received anything. After a few days, however, the energy did filter in.

One thing that had been stressed to them was to be sure to rest, especially during the transition stage, as their bodies adjusted to living on Light and not on food. Ideally, they would have someone taking care of them as they lightly puttered around, taking time to adjust. But it wasn't going to be like that for their busy lives.

Back at home over the next two weeks, they continued their work on the house and other activities, though their energy was low. That was a normal fasting experience, and they knew it was a process to switch over to taking nutrients from Light. Mother Mary told them that it would take a few more weeks to undergo the full transition period, during which the cells that couldn't take the leap to the Light would find their way out of the body, and the others adjust. She suggested resting as much as possible.

A few more weeks! That was disappointing. And since they were right in the middle of building their home, it was difficult to take time for rest! After two weeks had passed, Antera decided she needed to speed up the process. One night before sleep, she put her hands on her abdomen and talked to all her interior organs, telling them that she wanted them to completely purge themselves of any toxins or waste they were carrying. The very next day she felt absolutely horrible, as the purging accelerated. She could hardly stand up without falling over. And she thought her body was clean! Clearly some very deeply buried toxins were coming out.

This period of time was especially hard because they didn't want to worry any of their family and friends, so they decided not to tell most of them, and to pretend like they felt fine. Maybe after a few months without food they could be told, as it would then be apparent that they were fine. Most people have the idea that humans can only go without food for about 30 days. But when two of their sons visited, they couldn't keep it from them. The reactions were not what they expected. One said, "Wow. That would be a dream come true, and so freeing not to have to eat again." The other said, "But why would you want to do that? Eating is one of the pleasures of life! I definitely DO NOT approve!" To ease their son's worries, a deal was struck that they would see a doctor for a physical after two months.

After about three weeks, Antera reached bottom. One day she was so weak that Omaran came home to find her up in the loft, crying and laughing at the same time at how pitiful she felt. She had been trying to change the guest bed for almost an hour and had only barely gotten the sheets off and wrapped around her. Omaran was a bit alarmed and carried her downstairs, then finished changing the bed. Antera cried for a long time, literally releasing all the suffering of human existence and all she had gone through to become one with the Divine Presence again. She gave up everything, including her life, to the God-Force, surrendering completely. Afterwards, she felt much better. Over the next few days, her strength and health started improving, and it seemed she was over the hump.

Omaran was working hard physically the whole time, making the very complicated passive-solar foundation for their home, plus working his other construction jobs. Over the weeks, he lost some weight and his energy slowly waned. Antera became concerned when several times he completely blacked out, finding himself on the floor without knowing how he got there.

As he described it, "It's the strangest thing I've ever experienced. There's no lead time. I don't start getting dizzy or lightheaded or anything like that. To me, it's over before it begins and I'm on the floor with no idea how I got there. It's not at all like standing up too quickly. It seems like my brain just shuts off and that's that."

As his body got weaker, he was forced to face a powerlessness that he had never known. His iron will and powerful body had never failed him before. They both hoped he would hit bottom and then start improving like Antera had.

14

Throne

One late afternoon they decided to take a short hike, making it an easy one because Omaran was still working hard physically on top of the fast, half days with the remodel for Vince and Mariah, and half days on their own property. Staying relatively low in elevation, they were both drawn to explore where a particular road went, so they parked Tan Man along the main highway up the mountain and started hiking down an old dirt road. It was unusual for them to hike downhill first, because that meant hiking uphill to get back, and they preferred the other way around, but they didn't think they would go far.

After only about a mile, Antera glimpsed something unusual through the trees to the side. It was a strange-looking rock formation that drew her attention. In fact, for some reason it reminded her of a huge chair, or throne for a giant. She pointed it out to Omaran, and they decided to leave the road and walk over for a closer look. It was a large outcrop with a bench that was flat and large enough to sit or lie on, covered with soft pine needles.

This was too inviting to pass up, so they climbed up and sat on the large chair and closed their eyes to sense the energy of the place. Antera immediately found that she felt very much at home, like the energy was completely compatible and nurturing to her. Omaran felt a burst of white Light surround him. They both had the distinct impression that it would be nice to lie down here and take a nap.

Antera called on St. Germain to see if he could tell them about this place. He etherically appeared, but said, "It is not me you should ask. Look around you." And he faded a small distance away to watch.

She looked around with her inner sight, and noticed there was another being there, so large she hadn't even noticed him before. He was surrounding them with his presence.

"Oh! Hello. Who are you?" she asked.

"The Guardian."

"What do you guard?"

"This place."

"We like this place, it seems special," Antera said. "Why were we drawn here?"

"Open your hearts and you will enter."

"Enter to where?"

He was silent. When Antera shared this with Omaran, they decided to sit and see what would happen, concentrating on opening their hearts, which was always good to do. After a few minutes, Antera went into a void of some kind, an open space with no movement. Then she and Omaran traveled inside the rock with their consciousness, and found themselves in a large chamber, spherically shaped. There was indeed a throne in here, with someone sitting on it.

He presented himself as the King of the Ancients, and gestured a welcome. The King did not look like what they would have expected, had they known the Ancients had a king, instead appearing rather round and very light skinned. There was a twinkle in his eyes, as if this meeting was very amusing. He didn't volunteer much, but observed the couple closely.

Antera asked, "Are you part of the group of Ancients we met at Lords Rock?"

"Yes. I am the ruler of that community," the king answered.

"Where are we? What is this room?"

"This room is underneath the rock where your physical bodies are sitting. It is called a waystation. From here we can go many places." He pointed to various doors along the curved walls.

She looked around, but besides the throne and the doors, the room was empty. "So, why are we here?"

"You came to my attention, and I have been watching you do your land-healing work. I wanted to meet you. You seem to be different from other humans on the surface. I am pleased with the energy work you are doing to help the mountain."

Omaran said, "Thank you! Is there another place we need to visit soon on our hikes?"

The king laughed and pointed up, saying, "The top!"

Antera clarified, "You mean the top of the mountain?"

He laughed again. "Yes!" Apparently he thought it was very funny, perhaps because of the enormity of that undertaking, and how easy it was for him to say but hard for them to do!

The king became silent and more serious then, and other Ancients quietly appeared around him. These beings looked more like the ones who had appeared at Lords Rock—tall and lean.

One said, "We are here to give you a gift. It is a transmission that will help you in your land healing, bringing it to a higher level, by awakening abilities that have been latent in you. Just having this set of frequencies in your energy bodies is sufficient, you won't need to do anything consciously with it. The energy is intelligent and knows what to do."

Antera and Omaran nodded in understanding and agreement, and felt a gentle flow from these Ancients into their hearts.

And that was the end of the meeting. The Ancients faded from view and Antera and Omaran were back in the void, then in their bodies. When Antera opened her eyes, it took a few moments to get back fully. The physical world looked like pulsing, moving energy rather than solid 3-D objects.

They looked at each other and both exclaimed, "Wow!"

15

Cone

A week later, Antera had just closed all the programs down for the day and was looking at her computer screen. Her wallpaper was a picture of the mountain. She thought how funny it was that many people in this town had pictures of the mountain they lived right next to, and would even wear T-shirts of it. Of course, both Antera and Omaran had Mount Shasta T-shirts, and there was a picture of Mount Shasta on their living room wall. Mount Shasta was certainly well-loved.

Something caught her eye, something strange in the image of the mountain on her computer. An area on the picture was actually pulsing, getting smaller and bigger, like it was trying to get her attention. At first she blinked and thought she was imagining it. She looked away and back again . . . still pulsing. It continued for several minutes. When it did stop, she thought it was pretty weird and decided to shrug it off as one of those unexplainable things, a trick of sight or imagination.

She found that she couldn't really let it go, however. It seemed to stay with her. So after Omaran went to bed early that night after a physically hard day of work, she took the opportunity to get out the topographic maps and see if she could figure out where that spot was on the map. She told herself that she didn't think it was significant, but that she was simply curious.

Its location wasn't clear from the map, so over the next couple of days she found herself looking up at the mountain whenever she was out, from different vantage points, trying to figure the exact position of the place. It looked to be quite a ways up the slope, and she decided not to tell Omaran about it, because knowing him, he would take it as an invitation from the Masters to go there. The area was still covered in snow, and she did not think they could make it there easily without crampons. Plus, she was certain that there was no trail.

Somehow on Saturday evening, when discussing the hike they were planning for that Sunday, Antera couldn't hold it back any more and so let it slip that she had seen something unusual on the picture of the mountain on the computer. She knew he was better at locating areas in the real world than she was. Omaran was instantly alert, and wanted to look at the screen right then, and impressively, was able to figure out exactly where it was and how to get there.

"I thought we might be heading that direction tomorrow, and now I know for sure."

Antera said, "I don't want to go there until the snow has melted, so it will be easier to hike!"

"We can do it!"

He couldn't sleep that night, which was unusual for him, as he could sleep practically anywhere, anytime. It felt like there was an energy pulsing through him that was keeping his mind focused on that spot and going there. He was feeling very excited and good, though, without knowing why. They had been on so many hikes, and never had this happened before they even went.

The next day, he told Antera they needed to start early for the hike. She was in her period and had a slight headache, and made it clear that she really didn't feel up to a major hike.

She said, "I'll go explore the area, but not go all the way up."

"Okay, no problem. Let's see what happens." Of course, he secretly hoped she'd make it anyway, as he was really being drawn up there.

They drove up a very rough, rocky road as far as Tan Man would take them. Omaran was constantly amazed at how well the truck always did without four-wheel drive. They set off on foot, up a steep gradient, starting at about 5000 feet elevation. Antera was not going as fast as usual, trying to keep her heart rate down to minimize the pounding in her head. But she found she could go at a steady pace as long as she took it more slowly than their usual uphill speed.

It was quite warm. As they went higher, snow patches started appearing along the road, so Antera picked up handfuls of snow and put them inside her hat to slowly drip down over her face and neck, keeping her cool. It seemed like only a few days before, it had been winter temperatures, and it felt like they had skipped spring altogether and gone straight to summer!

Before long, the old dirt road was completely covered with snow and the challenge of figuring out which way it went presented itself. Omaran was very good at seeing the trace of the road through the trees and very confidently led the way, when Antera had no idea what he was looking at. All she could see was snow and forest. He repeatedly said, "The road goes that way," and she had to assume that he was looking at the energy trace of it rather than anything physical, although he claimed otherwise.

Along the way, tired from stomping in the snow, they stopped for a rest on a cedar stump. A man's voice suddenly yelled something from the left. They couldn't see anyone.

"Did he yell help?" Antera asked.

"No, I think he called a name."

"He must be looking for someone."

Then they heard more yells from another direction, probably answering. They had never seen anyone else while out hiking, so Omaran yelled back.

The man was on back-country skis, and came closer to talk. He was on a search for a missing man who had climbed the mountain the previous day and never returned. It was his partner who had also yelled. Omaran told him they'd keep a look out for the man as they hiked, and the skier continued on. After that, Omaran started thinking that maybe they were being drawn up to that spot because that was where the missing man was.

Continuing on, Omaran thought that this hike, perhaps more than any other so far, required him to really feel where they were being led. They were going across snow-covered areas without trails or physical clues, yet he felt sure in his heart that they were on the correct path. He followed his intuition without second-guessing, trusting more than ever that they would end up where they were supposed to be. It was exciting, he thought, to be led to a new place, not knowing for sure where they were going. Was this enhanced ability to follow the Masters because of the recent transmission from the Ancients?

When they got to where the road ended on the topo map, Omaran felt drawn straight up the steep snow banks to the top of the ridge, which should put them right at the place that had flashed on the computer screen. Antera said she'd go as far as she could, but going to the top was out of the question, especially since the sun was already getting low in the west. She estimated that her body was running at about seventy percent. They slowly climbed up a small ridge rather than up the snow bank.

At one point, noticing how low the sun was and realizing they would be hiking back in the dark even if they turned back right then, Omaran said, "It will take another 20 minutes to reach the top. Do you want to turn back?"

Antera said, "Let's go for it," without knowing why she said it.

To come so close and not make it seemed a shame. The last part was the steepest, and Omaran, after the Black Butte climb when she had started sliding, was rather protective, giving her his hand to help her up as much as possible. She did not refuse this help and tried not to take offense.

Finally they were at the top of the knoll, probably over 8000 feet elevation. Omaran yelled out a big "Hello!" thinking that if the missing man was here, he'd hear. He immediately felt it was the wrong thing to do, and that they were entering a sacred place and should be quiet. He looked embarrassed. They started whispering.

Knowing that they shouldn't stay long, they quickly found a small patch of dirt around a large fir tree and sat, to see if St. Germain would say anything about what was going on here. As soon as Antera closed her eyes and tuned her attention to the Masters, she heard just a single word.

"Wait!"

A circle of Masters was there, and they were obviously in the middle of a ceremony, all focusing their intent on something. The humans had been invited to join them, but had arrived a bit late. So they sat in silence for a few minutes, growing colder and colder, and not exactly knowing what they were supposed to be doing or how to participate. As the intent of the group got stronger, they could see that the Masters were creating something in the center of their circle. There was a cone-shaped form around the group, with the point up. The energy being generated by the group was intense, and the couple were both feeling rather dizzy, so Antera couldn't sense anything else. They just sat and took it all in the best they could, then when it was finished, they felt the urgent need to leave. It was almost dark, and it was a long way back to the truck.

St. Germain said, "Thank you for coming. We held the ceremony as long as we could but we did not think you would make it all the way up here. This is a very special place and I will tell you more about it when you come next time and can stay longer, but it is already time for you to leave. We will help you find your way back and you will be fine. I will talk to you soon."

Since they had taken in a lot of energy, they weren't fully in the **third dimension**. Somehow, they managed to scramble to their feet and practically run down the cliff, straight down the snow bank. It felt like flying. The sun had already set and there was probably only 30 minutes of light left. Luckily, the moon was half full. They pushed their bodies to the limits, because they knew it would get harder and harder to see their tracks in the snow, and retracing these was essential for finding the road. In the dark, even Omaran wouldn't be able to see the road under the snow.

He thought, talk about walking in faith! Each step was an act of faith, because they had no depth perception, and couldn't see the ups and downs of the snow surface, which they had been very careful of on the way up. Going at high speed, they just plowed their way down, with no time to think about where they may suddenly sink in deep or slide.

Several times, Antera found herself thinking that she couldn't take another step, and if they could just slow down she'd be fine, but then the reasoning voice came up in her mind and said that if they didn't keep going, they may really be in trouble, perhaps ending up lost like that other man. Overnight on the mountain at that altitude was not a good idea, and neither was getting lost. That was enough to keep her going beyond her body's limits. Just when she was about to say she really couldn't take another step, the snow ended and the dark-colored dirt of the road appeared ahead.

It was good to be able to follow the road, but walking on the rocky dirt actually turned out to be much harder. While walking on the snow, there was enough reflection so they could see easier. Here, the rocks on the road could not be seen at all. It was completely dark. They decided that it wasn't going to get any darker, so they slowed down to a more careful pace, stumbling now and then over the unseen rocks. When, after what seemed an eternity, they reached the truck without anything more major than bruises, they were very thankful for all the guidance they had received. It was truly a miracle they had made it back!

There was only a slight delay when Tan Man got stuck in the deep sand. Antera stood on the rear bumper and bounced, and Omaran was able to coax it out.

The next day, Antera tuned in to her guidance to see if there would be more information about the ceremony they had attended but almost missed. It was often the pattern that while they were in the intensity of high energy, she couldn't maintain her focus to get information, so she just went with the flow and hoped she would be told more about what really happened later.

She was told that the ceremony was attended by St. Germain, other Masters, and a group of the Ancients, including their king. The cone-shaped form they created was connected with the pyramid at Lords Rock and spherical forms that the couple had experienced at other places around the mountain.

As humans, they were told that the two of them were involved in the creation process, and simply needed to be there physically to help ground the energy into the physical. The perceived pulsing of that area on the computer picture had been their invitation, so to speak. The importance of the work was emphasized, as well as the need for urgency, or they would never have done this so early in the year before the snow melted. They felt good about their adventure.

16

The South Side

Their job to create a Light Field around the mountain, which they had started the year before, would eventually take them all the way around it. In the process, they visited some beautiful places, but they had so far avoided the south side because the energy felt so different there. So naturally, they were asked by the Masters to go to that side next.

They got out the topo map and set out to explore. As usual, they didn't know where they were going, but they headed in the general direction of the south side, toward the small town of McCloud. The map turned out to be quite old, because they came across many more dirt roads than it showed. They decided to head for McGinnis Springs, which they had visited years ago, found what they thought was the road to it, parked and started walking. They quickly got sidetracked.

"Isn't there a place for people to ski on this side of the mountain?" Antera asked as they walked. It was hot, and they had started out earlier than usual because of the long drive, so it was bound to get hotter before it cooled off.

Omaran was sweating under his hat and on his back where the pack rode. Knowing that Antera always needed twice the water he did, he was already deciding that he would cut his drinking so she would have enough. Maybe they should have brought more. His pack was heavy and he always insisted on carrying most of the weight, because he could.

He said, "Yes, I've heard that. And I saw a hill that looked like it might be a ski slope from higher up on the mountain once. It was bare on one side. But I didn't see it on the map."

A few minutes later, they came to the top of a ridge and had a shocking view. They both stood still and looked with amazement at two hills next to each other, both with huge scars where trees had been clear cut for skiing in the winter. There was no snow this time of year, and the bare spots looked so out of place on this sacred ground, that all they could do was stare silently for a while.

Omaran finally said, "Wow. There it is. Looks like we have some healing to do here."

Antera nodded and they headed down and across the valley for the bare hills, forgetting about the spring, their original destination. She could feel her hands starting to buzz, as they often did when healing energy was being drawn through.

At the bottom of the valley, they looked up at the first hill, which they later learned was Douglas Butte. There was no visible trail or easy way up to the top. The ski runs were very steep, the advanced black diamond kind.

"I think we need to climb it," Omaran observed.

Antera protested, "How? It looks too steep to climb, much steeper from here than it did from the top of the ridge."

"This is the only way, straight up."

Of course, they went. It was grueling, hot, and the steepest slope they had climbed so far, with loose rocks and gravel making it even more challenging. It was slow-going, and they both had to pause occasionally to slow the breath and heart rate.

"Do you think we are out of shape? I'm not sure we will be climbing the mountain again if we can't even do this one," Antera commented.

"Hmmm," was all Omaran could manage as a reply, as he tried to catch his breath. His energy was still low from not eating, and he hoped his normal vitality would come back soon.

They did plan on going to the top of the mountain to complete the Light Field, if possible. This was a way to get ready, for sure. It took what seemed like a very long time to make the ascent.

When they reached the top, they both looked around and started feeling disgusted about the litter all over the ground. Cigarette butts, coffee cups, bottles, and miscellaneous trash was scattered everywhere they could see.

"How could people just throw all this stuff down while they are riding the lift?" He said, revolted.

"They should have cleaned it all up when the snow melted."

"Unbelievable! What kind of mentality allows this?"

"Hard to imagine," she said. "But we are here to heal the land, not add bad energy to it by judging." She took a deep breath and deliberately let go of that attitude.

Omaran agreed, and they sat on a rock past the end of the ski lift, closing their eyes and concentrating on opening their hearts to allow the God-Force to flow through. Their hands were buzzing strongly, and they put out the intent that whatever was needed for this place would be drawn through them.

After the difficult hike up, they were both thinking that they wanted to take full advantage of being there, so they wouldn't have to make that climb again anytime soon! Antera could see St. Germain etherically, but he was a bit dim. He relayed to her that he wasn't penetrating the area with his full presence because of its need for healing.

"The area has stabilized somewhat since the original intrusion of the ski business years ago," St. Germain said. "These hills are aligned along a major ley line. There used to be a vortex of energy here that took energy in and out of the hill. This we had to deliberately plug when the ski activity started, so the energy would not be polluted. The new vortex we created is off toward the back side of the hill. If you can get there, your help would be greatly appreciated in opening that and making it more stable."

Antera and Omaran agreed, got up and found their way through the thick brush and patches of snow to the area indicated. There was a large boulder nearby that had what looked like a perfectly-formed seat on it, with a backrest, and as comfortable looking as any rock might be.

"We can sit on the chair rock and be comfortable but in the sun, or we can go into those trees in the shade and sit in the brush," Omaran said, outlining their options.

"Let's go for comfort."

They climbed the boulder and situated themselves. St. Germain led them to send their grounding cords deep, and to open upwards. They were to act as conduits for the energy.

"Hold steady," St. Germain said.

They sat there for a while, observing. They were sitting on a large ley line that came directly from the mountain, and by helping to stabilize this vent the energy could be balanced and maintained. At first, the flow of energy from below was minimal, but it slowly built into a wild tempest of spiraling, spinning energy. The upward venting from the hill gradually increased to the limit of what they could physically handle. It felt like a huge river of pulsing energy surging through their bodies. It took about 20 minutes to stabilize into a smoother flow. When it became less intense, they knew their work was done.

St. Germain thanked them, and before he left, he showed Antera a picture of herself playing a wind instrument, a recorder or wooden flute of some kind, saying that those were the frequencies that would help heal this area and open the energy flow. She didn't have a flute or know how to play, but the idea of playing sounds to help heal the land sparked her interest.

"I want to get a wooden flute," she said out loud to Omaran.

Omaran was used to these out-of-the-blue kinds of comments from her, and simply said, "Okay."

The hike down was quick, as they partly slid down a steep snow bank on the north side. The sun had gone down and it was fast getting dark. They both commented about how they always seemed to have to hurry back from hikes because of darkness. It was as if the setting sun was their signal to leave. No matter how many times they had talked about it, they still ended up walking in the dark, trying not to stumble over rocks they couldn't see.

17

Hitchhikers

A week later, they went back to the south side, knowing there was more to do there. Exploring more of the same area, they did finally end up at McGinnis Springs near Panther Creek. It is a series of small brooks bubbling out of the ground and interweaving through a meadow, full of skunk cabbage and grasses. The mud was deep, and they both sank in to their calves once, after which they were more careful. Their given task was to simply sit in a couple of spots there and bring up the vibratory rate.

As they sat, they sensed the energy of the place as pleasant but not strong. After projecting the energy coming through them into the springs, the energy of the place amped up very tangibly, but slowly, until there was quite a powerful, vibrant presence. It felt to Antera as though the life-force energy of the place had been enhanced, and the trees, plants, and water soaked up the energy that had been sent and then sent it back out, creating a positive feedback loop for all life forms, including humans. It was the first time Antera was so aware of the details what they were doing, and how the process worked when they were intentionally allowing energy through to raise an area's vibration.

The third venture to the area took them up Coyote Butte, the other ski hill. They slowly trudged up the steep slope that had been denuded for skiers. The many small rocks rolled under their boots, so they had to carefully place each step to avoid sliding. Fortunately, it wasn't as long a climb as Douglas Butte, and they reached the top when the sun was still two hours from setting. There was a hut at the end of the ski lift, but very little plant life. It had been much more desecrated than the other hill, in fact it was practically bald . . . sterile. There were only a few trees, so they chose a large fir to sit against.

As soon as they sat, Antera started receiving messages and information. They were not asked to open a portal here, but instead their job was to walk back and forth in the direction of current in the large energy conduit underneath. The ski activities and all the people left a lot of astral energy, which was percolating down and polluting the river of energy in the ley line. They needed to clear the hilltop of the remaining energy, and help free up the current flow.

"It would be useful if we came here and did this periodically, like every year," Antera told Omaran.

She was shown a very large river of red energy flowing from the mountain through the string of hills toward the south and on into the distance, and learned that this river changes color, or frequency, from time to time depending on what is needed. Some beings were clearly seen in the river of energy, using it for transportation and for sending messages, but she wasn't told who these beings were. It was fascinating to watch, and she relayed it all to Omaran.

Suddenly, the Spirit of Mount Shasta dramatically appeared as a huge white and silver form above the peak. He shouted at them, "This is for you!" He laughed as he rolled a giant white ball of energy like a snowball down the slope, which disappeared just as it reached them. Before there was time to even greet this mighty being, he disappeared.

Neither of them really understood what had just happened. The ball of energy was very visible, yet they hadn't felt any impact when it arrived. They had been given many gifts of energy in the past, and they generally were very tangible. They sat in silence for a while, and suddenly Antera completely understood.

"Oh, wow! I get it! That was a gift of knowledge hurled from the Spirit of the Mountain. I suddenly have a new understanding of how the mountain works."

"Well, tell me!"

"I saw the mountain from an overview, taking in energy with its giant vortex, which spins one way then another, drawing in energy from above then below. It is as if the mountain is breathing, in and out. The energy is collected in the mountain, then sent out along these giant ley lines, this one to the south where we are sitting, the one to the west that goes through Black Butte, and others we will find later.

"The energy really needs a place to go, and if the energy lines are clogged, blocked, or polluted, as this one in the south has become due to the ski activity, it causes problems. The system needs constant tweaking and clearing to work at maximum efficiency. It makes perfect sense to me now!"

"Yes, that is very useful to know." Omaran was thrilled, and waved to the peak, mentally giving thanks. "What a great job to have!"

"We better get to work, then."

They got up and started doing the clearing, both of them walking back and forth, Omaran using his special land-healing crystal and Antera using her hands. The wind had kicked up, and she was very glad to have thrown a turtleneck into the pack at the last minute. Even with three layers, it was uncomfortably cold, but in their dedicated way, they set aside thoughts of cold while they worked. When they both felt the clearing of the energy flow was finished, they packed up and started back down.

After the steepest and most difficult part of the descent, they hiked on the trail toward the truck. She didn't know why, but Antera felt blissful, joyful energies coursing through her as they hiked, and her body felt very energetic and light. Walking faster and swinging her arms, she started singing songs of praise.

But when she looked back to see why Omaran wasn't joining in, there he was, quite a ways behind, lagging and looking anything but joyful. She could see that his energy was clouded over, so she stopped to wait.

"Are you all right?" she asked when he caught up.

"Well, I just can't walk that fast because these new boots are uncomfortable," he snapped.

He was obviously upset, but she knew it wasn't about the boots, so she toned down her enthusiasm to soothe him. "Love, you walk at your own pace, and I'll wait once in a while. I have so much energy that I could run."

She skipped ahead and stopped to sit on a large, flat rock. He joined her and closed his eyes for a moment. He explained, "I was feeling upset about the boots and about all the trees that have been cut here. Then I remembered what St. Germain told us once, that when we are hiking, if we start to feel crummy, to stop and transform the energy immediately, because it may be negative energy in the area we are picking up on. So maybe it has nothing to do with the boots."

This was a big step for him to be in touch with his emotions and not let them control him. But she didn't say that. She said, "Would you like me to clear your energy field?"

"Yes, that would actually be wonderful," he said, and she was very glad to be able to put the large flow of God-Force moving through her to good use. She literally jumped up and sat behind him, placing her hands on his shoulders. Immediately, she sensed that he had picked up some dark entities on the hill while they were clearing the land, and those beings were feeding on some destructive thoughts he had.

She said, "Looks like you've picked up some hitchhikers . . . I'll just help them on their way."

She commanded them to either transform to the Light or go away, and they complied. He lightened right up, and she let the Light flow to him, soothing and enhancing his field.

"Wow, that was similar to the Black Butte experience, but this time I was able to pull myself out of it much quicker," he declared. "With, I might add, an incredible bit of help from this amazing redhead I know."

He looked much better, and was glowing again as the hike continued. The experience really got him thinking about why he had picked up astral beings.

"I wonder why I am still susceptible to those beings, after all the work I've done on myself," he said aloud.

"You know, they feed on harmful thoughts and emotions because that is what they resonate with. That is one reason why it is so important to be conscious of and in control of our thoughts always. Like attracts like," she said, matter-of-factly.

"Yes, yes, I know. But now it is more than just words. The concept is more tangible, so I think I've learned a valuable lesson."

The ground was littered with many coins along the way back, which they picked up and gave thanks for, even the pennies. They guessed that skiers must drop them and lose them in the snow in the winter, but secretly Antera wondered if the Master Germain wasn't involved, because surely they would have seen them on the way up if they had been there!

18

Mackenzie Peak

They still hadn't formed a big enough Light Field on the south side, even after all the clearing and stabilizing work in the ski areas. The Red Butte field wasn't quite large enough or far enough south to cover that side, so Antera and Omaran wanted to make one more trip.

It was July, and hot, so they started out early, in Tan Man, for the long drive. They had seen another small mountain on the topo map, south of the ski peaks, called Mackenzie Peak, so that was the destination. As often happened, what looked promising on the map turned out to be daunting in person. Several roads were tried, each looking like it may offer access, but every side was prohibitively thick with manzanita and other large bushes. There seemed to be no easy way up, so they settled on the western side and pulled off the rough, dirt road.

Getting out and looking up at the large bushes, they stood there a few moments. Omaran said, "I will lead. We may have to use the bushes like a rope and pull ourselves up the slope."

"I will follow you if you really think we can get through," Antera said doubtfully.

After an hour of pulling themselves up the steep hill, they came to a boulder that was large enough to give them a reprieve from the foliage and a vantage point. Climbing up, they were disappointed to see that they probably had another two hundred feet to the top, which wasn't much higher, but meant a long struggle in this steep slope and thick bushes.

"I'm not sure I can make the peak," Antera stated flatly. She sat down on the boulder to drink water.

"I wonder if we have to be at the peak to do the work. Maybe we can do it here. At least we are on the side of the peak. That's it, just over there." Omaran was also tired, hot and thirsty.

"The others have been at the peaks."

Omaran sat next to her on the large rock. "Can you bring St. Germain in and ask?"

"I'll try." She closed her eyes and shifted her position to face away from the sun, which was intense even through her hat and long sleeves. Taking a few deep breaths, she tried to relax and ignore the sweat trickling down her face.

A few moments was all it took. "The Spirit of the Butte is here. She has very different energy than Black Butte, because she is more feminine, and Black Butte is very masculine."

Omaran sat up straighter and opened to the energy of the spirit.

"She says that this hill is a lookout between the two mountains, Shasta to the north and Lassen to the south. It acts like a filter and processing center, like a valve to make sure the energy only goes in one direction, out of Shasta. At least that's how it works now. She controls all that flow, and has been working very hard to filter it because of all the pollution from the ski hills. Apparently we have helped her immensely in her work by the land healing we did there, and she is grateful."

"Tell her it is our pleasure to do this work," Omaran said.

"She says that it is quite all right that we are where we are and didn't make the peak. We can do the work here. Just by being here, we are opening the flow of this ley line. She wants us to go ahead and build the Light Field here, then connect it to the ones on Red and Black Buttes. That would more firmly anchor in all the energies, and purify them.

"This being's essence is about clarity. She calms down and clarifies the energy coming from the mountain, which is very raw. She puts it through a filter to make it more pure and clear, before it goes out the rest of the way. At least she oversees the process. Our force field will help protect the energies even more."

Omaran said, "Does she want us to call her Clarity then?"

"She says that would be fine."

They made the Field together, drank the rest of their water, and slid down the slope to the truck. Finally the south side was flowing smoothly again, and the Light Field was strong!

19

Triple Seal

Antera and Omaran really wanted to complete the Light Field around the whole mountain this year, connecting all the forms together, despite being so busy with building their house, and not eating. It would be so good to get it done before they moved in, so the energy of the area would be uplifted!

So two weeks later they managed to get away for a day and go to the north side of the mountain, where they were given two possible areas to do the lightwork. Choosing one trailhead they had been to before, they bounced along the washboard road, so rough that it felt like every bolt in Tan Man would shake loose.

After finally making it in one piece to the place they wanted to park, they started out on foot along a trail for a short distance, then veered off across country toward a place they had named Triple Seal. How Omaran remembered the way there after only going there once many years before, was a total mystery to Antera.

"Are you sure we're going the right way?" asked Antera. She didn't want to doubt him, but there was no trail and all the terrain looked similar to her.

"Heh, heh," was all he replied. Sure enough, after a couple of miles of easy uphill, they arrived.

The destination was a wide valley between hills with an energetically unique presence, either because of some rock structures created there by unknown people years ago, or because it was already a power spot, and

119

that is why the area was selected for the structures. Antera and Omaran stopped at the entrance of the valley and took it in before walking, to honor the spirit of the sacred place.

They nodded to each other and, after finding a tree with some shade to deposit their packs, took the time to walk around the rock patterns, gathering the energy. As Antera was walking in a meditative state, a rock called to her. She turned her head to look at it. This kind of thing happened often to her, and special rocks seemed to get her attention when she least expected it. This one was light grey and rectangular in shape, a volcanic rock like all the others, with nothing obviously special about it. Then the rock told her it was for the cornerstone of their house!

"Oh!" She picked it up. It was heavy! "My Love, would you mind carrying this rock back?" she asked sweetly.

"What? It is too big to carry all that way!"

"It says it is the cornerstone!"

"Ah. Well in that case, I'll be happy to, Dear."

He walked over and hefted it, carrying it over to his pack. Relieved that they had finally found the right stone, he realized that he had been worried about that and now could relax about it. However, he still had to carry it several miles back.

They resumed their walking meditation, which took the better part of an hour, after which they rested under the shade of the fir tree.

"My gosh, I love this place!" Omaran said contentedly. "We're going to have to camp here some time."

"Me too, and that would be lovely. Well, where do you want to create the Light form? I don't think we want to do it here in the valley."

"I was thinking the same thing," Omaran answered. "We don't want to change the energy that is already here, just maybe purify it if needed." They looked around at options. "How about going up on that ridge?"

"Sure. I just need to drink more water first."

After a short time, they climbed the ridge, found a nice shady place to sit, and did the work. Immediately afterwards, Omaran slid down to a horizontal position to be more comfortable. Antera took his lead and did the same. Sitting out in nature was always uncomfortable, and for the most part they had learned to ignore the sore spots on their bodies for short periods of time in meditation or lightwork.

When they got settled, Omaran started drifting off to sleep in the way he often did. This was another thing about him that Antera found mysterious. Her body had to be very comfortable before she could even think about sleeping. But he could wink out in a few seconds any time of the day and practically in any position. What a talent!

She thought about the time, early in their relationship, when he had tried to teach her to go to sleep more quickly. They had been in bed then, and her body was restless, not getting comfortable enough to relax.

She had asked him, "How do you just let go and fall asleep so quickly?"

"It's easy," he had answered. "I'll show you, just follow me and do what I do."

She had gotten as comfortable as possible, then said, "I'm ready."

"Good. Close your eyes and relax . . . take a deep breath."

She breathed. "Okay."

"Now . . . follow the lights . . . ."

"Lights? What lights?"

"Huh?" He had already been dreaming, after one breath! And he was gone.

Now, as she listened to his breathing getting slower, she knew he was heading to sleep. She could feel St. Germain nearby and wanted to get some information on what they had done, if possible. "I think we should get some feedback about this area, don't you? St. Germain is here."

Omaran opened his eyes and said, "Yes! Do we have to sit up?"

"He says it's quite all right if we want to lie down and be more comfortable. I asked him if he could tell us about the energy lines here, and how the energy flows from the mountain. He says the north and the east sides don't have as distinct an energy flow outward as the west and the south do. It comes out and branches out more quickly. But there is a line of energy from the north part of the mountain down to this spot and on north. The flow comes through this spot and then branches out to other places. That's why this is an important location. The energy here needs to be clarified and purified and differentiated before it goes to another peak in the north-northwest."

Omaran asked, "A peak far away, up in Oregon?"

"Yes, way up . . . . This has become more and more a sacred spot because of what people have created here. It originally was just a place where the energies branched out, but now it has become more distinct, a power spot in itself. The main ley line is not a straight line, it kind of curves around, snakes out."

Omaran asked, "Should we go to one of the other peaks this energy flows through?"

She paused, listening. "He says later if we want, because really this is all we need to do here on the north side. By creating this Light Field it is programmed to purify and protect this place as well as connect it with the others. At least for now, this is all we need to do here. The important thing is to make the Light Field on the east side to they can all be connected."

"Okay, then," Omaran said. "Our next big hike will be to the east!"

Again she paused. "There are three beings in charge of this place and who will host the Light Field."

"Do they have names?"

"They just want to be called the North Trio."

After they got home, Antera washed the cornerstone, and left it to dry. The next day she painted it with a golden mean spiral, so it would be ready to go when Omaran poured the foundation.

20

Ash Creek Butte

Anxious to complete the project, Antera and Omaran found time to go out just a week later, to find a peak on the map called Ash Creek Butte, on the east side of the mountain. They had never been there, and it was a long drive there and back, so they got up early and headed out in trusty Tan Man. Going in from the south, and trying to identify dirt roads from the topo map, they made their way closer. No trails existed, but they drove as close as they could, finding that it was as steep as Mackenzie Peak and just as thick with manzanita bushes. After more exploration, and one unsuccessful attempt at climbing that resulted in many scratches on their arms, they finally found a place they could climb that wasn't completely impenetrable. However, this was the steepest slope they had climbed so far!

"Wow, 20 steps and I'm at my limit," gasped Omaran. "If this were any steeper we couldn't do it." They were both bent over, trying to take in oxygen. They had to climb by side-stepping as high as they could, for a few steps at a time, then resting.

"We just have to make it up this first steep part, then hopefully it will get easier."

Omaran was thinking that it couldn't get any harder, but he didn't have enough energy to say it. He knew that not eating may be a factor in not having his normal energy, but he also was amazed at how well they were both doing without food.

Once they got up to the top, which they could not see from the truck, they found themselves on a ridge. It opened up, as the manzanita here was the shorter variety often seen at higher elevations. Only one or two feet tall, it could easily be stepped over. Whew! They sat down on some rocks to rest and drink water after the difficult, hot climb.

"We're on the edge of the caldera!" Antera declared.

Below them was a depression, partially filled with a lake—the part of the volcano that had collapsed after an eruption a long time ago. They could see that the highest point, their goal, was on the other side, directly across.

"It looks like we can follow this ridge right around to the peak," Omaran observed, pointing around to the right. He looked down to the left. "And next time we come here, maybe we can walk the whole way up the ridge from where it starts down there toward the north, instead of climbing up this side."

Antera nodded. "It is beautiful."

After their short rest, they hiked around the ridge up to the peak with little difficulty, taking about an hour as they boulder-hopped and followed animal trails. At the peak, the rock formations were unique and colorful, and they marveled at what nature had created. Scouting around, Omaran found another can with a notebook, so they wrote their names in it, noticing that few others had signed it.

Settling down to do what they came to do, they created the Light Field, then stood up and connected it to the four others: the north side, Black Butte, Red Butte, and Mackenzie Butte. They could see very far from here, with the majestic view of the east side of the mountain right in front of them—a different view than they had seen before.

The Spirit of Ash Creek Butte made herself known to Antera, saying that her name was Jade, and that she was very happy she had been chosen to host this energy and connect with the others. The hosting spirits of the other areas now had easier communication with her. It was as if they had never met! They were all very excited to have this connection now.

Thusly, the Light Field was tied together around the mountain, and the project was complete for now, unless they decided to go to the top at some point. They were very glad to have completed it at last! Energetically, they could feel that the energy of their favorite volcano was vastly improved and flowing in healthier ways, bringing higher consciousness to the entire planet.

21

Let's Eat!

Without food, spiritual and psychic sensitivity is always enhanced. Connecting to guidance, seeing and feeling energy flows, and intuition are all so much easier when the body isn't spending so much energy processing food. Antera and Omaran were both loving being so tuned in and aware, and with so little effort. It was very clear why all the great Masters of the world had gone long periods of time without food.

However, in mid-August, after the sixth week of eating no food, Omaran was still not recovering, and he didn't have the strength to continue their hiking together, putting all his energy into the house construction. Antera was feeling good and sometimes took hikes without him as her strength came back. On one of these hikes, along one of her favorite trails to a place called Horse Camp, she thought she saw a purple light in a grove of trees to the side of the trail. Dismissing it, she continued hiking. But a few steps farther she saw it again, and decided to investigate, taking a detour to the grove and sitting on a rotted-out log to see what was going on. No source of light was visible, so she closed her eyes and tuned in.

Immediately, a voice said, "Omaran's life is in danger." That got her attention! She asked for clarification.

"If he doesn't rest he will lose the body." She asked more and was told that she should watch him, do all she could for him so he could rest more, and go with him every day for a while to watch him work on the house, to make sure he didn't work too hard, and to send him energy while she worked on clearing manzanita.

When she shared that with Omaran, he reluctantly allowed her to do everything she could for him, and he rested more. But Antera noted that he didn't really know the meaning of the word "rest," because he had never needed to before! Even with this attempt, his body was still going downhill, and continuing to lose weight.

Antera wondered if he would need to go back on food. One evening, she called in the **Overlighting Deva of Healing**, a deva with whom she had grown familiar, and who had given much useful advice for their bodies since they had been on the fast. The question was whether Omaran should go back to food . . . and the deva told her, "Not yet." Maybe there was still a chance he could make it. The deva gave him an exercise to do several times a day to bring the Light into every cell and nourish them. This he did diligently, and it seemed to help for a while.

A solar eclipse was coming up, with a very special alignment of stars and planets at the same time. The Order of Melchizedek had asked them to camp on the mountain for a few days to help stabilize and balance the energies coming in. It also would give Omaran a few days away from work. He was so weak that Antera did most of the preparations and carrying of equipment to their favorite campsite. At the time of the eclipse, 2:30 am, they woke up, lit the campfire, and held the Light steady until about 7:00, by chanting, meditating, and drumming. Afterwards, they collapsed into bed for a long nap.

Omaran rested over the next couple of days, but instead of turning a corner and feeling better, he seemed to get weaker. He had lost so much weight that Antera became more alarmed. She did not tell this to Omaran, but it was clear that his body was not being fed, whereas her body had stopped losing weight after the first three weeks, when she had stabilized.

Their last afternoon at the camp, while Antera was meditating, the Overlighting Deva of Healing told her that she and Mother Mary would like to talk to Omaran directly. Antera helped Omaran get comfortable, and Mary got right to the point.

"Omaran, your body will have to go back to food. Your reserves are gone. And though you have come very close to living totally on the God-Force energy, there is not the reserve to carry you the rest of the way. I highly recommend that as soon as you get back home, you start on light foods.

"I want you to know that all the gains you have made throughout this period are permanent, and you will still have a strong connection to guidance, even after going back to food. These are very permanent lessons and insights and gains that you have made. Because you had to work so hard physically, and you depleted your reserves in your work, this is by far the best path for you.

"Do not in any way think that this was a failure! This was a very successful time for you! You have gone through and processed so much during this period of time that it will always be with you, and there is more in store. But you need to replenish your strength or you will not be able to survive, much less do all the work you have planned the rest of this year.

"I would also like you to treat everything you eat as sacred. It will be like eating for the first time, like being a baby. You have undergone a rebirth, you have died to much of yourself that is not God-based, and you are reborn. So you are feeding all new cells as you build them up and allow them to multiply again. Think about what that means. As you build up your body again, and create new muscle, new tissue, these cells are being born of the Light of the Divine. And everything you eat is feeding these new cells as well as the old ones, and encouraging the God Presence in every part of your physical continuation.

"It is also a good idea to check with your body before you eat anything or decide what you will be eating, to make sure you are eating exactly what your body needs. In this way, you become much more conscious of what you are eating, much more conscious of the whole physical experience.

"Antera, it will be your challenge to NOT eat while Omaran eats. We would like you, if you choose, to stay off food while you are tending him and cooking for him. If this is too difficult, you may also go back to food. But so far, your body is handling the change fairly well, and if you choose, you may stay off food for now.

"You are both so blessed, so very, very blessed! All of this has been for the higher good, even the pain you have gone through, all for your own mastery. It is such a blessing on the planet to have you here."

After they got back home, Antera started making food for Omaran—very slowly at first, then ramping up as his hunger returned. Omaran was initially very disappointed to have to go back to eating after 56 days without food. But as he started food again and slowly built up his strength, he went through an intense period of growth, with lesson after lesson and insight after insight. It seemed like lifetimes of lessons blew through in the first few days.

His heart was blasted totally open, and he let go of everything, surrendered everything in his life to the Divine. All the lessons that he had been taught over the past few years, he finally GOT at a deep level of experience, whereas before they had been mostly words and concepts. His was the deepest and most profound awakening Antera had ever witnessed.

All his life, if he wanted to do something or learn a new skill, all he had to do was set his mind to it, and it was done. But with the loss of his physical strength, then some of his mental faculties, about all he could do was sit and watch others do things. His attachment to having to DO all the time broke down, and in a sobbing fit he acknowledged to himself and the Divine that he couldn't do things by his will alone anymore. The relief! The joy! The ecstasy! For the last 30 years, his deepest core wish had been to have the courage to live his life on faith alone. Finally, with all reserves gone, his body withering away, he was able to let go and commit to the will of God-Goddess. He had to have everything taken away to learn this powerful lesson.

Antera nursed Omaran back to health. He ate large quantities of food, enjoying each bite so thoroughly that Antera was entertained just watching him eat. When he held his hands over the food to bless it before eating, she could see a large ray of Light shoot down from above onto his plate, filling it with life force.

One time, when he was chewing the same bite for what seemed to Antera to be minutes, she asked, "Are you having a hard time getting that bite down?"

His response was simply, "I'm just enjoying chewing and tasting so much I don't want it to stop." It was common at first, for him to take more than an hour to eat each meal.

She had fun shopping for the most high-energy produce, because in her enhanced-sensitivity state, she could easily feel and see the energy, or lack of it, in the plants. Preparing the food and watching Omaran eat made her look forward to eating again. She knew that it would be too hard to continue without food if he wasn't doing it with her. After 63 days without food, she got the go-ahead to start breaking her fast. It was wonderful to taste again!

22

Chickens in the Pantry

"I think I'd like to have chickens," Omaran said one evening as they were relaxing after a late dinner.

They were sitting in the small living room of their rental house, where they always ate, due to the lack of a dining room.

"Really? Now?"

"Yes. I'm thinking about how good fresh eggs are, and we may need to get chicks this fall to have eggs in the spring."

"Are you thinking about chickens because you have been so hungry since breaking your fast?"

"Maybe."

"Neither of us has raised chickens before. But it can't be hard. It is getting late in the year, so if we do get them it will need to be soon, so they have time to grow before winter." Antera thought it may be better to wait until next year.

"We would need to plan out where their yard will be at our new house. And that permaculture system your sons were talking about would make the garden grow better and make use of the hens."

They had discussed the system, which had two fenced areas with the chicken house in the middle, so chickens would be kept on one side and the vegetable garden on the other, and switching each year. The chickens would eat bugs and fertilize the soil, preparing for the garden, and at the end of the season they would clean up the garden area. It seemed like a workable system.

Antera agreed, always excited to try something new. "Okay, let's do it. I'll get a book and figure out how to raise them. I guess we can keep them here in our house until they grow up and need a real house outside."

The fact that it was illegal to have them at their house in town didn't stop them from moving ahead. She did some research and ordered a batch of chicks through the mail. There were only two breeds that could do well in the cold winter temperatures on the mountain, and they had decided on Barred Rock. The minimum order was 25, so they could huddle together and stay warm during shipping. A few days later, the post office called to say they had a box of chicks. Antera could hear loud cheeps in the background of the phone call, and rushed down to get them.

There were 26 of them, tiny, black fuzzy balls, one day old. Antera put them in a big cardboard box in the pantry with a heat lamp on to keep them warm. They were so cute and full of joy! The plan was to keep them there for a few weeks, then move them into the basement until they were big enough to go into a coop on the new property.

It occurred to Antera that there may be a nature spirit who was in charge of all chickens on the planet, so just in case, she asked to be guided in their care by the Chicken Deva. Indeed, she soon found out that not only does this deva exist, but she was delighted to have a connection and a say in the chicks' care. Antera felt her strongly, and had never been so intensely guided about anything before. It seemed that every few days the deva was telepathically telling her of something else the chicks needed, or warning her about a condition that wasn't suitable, keeping Antera busy with upgrades to their food and water. Whenever she went on a walk, she'd be asked to pick some fresh grass or plants to bring back to them. Several times she was warned that the plants she had selected were not suitable for one reason or another, sometimes just because of where they had grown.

The deva's guidance was sound, because they grew healthy and strong, bigger and bigger and BIGGER. The couple had never seen anything grow so fast, not even plants, and they were astounded. Another box was taped on and a doorway cut between to give them more room, then another, and another. After four weeks, they were big enough to discover that they could fly up and perch on the edge of the boxes, and it was clearly time to put them in the basement. The dust they raised in their incessant activities was also becoming intolerable.

Antera spent most of a day cleaning out the basement to make room, but then got a clear message from the Chicken Deva that the basement was not an acceptable place for the chicks. Looking around, she noticed that some of the paint was chipping off and the cement was a bit old and crumbling, and realized that they may eat those things and that would not be healthy for them. Plus, they needed fresh air and sunshine.

"You're not going to like this, but . . ." Antera got Omaran's attention with that phrase when he came home for dinner, and told him the chicks couldn't go in the basement. They needed a new plan. The earliest the chicks could go outside was two or three months old, so they decided the only option was to keep them in the pantry until Omaran could build them a proper coop at the new house.

"I can get more boxes, and fortunately, this pantry is almost room size. I'll just do a quick in-house-chicken-remodel-room." They both thought that was funny.

So in came the biggest box they could find, the one that a bathtub had come in for the new house, and it was crammed in, cut, and duct taped on, effectively dedicating the entire pantry to the chicks. All human food was taken out except for the canned goods. They hung a blanket over the doorway to minimize the chicken dander in the rest of the house.

The chicks continued to grow, every day visibly bigger, and before it seemed possible, there were 26 full-grown chickens in the pantry! As Jeen put it one evening when she and Michael were visiting, "I've never known anyone who had livestock in their house before!" They decided not to invite friends over any more.

The dust they kicked up with their constant scratching started covering not only that room but the whole house, even with the doorway covered, building up faster than it could be cleaned. Chicken wire was added around the boxes so they wouldn't get out. Not long after that, they started perching on the top of the chicken wire, and shortly afterwards, there was evidence that they had been exploring outside the pen! The situation was a bit out of control.

Every time Omaran peeked into their room, all activity stopped, and there was sudden silence as all eyes were immediately trained on him. Twenty-six pairs of eyes looking his way made him think he had just stepped into Hitchcock's movie, *The Birds*. An ominous feeling indeed.

Despite the inconvenience, the joy these animals brought was delightful. There is nothing like raising babies of any kind. They ate out of the couple's hands. And who would have guessed that a being called the Chicken Deva would be so influential on their journey!

23

Marathon

Through the summer and fall, Omaran had worked very hard on the house, feeling appreciative of his strong body. The construction help he needed continued to come along as he needed it, as long as he kept himself in the flow. It was a really good challenge for him, he knew that, because if he ever succumbed to negative thinking, the effects were immediately apparent. Obstacles and problems came up.

During his entire building career in the Bay Area, he had never fired a single guy. Not wanting to hurt anyone, even at his own expense, he had always given them another chance. This trust in his workers had generally turned out well. Being around Omaran's energy and understanding did have an impact on them, and in time they had often thanked him and expressed how much it had meant to have his trust. But for his own house project it was quite different.

"I just put an ad in the local paper advertising for spiritual carpenters," he excitedly told Antera when he came into their rental house late one afternoon.

"Ah," was all Antera could muster.

"I feel good about this! Look where we are, we live in Mount Shasta! There have got to be some guys here who are both in construction and spiritual."

"Well, I guess you're going to find out," mused Antera.

"Oh, this will be great, you'll see, it will make everything so much smoother. We can get some good energy going into the house right from the beginning!"

Three days later he met two guys, one at a time, at Has Beans, a coffee shop in town. He decided on one of them, but the second also seemed a possibility so Omaran kept his phone number just in case.

"The first guy is going to start tomorrow," he told Antera when he got back to their house. "Maybe we can get this moving a little quicker now."

The guy showed up in the morning on time, and Omaran saged both of them, then led a quick connection with the land, grounding them, and set the intention for the project before starting work. That went well. Unfortunately, it became apparent very quickly that the worker had quite exaggerated his skills. Omaran's disappointment must have been pretty obvious, because the carpenter started getting very nervous and made a couple of small mistakes. At the end of the day, Omaran told him—with great difficulty—that it just wasn't going to work out.

That evening, he called the second guy, who said he could start the next morning at 8:00. As it turned out, it seemed he meant he could start his day at 8:00, but he didn't get to their house until 9:30. He lasted three days and Omaran finally had to tell him, with a little less difficulty, that it wasn't going to work. In the first week he had fired two guys! By the time he got to number seven, he didn't think twice about it.

It seemed that "spiritual" and "hard worker" didn't really go together, so he pulled his ad that looked for a spiritual carpenter and changed his requirements to an experienced carpenter. As he talked to other guys in construction he became aware that he wasn't the only one having a problem finding good workers. In this rural area, the most important and often the only criterion to getting or holding a job was simply showing up. By referral, he did finally find two young men who lasted.

The goal was to get the house closed in before winter, when there would be rain, snow, and cold, generally starting in October or November. The interior work could be carried on through the cold times as long as it was finished enough to be heated. Omaran asked the elementals for a bit of a reprieve this year so the cold would start later and give him time to be ready.

One critical aspect of Omaran's planning schedule was getting the exterior painting done while it was still dry and warm. One evening, as Antera massaged his sore back muscles, Omaran mentioned this to her.

"Maybe I could do the painting!" she volunteered. "I'm not strong enough for much else now that the real building is going on."

He sighed as his muscles relaxed. "Well, that would certainly save us a lot. Probably about $8000, in fact. But are you sure you can do it? It is hard work, and you'd have to stay ahead of the crew. You are still working almost full time for Byron."

"How hard could it be?" She pressed her thumb into a hard, tight lump of muscle next to his spine and held it there.

"That hurts!"

She backed off the pressure a bit, thinking that men were such babies when it came to pain, then continued, "Anyway, I'd like to be able to charge up the paint with the **Golden Ray** energy while it is being applied."

Ever since they had purchased the property, St. Germain had been guiding and encouraging them in using the Golden Ray almost daily. Omaran considered how cool it would be to put that into their house through the paint. The muscle in his back relaxed.

"That is a great idea. Hmmm. I wonder if you could paint the siding before it is put up. You know, that would make it much easier. The house is very tall, and painting in place would be very high for the second story, on scaffolding."

"Sure. Well, could you bring the siding here? Maybe I could paint here, that would make it easier for me." Her hands were sore from the massage so she finished and stood up.

"Ah!" He rolled over to his back, feeling better. "That is a great idea! I've been wondering what to do about the dust over there as we are painting. There is so much dust and the wind is constantly blowing." His mind went into planning mode as he thought about how to set up sawhorses with boards on them in the driveway. It just might work . . . .

So Antera became the painter. Omaran set up the driveway, and started her off with as many siding boards as he thought his crew could put up on the house in one day. Two coats were needed, but it was warm enough to dry quickly. She used a small brush rather than a roller, since the boards were not very wide, and this made it easier to chant and infuse the paint with energy.

She went at it exuberantly the first day, excited about her new job. But after only a few minutes, her wrist and elbow complained loudly in pain, saying that they were not cut out for this repetitive motion. She stopped and reassessed. This certainly was not okay—she had only just begun!

She had always been able to work with her body, and her body had always gone the distance for her. She encouraged her body to get used to it because she was committed, and to build whatever muscles were needed to do the job, then worked through the pain.

In the past, whenever she needed her body to do something difficult or demanding, Antera would make a deal with her body, giving a warning ahead of time if possible, and promising that she would do something special for the body afterwards. Over the years, she had learned about the **body elemental**, the nature spirit in charge of the body who constantly maintains the form and its functions. This was the spirit she was able to talk to and bargain with. She and her body elemental had developed a good working relationship over many years, and they had made it through times when extra effort was required.

"Listen up, please," Antera said out loud to her body elemental, hoping the neighbors could not hear as she stood on the driveway. "This is the deal. We need to paint hundreds of these boards for our sacred house project. You will love living in this house we are creating! Your reward will be the finished product. I know you have never painted before, and these are new motions for the arms and hands, but you will get used to it and we can do this! Afterwards, I may never paint again. So please do this for me for a few months."

The body elemental, however, was not convinced and did not think the body was cut out for this kind of work, and every day complained a few minutes after starting. Antera was determined, however, and overruled the protests, hoping adaptation would happen. Her job was not only to paint, but to infuse the boards with the spiritual energies and Light of the Golden Ray. This forced her to meditate and concentrate these energies into the paint as she applied it—quite an exercise in mental focus, four hours a day! Not caring about what the neighbors might think, she chanted and sang out loud as she visualized with strong intent. Those boards were shining brightly by the time she was done with them, and the pain was forgotten.

After a few weeks of this, she noticed that her hands were very numb at night, interfering with her sleep because she had to hang them over the side of the bed and shake them to get circulation in there. She researched the symptoms and it seemed to be a bad case of carpal tunnel syndrome. The way to heal it was to stop doing what caused it, but that wasn't an option. She had to keep up with the boards as new ones were supplied each day for painting, and the finished ones were taken to the building site.

Fortunately, her guidance sent help. One day, she was out doing the meditation-painting, when a young woman walked up the driveway.

"Hi," she said. "I want to tell you about magnet therapy."

"No, thanks," was Antera's immediate reply. "I don't need it."

"Ah. Well, please take my flyer in case you want it someday."

The woman walked off. Antera thought it was a bit odd, because in this small town there just weren't any solicitors. She set the flyer aside and continued with her work. When she did look at the flyer that evening, it said that the magnets were good for carpal tunnel problems! She asked her body elemental if this was what was needed, and got a strong yes. So she ordered one the next day, and wore it on her wrist day and night, for two weeks. The numbness went away almost entirely. What a blessing!

This made it possible to paint nearly every day for several months, on top of all her other work, meaning 12–14 hour days, seven days a week. Her body elemental did a fantastic job, coping with the new activity, and Antera kept promising that it was temporary and she would get back to a more normal lifestyle when the house was complete, praising her body. Bodies love to be praised.

She got one day of rest when Jeen heard about Antera's job, and decided to give her a little break. Michael and Jeen had moved to Redding, only an hour south, so Jeen came up and spent the day painting the daily quota. She even chanted the entire time, infusing the boards with good energies. She was like an angel and Antera was very grateful.

It also turned out that Omaran's request of the elementals was heard, as the winter weather came later than usual that year. The paint needed at least 50 degrees to dry properly, and of course it also needed dryness, and the weather complied. Plus, the roof of the house obviously needed finishing before any rain. Into November, the weather was still perfect for panting and building.

The chicken situation in the pantry finally could not be tolerated anymore, as they were full-grown and desperately needed a real home. The roosters were starting to crow, which wasn't good. So despite the rush to complete the house, Omaran took his crew off the house for a few days to build a hen house with a small fenced yard. The Chicken Deva had input for the location and other details of the hen house, of course. Omaran wanted it to match the main house, so it was made with the same siding and the walls were insulated for warmth. His construction workers joked about it, calling it the "Taj Mahal of chicken houses." One of them said, "If this doesn't work out for the chickens, maybe I could move in."

The chicks were joyful about their new digs, and real dirt to scratch in. However, a few days after moving the chicks, Antera went out there one morning and was shocked to find one of the pullets dead in the corner. She stared at the body, not knowing what to do. Never having actually touched a dead animal, her first thought was to go get Omaran to deal with it. But she decided not to shy from it and picked up the dead body by the feet, carrying her out respectfully. They buried her with a blessing.

The cause of death wasn't apparent, and they were concerned that there may be something in the environment that wasn't healthy, so later Antera asked the Chicken Deva what had happened. She said that it was an accident. The birds had gotten scared by some noise during the night and panicked. The dead one had fallen and was trampled by the others. It was sad, but they both were grateful for the opportunity to make peace with the death of their chicken.

One other thing about the chickens that really had Omaran worried was that half of them were males, and they only wanted to keep two roosters, so butchering the others was looming darkly on the horizon. Antera had told the chicks all along what their purpose in life was, that some of them would be feeding humans or animals with their bodies and others with their eggs, and that they were blessed in this service. So there was no misunderstanding with them, and in theory, it was a good plan.

But talking about it and doing it were two different things, especially after having them like pets in the pantry for months! Antera sincerely tried to convince Omaran that butchering was a man's job. When that didn't work, they tried to find someone else to do the killing. Two people volunteered to kill the roosters in exchange for the meat, but that fell through at the last moment.

Omaran finally decided he wanted to kill the roosters himself, because he could do it with the right blessings and attitude. And he did, though it wasn't a pleasant job. Antera gutted and de-feathered them, also not pleasant. But it was done. Afterwards, Antera heard Omaran muttering to himself, "Next time we better get almost all hens."

The new house was almost finished on the outside, and the painted siding was in place. But Omaran noticed that, even though he had been careful in moving them, the boards, simply by being next to each other, had gotten slightly scratched. He didn't want to say anything to Antera after all the work she had done, and the pain she had endured, but he knew he had to.

"Love," he began, "we've been very careful, and we didn't slide the boards against each other as we moved them, but they still got scratched, and I'm afraid they're going to need another coat of paint in place."

She was silent for a moment. She had been so happy to be finally finished with the outside painting. "Oh, man. Are you sure? Three coats?"

"I'm afraid so. Can you do it?"

She let out a big breath. "All right, I will give them one more coat in place, but I will need scaffolding. I can't do the second story on a ladder."

"Great! No problem!" Omaran was relieved, because if she didn't do it, it was another thing he would have had to tackle.

Antera did a coat over the whole house in place, with her small trim paintbrush. The scaffolding for the top floor was very high, and swayed with the gusty winds, a new and thrilling experience for her. It took special concentration to infuse the energies and not fall off. She took it all as a challenge in concentration and balance, and didn't look down.

The days were getting shorter and shorter, so they were both working late into the night. By the time the outside was finished, Antera went immediately to the inside painting. By then she was tired of chanting and focusing so hard on putting energy in, and decided to go for the fun music, turning on a classic rock station as soon as the crew left for the day, and that gave her more energy and rhythm to continue the marathon.

Antera never realized how many doors a house has until she had to stain all of them, both sides, three times. In fact there were a lot of things about houses she never noticed before, and suddenly they were making quick decisions about such obscure things as porch lights and tile and sink fixtures. Neither she nor Omaran was even slightly domestic, but they did their best at these house details, knowing that as soon as they moved in, they wouldn't pay them any attention again.

Omaran had never worked so hard in his life. He was a great planner, and managed the workers well, but did as much of it himself as he could, to save money. He was working very long days, and it paid off. As winter approached, he felt more confident that all would be in perfect timing. Somehow he always had enough energy for the project. It seemed like energy was being supplied from the land itself, as well as from the Masters, while he worked.

Omaran brought it up one day as the two of them had a lunch break together in their future bedroom. "You know, I've been thinking about it, and I shouldn't have this much energy, not working these hours and this hard. I know my body pretty well and what it can do for me, but I've never had this kind of energy and strength."

"Me neither. I knew I had to finish all the painting both inside and out, but that didn't mean that I was going to be able to. I've been thinking about that too."

"Yeah. It's like that same energy that felt so raw and uncomfortable at first, is now energizing us. It used to tire me out, and now I guess something switched in my body and I'm used to it."

"Yes, maybe the long fast caused us to adjust to the energies of the mountain, and now the energies are powering us up!"

"Wow, it is really great, isn't it?"

They finished their lunches and went back to work. While he worked, Omaran was also thinking about what **Jeshua** had told them the night before, that what they were building was not only a home. Neither of them had really understood the extent of it until Jeshua had explained.

Omaran could still hear his words: "If you look at the home you are building from a higher perspective, you will see that it rises up and up, far above the surrounding landscape. It is a very high tower that has been built here etherically, like a beacon of light. It is an anchor point for tremendous Light energies. Even though you have made mistakes in the building of this temple, the energy is very much intact and there was allowance for some mistakes in the basic plan. So you are still within the bounds of what is acceptable for this temple."

That had made Omaran feel better, because he knew he hadn't always kept his mood perfect. He had gotten frustrated sometimes, and even though he started each day on the site by setting intention and prayers with his workers, their minds were certainly not under his control. If some mistakes were allowed, he was off the hook! It was a major relief for Omaran.

24

Ceremonial Grove

While the building was going on, Antera was in a hurry to put some trees in because they took so long to grow, especially a circle of sequoias for a ceremony area. But though the well had been drilled, it would be a while before the water was available because it was not clean or plentiful, and planting trees that would need water most of the year wasn't reasonable. Still, after overcoming his initial resistance, she managed to convince Omaran to get the eight trees, which would be so important for maintaining the sacredness of the land.

Once again, they dowsed to find where the sacred grove was supposed to be, and this time they both felt very confident in their dowsing abilities. When they found the place, they started constructing a medicine wheel, which is a sacred structure in the Native American tradition. This was laid out on the ground using rocks collected from around the property. The wheel was a circle with a cross in the middle, the symbol for Earth, and it was aligned with the four directions. They had built a smaller one in the back yard of their Mill Valley house and used it for ceremonies for years, and they loved the energy it provided. Just by creating these wheels, the Earth energies are balanced, making them ideal places for sacred work.

After calling in a special request at a local nursery, a shipment of sequoias came in. Antera and Omaran went to pick out their eight new trees. Rob, the nursery owner, whose reputation as a plant expert was well known, was there to help them. He apparently had lived alone in the forest for two years, and was very attuned to the energy of plants.

"Don't look at them physically," he said as they were choosing. "Sense which ones really want to be with you."

Surprised, Omaran said, "Oh. Okay," and started sensing with his hands instead of looking at their physical attributes. Antera watched.

"No, not that one," Rob said. "See the energy reaching out to you from this one? That's what I'm talking about. If they want to be with you, they send their energy to you."

Omaran closed his eyes and sensed. "Yes, I feel it."

Once tuned in, he could definitely tell which trees to take. They knew whether or not they wanted to go home with the couple. Finally the eight trees who had selected to go were loaded in the truck.

"That was interesting," Antera commented as they drove away. "I wonder if he does that with all his customers. I mean, not everyone can sense energy, for heaven's sake!"

"Well," Omaran confessed, "I might have told him we were getting them for a spiritual project."

"Ah, I see. That explains it then."

The eight trees were planted in a 40-foot-diameter circle, at the cardinal directions and between, to eventually create a secluded circle around the medicine wheel to define the ceremony area. To water their new sacred grove trees, Omaran filled two 32-gallon trash cans from their house in town, drove them out to their property, and from them filled two 5-gallon buckets, which he carried by hand out to the trees. It was a lot of work, but Omaran really loved it. He felt a deep connection to the trees.

The sequoias were three to four feet tall, and every time he poured water around them, Omaran told them how happy he was to have them on their property and that someday they would be taller than him. As it turned out, that happened in only a few years, as they grew quickly.

After the ceremonial area and trees were established, the first ceremony was held in the new grove, to consecrate it with the energies of the Order of Melchizedek and the Christ Light. A small group of people attended, with others joining in from a distance. A tremendous flow of energy was opened up and poured into the circle and the people. They took turns going into the center, where the energy was strongest, some of them to receive initiatory transmissions, and others to re-energize their connections to the Masters.

The small sequoias held the energetic space very well throughout the ceremony, delighted to join in for the first time. They knew exactly how to do this, and at the same time receive their own blessings. It was a powerful start to the sacred use of the land.

Later, Mary told them, "The Cosmic Christ energy that you activated in your ceremony is now being held by the circle of trees that you planted. It is firmly anchored and held in place by the trees themselves. They each have a highly evolved being associated with them. There are twelve beings associated with the grove, the eight for the eight trees plus four others who are associated with the center point. These twelve beings are holding the energy of the Christ Light. They will always be there, as long as you are holding ceremonies. And over the years this energy will grow stronger and stronger."

Knowing that there were twelve beings in the grove, Antera and Omaran started greeting them every day and praising the sacred area so it would grow more powerful with each ceremony. It was a very good start to what they hoped would be decades of sacred use.

Though Omaran didn't really mind carrying the water to the trees, he continued to pressure the driller to finish the well so at least he would only have to carry it from there. The driller had left his pump in the deep well and said to run it occasionally and after some time it should clear up, but after weeks of waiting, he finally said it wasn't going to change.

When they heard that, Antera and Omaran called on a number of friends and family to send good energy to the well and visualize it healed, cleared up, and running freely. A couple of weeks later, the water was indeed clean and plentiful. The holding tank was full. When the driller saw that, he was incredulous, and said he had never seen a change like this. He pulled his pump out, removed his equipment, and left. It was quite an affirmation of the power of prayer and energy work. So, hoping it would continue to be fine, they decided to finish the well in the spring, when they would get a pump and build a pump house before they moved in.

25

Out of Hiding

It was a cold day in December, and Antera had worked most of the day in her office rather than going to the new house with Omaran. The monitor heater in their small rental house really only heated the living room, so it was not warm in the office, but she had bundled up in a thick cotton sweater and was feeling toasty enough except for her hands. Occasionally she went into the living room to heat them up at the heater so she could continue working at the computer.

It was late afternoon, and she decided to take a break and drink some herbal tea on the couch. Looking outside, a few light snowflakes delighted her and she smiled. It was their first winter in Mount Shasta, and her first winter in a place that had snow. It was magical white stuff, which fully enthralled her.

All day, she had been feeling the Masters wanting to talk, gently nudging her as she worked, and she had put them off long enough. With her hands on the warm mug of tea, she closed her eyes and opened her connection.

She heard them say, "It is time to come out of hiding. The world needs you."

That caught her by surprise. "What do you mean? I'm not hiding."

But as soon as she said that, she understood. Yes, she really had been hiding. This wasn't the first time they had tried to coax her out, either, and talk her into shining her Light more fully in the world. But there was something inside that kept saying to be cautious. If the opposing forces found her or knew who she was, she would be drawn into a battle she didn't want to fight.

"You are an official emissary of the Order of Melchizedek, and we think it is time to go to the next level of service. You are aware of the condition of humanity. You are aware of so much that most people know nothing about, the unseen forces and activities influencing the world, some for its betterment and some for its downfall. All your skills and vast experience could be put to more focused service."

She thought about her life, how she had been such a shy child, in part because she was so sensitive to energies in a world where most people seemed oblivious, and in part because deep down she had the feeling that if she was noticed, if the wrong people knew who she really was, it would be bad news.

Now, she knew that this deep fear came from experiences in past lives when she had gone out on a limb and those who oppose the Light had broken the limb off, along with her and her sacred objects and teachings.

"We are asking you to once again take up the Sword of Light."

She was still reluctant. "I'm already doing a lot for the good of this planet. Look at all the land healing we have done, and the group ceremonies."

"You know you have much more you could give if you so choose, if you were willing to shine your Light more strongly."

"Can you guarantee that I will be protected if I get more active?"

"No. But service does have its rewards. Think of it this way. If you decide to come back into battle, so to speak, you will be able to draw the fire from others who cannot handle it as well as you. This will alleviate much suffering, and you could eventually train others to do the same."

She thought about that. It was true that she had always been a guardian for many, deflecting **psychic attacks** for people who often didn't even know what was happening. Then there were the countless times people told her about dreams they'd had when she flew in at the last minute and saved them from some kind of disaster.

"I don't want to be in battle. I don't want to fight. I'm tired of fighting."

"We and this planet really need you. This isn't the old fight between good and evil. Taking up the Sword of Light again simply means shining the Light to your highest ability and owning your power without fear. But it is entirely up to you, and if you want to stay small to protect yourself, you can."

"I will need to think about this. I know you have been coaxing me for years, and I've been taking baby steps into service of the order. I feel strong, especially with Omaran at my side, but I know that I have held back from going to the next level, partly because I feel like I've been fighting to bring higher consciousness to people of this planet for eons . . . and I look around and wonder if it did any good."

They soothed her, saying, "You know that you have made a big difference. Even the times you failed, you inspired many. That is always worth it."

She thought about this in silence for a few minutes, while they held a space of support around her. Could she rally for humanity once more? Or was she done with that and ready to simply give in to the opposing forces, letting them hold people back in their evolution? Maybe it was better to just focus on her own enlightenment and not on everyone else. After all she had been through, why should she care?

Well, she did care. And, she realized, it wasn't in her nature to give up. She really wanted to further create the mystery school and teach others how to evolve quickly.

"Very well. I answer your formal call to take up the Sword of Light again. What about Omaran?"

"If you accept, you know he will be on board."

"Tell me what to do."

26

Y2K

The turn of the millennium had been looked forward to for a very long time in the spiritual community, because of the cosmic energies that were building and would peak around that time, and the resulting predicted changes in society and land. But as it approached, fear came up in the general public because of the Y2K computer issue. It seemed that computers had always used two digits instead of four for the year, and if they went from 99 to 00, it could cause big issues.

Antera was still working for Byron's company from a distance, and he had just published a book about Y2K. The worst case scenario was that all systems depending on computers would malfunction, which was pretty much all important services in Western civilization, including food distribution, power, and water, and that chaos would ensue while it was being fixed. People, especially those who lived in cities, were storing gas, food, and water, and making backup plans in case it got bad.

The process brought up for scrutiny the fragility of the systems most people depend on for their lives. A resurgence of self-sufficiency and the need for decentralization of food and power supplies grew. It was a wake-up call for many, and healthy for people to look more closely at their lifestyles and how separated they had become from the Earth.

As Antera and Omaran watched the concern growing about the turn to the year 2000, they were certainly glad they had moved away from the city. Because Antera had educated people about earthquake preparedness when she was a seismologist, she understood the need for everyone to have food and water on hand. It was second nature for her to always have backup stores. They both also had unshakable faith that no matter what happened, everyone would be exactly where they needed to be, to have the experience they needed to have. So there was no fear when it came to natural or human-made disasters.

But they had read some recent channelings from others that said Y2K was going to be a major disaster, a huge breakdown of society, and that there would be Divine intervention of some kind to save the cultures on Earth.

They discussed this on one Sunday morning, when they were taking a rare few hours off from work.

"You know, I don't really want the Masters to intervene. I want humans to figure it out for themselves," Antera said.

"Yes. I used to think it would be great if the Masters came here in the physical, or more advanced beings from other planets came, and showed us better ways of doing things. But now I'm not so sure I'd like that."

"I bet there really is a Prime Directive like in *Star Trek*, so others are not allowed to interfere."

"That would make sense," Omaran said.

"And I have great faith in human creativity and ingenuity. We will all get through this as we have gotten through so much before."

"Want to ask the Masters? I'd like to know if we need to be concerned, especially for our kids and other family members who live in the city."

"Sure, we can ask if there is need for more concern."

Omaran set up his chair across from Antera in the living room, purified the space with sage, and lit a candle for mood. They got comfortable, and beloved Jeshua came through Antera to give them blessings and talk about some general things, before asking if they had specific questions.

Omaran asked, "We heard that Y2K may be a little bigger than some people think, and there might be some kind of intervention from the Masters or extraterrestrials. I think we are pretty much set, but is there anything you'd like us to be aware of, or should we be concerned?"

Jeshua responded, "Y2K is only one manifestation of the energy changes happening on the planet. It is a way to prompt many people to get their act together and to give them a deadline. That's how it worked for you, is it not?"

"Well, yes. Just in case, we wanted to be here and settled before then."

"Otherwise, how long would it have taken for you to move and build a house like this?"

Omaran nodded. "Quite a bit longer."

"Indeed," Jeshua said. "Y2K has given many people the deadline that they needed to pull their lives together, make the changes that they have been wanting to make for some time, and provide for themselves a comfortable lifestyle through these transformations on the planet.

"Though many may not look at it that way, it is exactly what they are doing. Those who have denied that there is a need for action, are exactly where they need to be already. It may be that they have drawn to themselves exactly the experience that they need at a deep level. There has been so much Divine intervention already, that I do not see any new need at this point. We are all waiting to see how it will play out. There is much concern about the world and about how people will react to what is coming down. We also believe that humans are capable of making it through by themselves and without our assistance other that what we already give.

"We would have preferred for you to be in your new home before the solstice, because that is a time of energies climaxing. But things are as they are, and you've had to deal with some opposing forces to your building this temple. You have done as good a job as you could, and therefore you will be in it when you are in it. I believe that everything will fall into place for you this next year. Your spiritual jobs will become much clearer when you move into your new home. Until then it is enough for you to be building it and staying tuned in to the Divine forces as you build it.

"I leave you with the glorious blessings of the purest God-Force."

Antera and Omaran were relieved that Y2K probably wouldn't be as bad as many were predicting. Though they knew that many systems in the world weren't sustainable and would absolutely have to break down at some point to create better systems, perhaps that would not happen just yet.

They had wanted to finish the house by the end of the year, but even with the marathon work hours they were putting in, it wasn't going to happen.

One evening as they were sitting on a board between saw horses in what would become their living room, they looked around. The crew had left hours ago, and they were still working.

Omaran turned to Antera and said, "You know, I have a very simple dream."

"Oh? And what's that?"

"My dream is to be sitting in this room, on our couch, with all our work done, sipping tea, and completely at rest."

"It's dangerous to think like that at this stage."

"I know, and as soon as I stop this pace of working, I won't want to do it again."

So the new plan was to move in by the Spring Equinox. Once the outside was done, just in time for winter, they worked inside, quickly realizing that the house was really only half done, though the outside walls, siding, and roof were on. The marathon continued as they finished the details inside.

As the weather got colder, they had to stop their hiking for the year. In the process of creating the Light Field, they had learned about the flow of energy into and out of the mountain, and had done as much land healing as they could until next spring. They wished they could have done more. They asked for some feedback from Mary, and she came through Antera with her usual loving words of encouragement.

"I greet you, my dear ones. I greet you with my love, I enfold you in my embrace. Please open your hearts to receive my ever-flowing love and support for you.

"It has been quite a journey this year. Much of it to our amazement, and some of it very predicted. It is the choices people make that keep us on our toes, as we continue to help guide this planet into its new level. All the spiritually awakened people have been clearly called and many are working in service now. There have been surprise awakenings among people, and some very clear changes in the direction that we thought things were going this year. Nevertheless, the time has come for the greatest changes on the planet. And wherever you are, that is where you are supposed to be during these changes.

"The work that you two have done on the mountain and surrounding areas is sufficient for now, even though you did not have time to do all you wanted. It has much aided the energy going out to other parts of the planet. It has created free-flowing energy in places that were blocked, and has opened up a way for the Masters to send energy easily and unimpeded. The force field is so good already that no other forces are allowed through it, other than those of the White Brotherhood and the Order of Melchizedek. I advise you to keep up the work, keep the force field strong. If each of you, twice a week, puts energy into the force field it will maintain its strength at its current level."

Omaran said, "Thank you, Mary. That is good to hear. What about the balancing we did in the Los Angeles area? Has that helped?" He was speaking about a ceremony they and a small group had done to stabilize the area in southern California.

"The work you did in Los Angeles is also appreciated. That area is under tremendous strain and the danger there is from, in addition to the stress in the Earth, the forces behind it. There is no doubt that there will be earthquakes in this area, but the way they happen, and where and what time of day, and all the other variables that are possible, are what we are working to control. There are forces which are trying to create the greatest destruction possible, and we do not see that this will serve the highest good. Therefore we are trying to alleviate the destruction, and change it to a minor level.

"The land is purifying itself. All over the world, purification is going on. We have been predicting this for a long time, and the way these purifications come about and what areas are hit, have to do with the thoughtforms of the people, and the emotional-astral energy that they have put around themselves through their thoughts and desires. When the land is in harmony, there are no natural disasters."

"We are glad it helped," Omaran said.

These words of Mary reinforced what they understood in their training as land healers, that the balancing of harmful thoughts and emotions in the astral realm was essential in balancing the land and preventing disasters of all kinds.

He asked, "Can you speak about our house project? How are we doing?"

Mary said, "The house is coming along fine. If you spend five minutes a day charging up the land and the house and making sure that energy is flowing well, there will be fewer problems and it will go much more efficiently and smoothly. If you have to keep clearing it and spending time discharging energy that is not of the flow, then it will take longer. No matter how rushed you get, there is always an efficiency factor that comes into play that is much higher when you are tuned to the Divine nature of this project.

"There is absolutely no need to push yourself until you are completely out of your Divine Self, Omaran."

"Yes, thanks, I do know that," he said.

"Allow this project to have its perfect timing," Mary went on. "If you continue to affirm that the Divine Presence is completely in control of this project, and that it can only create perfection through you and the other people who work on it, then that is what will be created. There will be perfection, and there will be perfect timing with every part of it. You are building a temple. The temple will be built if you maintain a temple attitude.

"There are many lessons in this project, and you have been through so much. Allow the Divine Presence to work through you. And stop once in a while and take a few deep breaths!

"I am surrounding the entire property now with Light. This house will be the anchor point for the Golden Ray and for the energies of the Masters. But I again urge you, Omaran, to take whatever time it requires to maintain your clarity of thought and emotion, and immediately take a break if you find that you are getting out of the flow. You are not in such a rush that you cannot take care of yourself or maintain the energy that you are building. You are masterful at this, and you can do it! You can build the house and still maintain your Presence! Still maintain efficiency!"

Omaran was inspired and said, "I promise I will!"

"Also, please keep in mind that everything is being magnified intensely by the energies that have been in place since the eclipse in August. It is important that you stay grounded, stay centered at all times! Because this energy will take you for a ride if you're not careful. If you can stay tuned to your center, to your guidance, then it all will go very smoothly. If you can navigate the narrow path that is ahead of you that is perfectly balanced and harmonious, it will take you straight to your goals. It is only when you get distracted or taken off the path or forget to follow it, that there are problems.

"You are my beloved sister and brother. I would like things to go very smoothly for you. And in no way are you asked to work so hard that you cannot maintain your balance. I leave you with my many, many blessings!"

When the much-anticipated year 2000 came, the world watched to see if everything broke down and systems failed. Nothing happened. Not even any power outages! It was almost a letdown, after all the excitement. In many peoples' minds, it was hoped that this would stimulate some big changes that needed to happen. Antera and Omaran felt some of this disappointment, even though the Masters had said it would be fine, and they knew that disruptions could have stopped the work on their home.

Early in January, they checked in with Mary again.

She said, "Dear ones, I join you tonight and hope that I can shed some light upon what is happening within you, and within the hearts of all those on the planet, and within the heart of the planet herself.

"I understand your confusion and I hope to help you see that as this drama unfolds, all is indeed part of the Divine Will. There are no mistakes. But even we did not fully know what was going to happen. There were some fairly major shifts late in the game and some changes were made.

"Your concerns about the need to change all of these outdated and harmful ways of living are very valid. But please be patient and understand that the unfolding plan is as it should be and there are much greater changes that will occur. Also understand that because of the Y2K issue, there were many changes made in the minds and hearts of people. There was a reaching out to community, there were new thoughts about priorities. Just by conceptualizing change, some of the change wasn't necessary, because the shift occurred without it. It doesn't mean that many problems were solved, but there was a shift in the masses.

"Those of you who are at the forefront and have been awaiting major changes, are frustrated because you want the change to happen much more quickly. But we are at a point now where we are trying to pull up the vibrational level of the masses as quickly as possible. This may mean it cannot happen as quickly as originally planned, when we thought we would have to leave some behind.

"For you, it is not changing fast enough, but for the masses it is changing much more quickly than they can deal with, and so the pace has slowed. But bear in mind that the changes will happen, one way or another, and if we can gather many more people to raise their vibrations and open their hearts, then we will gain so much more. And we will have helped the planet in a far greater way than if only a few are able to bring in the new. The support of the masses is critical.

"That is why there was a last minute shift. For the awakened ones to shine, there must be plentiful support from the masses who are just waking up. And therefore we wait.

"Is there something else you would like to ask about this?"

Omaran replied, "You have explained it very well. I'm sure we are not the only ones feeling the frustration. But obviously the more people who awaken, the better for the planet. I guess we just need to keep on keeping on."

Mary said, "Yes, continue to keep your hearts open, and fan the flame of faith that all is going according to **Higher Plan**. Sometimes you don't know what the Higher Plan is, but you need to have faith that all is going according to it.

"Continue to release any attachment that you have to outcome. Because whatever you have attached to, will cause resistance. This is a time of non-attachment. This is a time to be free-flowing . . . a time of the moment. Making plans too long in advance is difficult now. The present moment is growing larger and larger in scope, and is changing. Every moment is a new moment, and has new parameters, new possibilities for the future.

"That is the challenge. That is also the fun of it, if you can look at it that way, if you can see your lives as a string of moments, each one unique. Then gradually you will give up the focus on the future and live right now in this moment . . . expanding your awareness such that you have true empowerment.

"Because there is only power in the present moment. There is no power in the future until you get there, there is no power in the past because you can't access it. Right now is where the power is.

"The lesson for many in this time, is to be totally open to the present and fluid in your perceptions of what will be coming next, trying not to overanalyze or predict . . . continuing to do your best, to keep your heart open, to do your service to the planet without expectation. Not without goals, but without expectation."

"Thank you, Mary!" Omaran said. "Your words are so inspiring to hear. I'm sure they are true for all of us."

"Ah, even among the spiritually aware, so few are ready. Many are undergoing tremendous spiritual crises, or having a need for healing that they did not even know was there. All that has been neglected is coming up to heal. Those who have not spent the time and done the work are having a difficult time, and your society does not provide you with the support, time and energy to deal with so many things at once, which makes it even more difficult for those who are having all of this need for healing come up so quickly.

"We had hoped that many more would be ready, would be able to sail through and lead the way for others. But many of them are still in need of healing. All we can do is send love. The work must be done by the human individual.

"You two are doing much better than most. You've had some challenges this year, but for the most part you are in smooth sailing. We are very pleased with that, and we know you have worked hard to get where you are. Now, because Y2K was mild, you have a reprieve to complete the house and to get firmly established in your sanctuary."

The experience was a good lesson in releasing expectations, and increasing faith in the **Divine Plan**. They both understood that even though they had been aware for decades, and from this perspective it seemed changes were much too slow, masses of others were just starting to wake up and needed time. Maybe years.

27

Precious Water

It was in February 2000, during a warm few weeks, when they once again turned their attention to finishing the well. Their timetable for moving into their new house sometime in March was looking good, and they would need water. Omaran set to work on building a pump house, and they bought a pump that the driller put down the well. But when the pumping began, the water was again sparse and full of sediment. The driller did not take responsibility for it, saying he had done what he was contracted to do and he was done. Paying for another well wasn't an option, so Omaran had another driller look at it, and talked with a lawyer. The lawyer pretty much said that there was nothing they could do, that they would just have to live with it.

The new driller said that what he could see from the surface looked like shoddy work. But the only way to confirm that the well was not drilled properly was to hire a video company to lower a camera down the almost 300 feet of shaft. So this is what they did. This plan was worth it, because it clearly showed that the well had not been drilled as deep as the driller said, and worse, that there was an obstruction and damage in the casing that wouldn't allow the pump to go deeper than five feet into water, explaining why the water had never been plentiful or cleared up permanently. Estimates from others said it would cost as much to fix it as it would to drill a new one. The original driller, after some legal pressure, gave them their money back based on the video.

But they still didn't have a working well! This was all frustrating for Omaran. He asked Antera to check with her guidance about what could be done. Water was obviously very essential. Mother Mary confirmed that there was plenty of water but it was deeper than the well would provide. She also said that there was one other option besides drilling another well. Omaran could go out to the well and pull up the water energetically, a skill he had mastered a long time ago in a previous lifetime. It was further explained that just because he was able to do this long ago didn't mean that he could just go out to the well, point his hands down and draw up the water. He had to learn from scratch how to do this again, working with the nature spirits, elements, and energy. This sure put him on the spot. The pressure was on!

Omaran was both excited to think that he may actually be able to do this, and nervous because of his doubts and lack of faith in himself. Who was he to think that he could move water underground? It seemed unbelievable. Yet somehow he knew that this was his challenge, and though Antera offered to help, he said he wanted to do it himself, so there would be no doubt that he was responsible for bringing the water level up.

"If I were you, I'd do the work without expectation. Simply believe it is done and let it go," Antera advised.

Easier said than done, he thought. Out loud he said, "Yes, I can do that."

For weeks, he went out to the well almost every day, and willed the water to rise, with little result. He didn't talk about it to anyone. One day he went out to attempt to move the water, and suddenly had the realization that this manifestation of water was really a manifestation of faith. Faith in himself! Since his spiritual awakening in his late twenties, he had always had good faith in God-Goddess, but faith in himself had been a challenge. Now he understood why this was so important for him to do.

This was a physical problem that could be fixed with a spiritual solution! But this made him feel miserable, knowing that this time he couldn't avoid the lesson, because without water, they couldn't live in their new house. So, he was face to face with taking responsibility for his own faith.

He had been working for years on moving energy in the land with his hands, and felt his abilities strong. But in reality, he had never really known for sure if he had been successful because there was nothing physical to measure the flow of energy. Now he would know for sure. There would be water or not. He appreciated the humor in the situation he had put himself in, and had an image in his mind of the Masters watching him and placing bets on whether he would overcome his doubts.

With renewed spirit, he went at it again, and intuitively, a process came to him and he knew just what to do. Calling in the Angel of the Property, the Well Deva, the elementals of ground and water, his **Higher Self** and guides, everyone he could think of to help, he then focused his mind on seeing exactly what he wanted as an end result, which was a full tank of water. The energies began building in his hands. When it was at a peak of power, he sent the energy down to the bottom of the well, and further down through the Earth into bountiful, flowing water. He mentally brought it up the well and into the holding tank.

After a few days of experimenting with this process, one day he went out to find the 600 gallon holding tank full! Keeping true to his habitual doubts, he thought it was probably just because they were running the pump more, and the system was starting to work on its own. Since there was now enough water, he thought his job was done and he stopped working with the well. A week later, the tank was empty. He began working on it daily again, and the water came. He slacked off, the water stopped. He went at it again, there was water. Over a few weeks' time, with this happening over and over, he began to see a pattern emerging, and in fact it finally eroded away his doubts about his abilities. There was no way to ignore the connection between the energy work and the result.

In spring, the house itself was finished except for some minor details inside and the carpet in the living room. They were very excited as they moved in at last. Water was greatly needed. Encouraged, he kept experimenting.

As the weather got warmer, Antera was thinking about more plants. She asked him, "It's so dusty here. Do you think we'll have enough water to support a small lawn?"

Omaran immediately said, "Are you serious? No way! I'm just glad we have water for toilets, washing, and a few trees!"

"You can get us more water," she said as she walked away.

"No more plants until I'm sure the well is fixed!" he yelled after her, but she ignored him, and that afternoon he saw her leveling an area in the back yard for a lawn.

In his mind, he sarcastically thanked her for her confidence in his abilities, and for giving him yet another opportunity for developing his faith. He continued working with the water, and as he did, his confidence did grow. But the nagging reality of it not being permanent, and having to do this work continually, maybe for years, just to have water, didn't sit well with him. When was the water going to work on its own? Every so often, he quit the work to see if it was okay by itself, but every time he did this the water decreased.

He finally asked Antera to talk with the Well Deva and see if more clarity was available from her. She did, and reported that the deva said there was currently a drought, plus a new bottling plant had begun pumping, and the water table had dropped because of both these things. The deva said that she didn't think Omaran would be able to raise the water enough to reach the pump consistently, and that to do it properly might take a long time, maybe years of work.

Omaran was relieved. So he couldn't do it after all? Suddenly he was off the hook. No more pressure! But they were once again without water, which meant carrying buckets of water into the house for flushing toilets and washing. And the more he thought about it, the more it ticked him off. What did the Well Deva mean telling him he couldn't do this? He'd already done it, and could do it again!

He went out to the well and resumed working, and the very next day the tank was full. Ha! That was when he realized that the tricky Well Deva knew exactly how to get him motivated again. This was turning out to be a very big series of lessons for Omaran, who wasn't ready to drill a new well yet because it would feel like he had failed. Fortunately,

Antera supported this and was willing to go through his process while they lived in their new house without much water.

He asked Antera to check with the Masters. **Djwal Kuhl**, a Tibetan Ascended Master, came through Antera to help him understand his process. Omaran asked him for more advice about the water situation.

"Yes, you do have a price to pay, a karmic debt. There was a time when you abused your power within the planet. This has made you very hesitant to use your power in this way again, to change the forces of nature, to create a miracle in the well, so to speak. Using the forces of nature is a very difficult thing to do ethically until you are ready for it, because the forces can be used for good, bad, or indifference. They can be turned against people, which is what happened before, and why you are so hesitant now.

"If you used your latent power, there would be no difficulty whatsoever for you to send your energy down into that well, and create the passage necessary to bring the water up in full force. You have that ability. But you have stopped it because you are afraid of what may happen elsewhere. Perhaps you may change the course of the underground river and then the spring will not flow on the other side of the hill. Or perhaps it will affect the wells in neighboring yards. You are very concerned about the effects.

"But what you are not allowing is that if you change things and call forth the I Am Presence within the change and bring forth the higher good for all, then nothing bad can come from it, nothing. As long as you specify that all of the effects are in the highest purpose, there is no other effect that can be created. If your intent is pure and your heart is pure, there is absolutely nothing that can or should stand in your way.

"The hesitancy and doubt you feel comes from this past abuse of the natural forces, of influencing the Devic Kingdom. Does this make sense to you?"

Omaran thought about it. "Yes, it feels right, and somewhere inside it really does make sense. I love the land and I know there is a part of me that is a little afraid of hurting someone else. I'm really glad you explained this, it helps a lot."

Djwal went on, "You, in the past, have had the ability to control underground water flow. You have proved to yourself that you still have this ability, and you have worked through many fears and doubts. The karma has been paid, through all the inconvenience of little water these last few months, and the hard work you have put in."

"Okay," Omaran said. He felt relieved that the karma was paid. "It is good to understand more of why I've been going through this. Thank you. I have more to think about."

After a few days Omaran told Antera he wanted to have a talk with her about the well—a serious talk. They sat in the living room of their new house, which had most of their furniture, but the floor was still concrete.

"I really do appreciate this incredible gift of being able to, apparently, once again move water energetically," he began.

"Apparently? You mean after all this you still aren't convinced you did that?"

"Okay, you're right, I know I moved water," he corrected. "It's been a great gift to have this experience. And I was able to release karma that I didn't know I had, by going through these months of not having much water while I experimented. I do feel energy in my hands stronger than I ever did before. But when I think about what the Deva of the Well said, I don't know if I can keep this up. It takes too much time to maintain it."

"Yes," she agreed. "It does take a lot of time, but what are our options?"

"Well, at this point, I'm leaning toward bringing in Len and letting him drill a new well for us. What do you think?"

Antera considered it. "What would it cost? And would there be any guarantee that the new one would work better?"

"Since we know the work on the first one was shoddy, and Len was the one who pointed it out, we can expect that he will do a better job. Right?"

"I know you like Len better too. If you feel you are done with this experience, and are confident you can move water underground, I'm all for drilling a new well."

Omaran was relieved. "Yay! I'll call Len tomorrow!"

28

Settling In

Now that the house was mostly complete and they had moved in, they needed to create more income so they could make the mortgage payments and actually stay in the house. In their usual way, they affirmed and knew they would be provided for somehow. Omaran started to look for some more remodeling work. His job with Mariah and Vince had lasted all the previous summer. He got a few other small jobs locally.

Antera was still working as much as possible for Byron, though it was difficult to do from a distance. Telecommuting at that time was not efficient. Slow dial-up internet was still the norm, and video calls were only in science fiction shows. Phone conferencing was expensive but sometimes doable with company meetings, and no one had cell phones, so even simple long-distance phone calls cost quite a lot.

Antera and Omaran were having dinner in their new dining room. The floor was a dark cherry wood, and they had put cedar half way up the walls. She loved the feeling of the cedar, and they had also covered the walls of the living room and bedroom with it.

She told him, "Byron wishes I could come down there to work, maybe four days a week. He hasn't found anyone to replace me." She looked at Omaran, wondering how he would respond.

"That's too bad. I'm sure he will find someone. I thought you were doing okay from a distance." He took a bite of his salad with fresh eggs from their chickens.

"It's limited, what I can do from here," she said. "I'm considering doing it for a while, as long as we need the income."

"Drive down there every week?"

"Well, didn't you say Jak is doing that?" They had met their neighbors, Jak and Kathy. Omaran liked to joke around with Jak, who had come over occasionally during the construction. That family had also recently moved up from the Bay Area but Jak continued to drive down there once a week for his job, while Kathy and the two kids stayed at the mountain.

"Yes he is, but I wouldn't want you gone so much. How many days would you be gone?"

"I was thinking maybe I could stay three days, sleep there two nights. I could do that if I left really early."

"But where would you stay?"

"I don't know yet. I'm just thinking we need the income, and that may be the easiest way right now. And the company really does need me."

"Hmmm, we can think about it," he said.

She took that as an agreement, talking to Byron the next day and asking if she could sleep right in the office if she brought a mattress. Byron happily said fine. So she began driving to the Bay Area once a week and staying for three days. She left at 5:30 am Monday mornings, spent two nights there, got home Wednesday evening around 11:00 pm, and still got in about 30 hours of work. There was no shower in the office where she slept, so she took sponge baths and managed to hide all evidence of her staying there during the day. It worked out well for everyone.

And they finally had water, water, water! The new well was flowing with plenty of water, so they planted almost 200 trees, many of them fruit trees, and started in with flower and vegetable gardens, as well as expanding the lawn to keep the dust down. They had found that dust was a big issue when living on a dirt road in an area with lots of wind. Antera had been hoping that they would be able to hang their newly washed clothes outside to dry, but as Omaran pointed out, they would have to wash them again because of the dusty winds.

As things finally began settling into a more normal schedule for them, and the couple got more comfortable in their new house, they decided they wanted to have some furry companions. A dog for protection, and a cat for catching mice, and both for the love of animals.

They got their mixed-breed puppy from a local litter they had found in an ad. When they went to see the litter, they both selected the same pup, out of six. There was no question which was going to be theirs. The mix was Belgium shepherd and lab, maybe with some beagle. They thanked the young girl who had shown them.

Antera said, "We have to get dog food and a bed and some toys, so can you keep her for us for a few days? We definitely want that puppy with the short tail."

The little girl said that she would be happy to and that the pup's name was Faith. Antera and Omaran both looked at each other and exclaimed together, "Perfect name!"

A few days later they went back to pick up their puppy, and the little girl said, "I just want you to know that I changed her name to Princess."

They thanked her, got their puppy, walked out to the car and both said, "Hop in, Faith." No way would they keep a name like Princess!

They found Samantha, their kitten, a week later in another local litter in Weed, the town just a few miles north of Mount Shasta, and they both chose the most energetic cat of the group, knowing she would have to hold her own with a puppy. She was very tiny, they could actually hold her in just one hand and they took her home with them right then.

So Samantha and Faith became the Golden Ray cat and dog. The Masters said that the animals literally carried those energies for their respective species, gracing the new home and bringing much joy.

The chickens were happy in their house and large yard, and the eggs had started arriving in spring, the most delicious eggs imaginable, from happy hens. They had kept two roosters so the eggs would be mostly fertile, since they had heard that was healthiest. One of the roosters was the biggest, alpha bird, who Omaran named Adam. Thinking that because he was the biggest he would be most protective for the hens, turned out to be a fallacy, however. When the hens were threatened in any way, he was the first one to hightail it inside the henhouse. Charlie, the other rooster, was close behind. The alpha hen was much tougher, and she was the one who herded the others inside, staying to fight.

But for some reason, people did bring out Adam's fighting nature. Antera found that she couldn't go into the hen house to get eggs without carrying a trashcan lid as a shield. Adam rushed at her every time, giant spurs first, his scary dinosaur eyes wild with a need to attack. She warded him off with the shield, but he came at her again and again until she got out of his space. Taking care of the chickens became Omaran's job.

Living on the edge of the forest was wonderful, but it did have its challenges. Some of the wildlife thought the chickens had arrived for their dining pleasure. The six-foot fences kept out coyotes and foxes, but a bobcat could jump over, grab a five-pound chicken in its mouth and climb back over easily and quickly. The strength of those cats was amazing. After asking around for solutions, Omaran installed a single electric wire around the top of the fence, and this protected the birds at last. At least until the bears found them later. Nothing could keep them out.

When it got warm enough, the couple continued their hiking and land healing work, reinforcing the Light Field the Masters had asked them to create around the mountain, which had been working since the last year. The next big hike would be to the top, if possible, but this was not something Antera ever wanted to do again, after their physically difficult trek there in 1995. So it was put on hold for the time being.

The house was getting more and more comfortable, and finished. It was so good to be in their new house at last! Compared with other places they had lived, this was so wonderful, the energy so expanded. Clearly, the projects would continue for years to come, especially the landscaping and grounds, but it really felt good to have a home they had created themselves.

They sat in the living room, so happy they had finally gotten a carpet installed, the last of the big projects. They had waited on that until there was no chance of soiling it in construction processes. Now it was a real room, comfortable and warm.

"I'm so happy the passive solar works!" Antera said.

Omaran looked up from reading the newspaper. "It is amazing, isn't it? It has been pretty cold outside, and we haven't needed a fire for a while. The big test will be next winter when it is coldest. But I think if it is cloudy, the woodstove will be enough heat."

"Thanks for building that, Love." She smiled at him, appreciating how hard he had worked on the house, and the extra effort to build the passive system in the foundation.

"You're welcome. I'm really glad, too. So," he continued, "I have some questions for the Masters, any chance you can channel one of these nights?"

"Okay, how about this evening?"

"Great."

After dinner, they got comfortable on the couches and lit a candle for soft lighting. As soon as she closed her eyes and relaxed to open the connections, Archangel Metatron was there and ready to talk.

"I greet you, this is Metatron of the Light! Bringing you the Light of the Great Central Sun, bringing you the purest Elohim energies to be with you tonight.

"Focus on the One Source of Light! On the mind of God! Focus your spirit, your consciousness, on the consciousness of God. The One!"

Omaran felt almost blasted by the power of this being. When Antera brought him through, her voice was loud and forceful.

"As you do this, you bring in more of this Light into your body and into your soul. And you build your connection ever stronger. You remember more about your origins, where you are going, your soul's purpose, and the destiny of this planet and this universe. Go for the Source, always go for the highest levels, which means you go full circle. For as you look farther and farther out to the Source of all energy, you come back to you!

"I come to you on wings of delight. We have always had a joyous connection and it has been a while, because you have been preoccupied with other tasks on the Earth level. And you have been working on your own healing. Now that your home and environment are nearing harmony and perfection, you are looking outward once again.

"I hope you don't think that the last couple of years have been wasted or have been holding you back in spirit, for it is far from the case. The work you have been doing is very essential to your path of service. You can only serve when you are in a space that is perfect for you. And this is what you have been creating, a place of perfection and harmony in all areas of your lives, so that you can free up energies to move forward into more service.

"Perhaps you have noticed how different it is living in this house compared to living in the last few houses that you have had. How much more expanded your energy is, how much more harmonious, more spacious, more Light. It is not only because of where you are, but because of what you have built. It may not be completely finished, but you can enjoy the fruits of your labor now.

"As the inner you expands more and more, the outer environment must reflect this expansion. You absolutely needed more space, not only inside but outside. You needed space! You needed land! You needed to have more space so that you can expand and so that no other people or beings are interrupting your full lightbody stance!

"The nearest people now are far enough away so they will not interfere with your energies, and this is essential for the work you are to do. My congratulations go out to you in earnest for creating this! A wonderful and most essential step to take so that now you can start thinking about what these expanded energies are going to do in the world. They are going out in force! They are going out to spread the Light over the land in all of their glory! Lighting up the world!"

"Thank you, Metatron, for that validation of our home here. It does feel good to have space around us. I can't imagine being in the city anymore." Omaran's heart felt very good. What they had done was quite an accomplishment.

As Metatron had said, now that they had space and a comfortable home, they could put their attention back on their spiritual center, and the mystery school the Masters wanted them to create, based on ancient teachings of the Order of Melchizedek. These teachings had been available in some form throughout the planet's history, through many mystery schools. The location on the slopes of mystical Mount Shasta was now perfect for a new school for the current times.

Would there be enough people awakening to be open to the teachings and to support the school? For years, the Masters had said that the masses were close to waking up, that they would be hungry for mystical and esoteric knowledge and experience. Antera and Omaran knew it was their mission to be ready to guide and teach these people when the mass awakening happened.

But the masses still seemed asleep! Yes, some had awakened from their slumber with the Y2K threat, but it seemed after only a few months, it was back to business as usual, with most people clueless as to what was really going on, and focused on the mundane, physical world.

When they discussed this with the Masters, they were told to build the center and school, and when the time was right, the students would come.

As St. Germain described it, "The Order of Melchizedek is behind this project, and all of your projects. With the center, we see a way of opening the doorways to the ancient knowledge and allowing it to permeate the culture.

"I know that you have been hearing for years about the masses awakening and needing your services, but I'm going to say it again. We do still see this happening, though it is not happening as fast as we had hoped. We still envision mass awakening. At first, years ago, we thought there would be a polarity and separation happening with all the people on the planet, into the very, very good, and the very, very bad . . . the dark and the Light separating—so that many would walk in the Light, but many would also remain in the depths of the darkness.

"But now that image has changed to where all will walk in the Light, all will become one with the God-Force energy. This is what the new meaning of mass awakening is. The pure Light essence reaching everyone on the planet, every single person alive! There will be a few who leave, because they cannot possibly be reached, but the goal now is to reach everyone living on the planet! This is why we keep saying there will be a mass awakening. It may take years, it may take a longer time than we thought, indeed it already has, but we still see it happening as a most probable future. And for that you are holding a focus."

With this encouragement, the couple carried on with the creation of the center and mystery school, as a non-physical place for now. They did ceremonies on the solstices and equinoxes, which only drew a few people in person, but hundreds of others who participated from a distance. Antera had been printing a quarterly newsletter for years, sharing messages from the Masters and the classes they were teaching, and the mailing list grew slowly.

29

Song and Word

In late May, Antera and Omaran went up on the mountain for a day of meditation. For many years, this had been the way Antera spent her birthday, in meditation in a natural setting. It was, after all, her most powerful day of the year, her personal new year. Omaran now liked to go with her each year, to where she found a nice spot that would be good for her birthday meditation. He would then leave her there, and find his own place nearby but out of sight.

Their dog Faith, who loved hiking as much as they did, came with them as they parked Tan Man and hiked to a place on the mountain they had never been. It was always fun exploring new places. It looked as though no one came to this area, so they would not be disturbed. In fact, since they didn't use the few trails on the mountain, for the most part they were always alone.

Once Antera found her birthday meditation spot, a cozy area with some large firs to sit under for shade and some flat places to walk around if she wanted to do a walking meditation, Omaran left her there. He settled about a hundred yards away, behind some large boulders. Faith was a bit confused, and at first went back and forth between them, trying to herd them together. Herding was a strong instinct for her, with her shepherd breed. After a couple of hours, she found a place on a knoll where she could see both of them and, satisfied, she sat there for a while like a sentry.

Antera could feel the power coming through her as she resonated with her time of birth, and with all her previous birthdays. She had kept a journal, writing every year, and it was good to review where she had been last year and where she was now, in terms of her evolution and priorities.

As she meditated, she thought about the struggle she was having. She had so much experience and knowledge to share, and yet she had been teaching small classes for many years. It wasn't about finding a way to get the classes more known. It was about the people who had not yet become awakened. Was she looking for an audience that simply wouldn't exist for years to come? Was she so far ahead of the times that her classes would always be small?

The Masters kept telling them that the mass awakening was coming, that many people would shift in consciousness, and the interest in spiritual subjects would increase. She believed them, but it had been so many years that her patience was definitely wearing thin. Why should she keep putting so much time and energy into all the free events they provided, and putting out the newsletter, and preparing classes, when so few were receptive?

"How long do you think I can wait?" she asked the Masters. "Why aren't people waking up? How long does it take? Will it take disasters for people to change their priorities and figure out what is real?"

She didn't listen for an answer, knowing what they would say. Pacing back and forth in her small area, over rocks and sticks, she vented her frustration. Maybe this planet would never wake up and evolve. She had been trying to awaken people for many lifetimes, and here she was, doing it again. She thought of her history . . . the many lives she had spent working her way up from a dedicated spiritual student to a teacher, in mystery schools all over the planet. How silly of her to think she could do it again this time, and even start her own school!

Deep inside, she knew this time was special. There really was a possibility for mass awakening because of the energies on the planet and the souls who were incarnated now. She had known this her whole life . . . and really, it was why she had chosen to be born when she was.

But it was a long time to wait! So far, being an emissary of a cosmic order really wasn't very fulfilling! Her Sword of Light was being underused!

Even knowing that her thin patience was as much about her past as the present, it still seemed like it was too long for anyone to wait. Maybe it was time to make a change.

By the time Omaran came over, saying it was time to go, and they started their hike back, she had made a decision.

"I don't want to teach any more. Since so many people are still asleep and it may be a while before anything changes, I just don't want to waste my time until the people are ready."

Omaran was shocked and concerned. He had never heard her talk like this. He had always counted on her to stay the course, to do the work no matter what, knowing big changes were going to happen soon. "What? You don't mean quit, do you?"

"Well, I'll keep some things going, but at a minimum. I want to do some fun things now. Time to create! Let's spend more time on our music! And I want to write!"

After his initial shock, Omaran agreed that doing some creative projects would be wonderful. But he knew that he really shouldn't speak much about this right now. Antera could just as easily change her mind again—in fact, he couldn't imagine that she would give up teaching and creating the mystery school. This was her core. She had been told as a young girl that when she turned 40 her highest purpose and true world service work would begin, and they had met when she was 40! Omaran knew that she was very serious about her decision, but he really didn't believe that it would last long, and it was just a matter of time.

Now that the house was almost done, they no longer needed to work such long hours. In fact, even working 30 to 40 hours a week to make a living seemed like a vacation! Lots of free time!

They went ahead with the music, and started working their voices with a voice coach, a delightful man with classical training named Donnelley. With his keen ear and effective techniques, he helped them whip their voices into shape after not singing for several years. They started working more seriously on a joint music project, a group of songs they had started writing years before. This was so much fun! They did their vocal exercises twice a day and noticed improvement individually and in their blend when they sang together.

Omaran was in seventh heaven when working on vocal arrangements and singing with Antera. One of his greatest joys in life had been when he was singing with a rock group in the 60s, with an off-Broadway show in New York and an album with Atlantic Records. He loved singing and arranging voices, but it was the complement of his and Antera's voices that truly moved him. Antera had an incredible voice for someone who had been a singer with several bands when she was younger, but never had formal training. With Donnelley's help, both their voices were blossoming. Music was becoming a big part of their lives for the first time!

When it was time to find a recording studio, they got referrals for two places, one in Grants Pass, Oregon, about a two-hour drive, and one that happened to be in their own town. Both were musician-engineers who had studios in their homes. After meeting both, they chose Terry, who lived only half a mile away. Immediately, they had a good connection with him, and Terry's open heart won them over. That, and his obvious talent as both a musician and engineer, playing both guitar and bass. He heard some of their rough songs and was moved by them.

To make it even easier, Terry had been converting an old, large garage into his office and recording studio, and he needed help finishing the studio. Upon learning that Omaran was a general contractor and carpenter, he suggested that maybe they could work out a trade. Omaran would complete the studio and Terry would produce their album. Ah, they were all in the flow!

Almost as soon as they started working with Terry, they knew that they had made the right decision. Not only was he excellent at what he did, but he felt like family. He was very creative, had wonderful ideas, and while every once in a while he and Omaran would have musical thoughts that went in slightly different directions, they always worked it out and both became more open to the other's ideas.

Later, when they had many of the songs from the album in rough mix, they brought in one of Antera's sisters, Janet, who was a recording engineer and musician, and had an incredible ear. Her feedback and recommendations greatly enhanced the product.

During the same time, Antera began writing a book about their experiences during the first few years after they met, and pored through her journal and transcriptions of recorded messages from the Masters for that time period. Knowing the difficulties he had caused early in their relationship, Omaran was a little nervous about sharing their story with others. He knew it would help couples with similar issues, but he really was ashamed about how he had acted at times. Antera said she wouldn't write anything he didn't approve, and that eased his mind.

After Antera had finished a draft, and Omaran had read through it, they discussed it with Mary one evening in late November, as they sat in their new living room. A fire was burning in the woodstove and it was cozy.

Omaran asked Mary about Antera's book, voicing his concerns about sharing behavior of which he certainly wasn't proud, but hoping that maybe it would help others. Mary assured him that writing the book had been a healing process for both of them, and would especially help him understand the pain he had caused others, and the dark forces he had allowed through.

Mary said, "And you cannot transform darkness into Light without fully going into that darkness and experiencing it to its very depths!"

By sinking into darkness and then making his way back, transforming it into Light, Mary said it made it much easier for others to find their way back. So by sharing the story, it would be very healing for many who read it.

"You have transformed not only your own darkness, your own pain, but you have transformed with it pain of many others."

Omaran had never considered that he might have been healing more than his own pain. He said, "I really want to transform all of this energy."

Mary went on to say that forgiving himself and making amends was the way to finish the healing transformation. She ended with, "And the Light shines brighter on the planet because of what you two went through, how you persevered and finally made it through."

179

"Thank you, Mary," Omaran said. "I feel the Light and strength increasing in me as you speak. Of course I will let it all be shared. What helps me a great deal is to know that others who read this might be able to learn something from what we went through, especially men. Very few men seem to have worked on their emotional bodies."

Antera decided to self-publish the book, since working for the publisher had required that she learn many skills. It was a process that she knew would take a couple of years.

The music project evolved into a two-person musical, based on the story of the book. Whenever Antera and Omaran worked on either, they could feel the creative energies flow. It was so good to take time again to allow the creative juices, after all the hard work of building a house.

Both the book and CD were highly supported by the Masters, and great fun. The Goddess **Isis**, a beautiful Being of Light who was very involved with the mystery school teachings they were developing, explained that the ancient teachings were coming out through both the music, in the form of frequencies, and the book in the form of words.

In the words of Isis, "The teachings of the Order of Melchizedek, which are being unlocked and unfolded for the new era that we are entering on this planet, are not new . . . but they will seem new. They are as old as the universe. Parts of these teachings have not been seen or understood for many hundreds and thousands of years.

"Now they are being prepared so that you and a very few others on the planet, who are aligned with this purpose of getting these ancient mysteries and truths out to the world, can bring forth your part.

"As you work on your music and writing, you are bringing through ancient truths and ideas in the highest and quickest way. By using songs and words you will unlock these mysteries for the public. Many will feel their hearts opening, they will feel the effects on their souls. It will awaken many souls."

30

Ancestral Karma

"Guess what!" Omaran said as he came through the front door and walked into the kitchen.

Antera looked up from chopping vegetables. "What?" They kissed.

"I got a small job at the Abbey making a platform for a stupa."

"What's a stupa?"

"Some kind of platform for a Buddhist statue. I think it will be dedicated to their founder, and to peace and harmony for the area. The monks are very nice people, so it will be a pleasant job."

Omaran had been looking for more work since finishing a few small remodeling jobs. The Shasta Abbey was a large retreat for monks, situated west of Black Butte, in a forested region. He was to build an octagon platform for the statue—simple, but it had to be very precise. The designer had made sure he understood the precision required.

The following Monday morning, Omaran packed up his truck with all the tools he would need to start the job. Everything was in, so he stepped into the garage to get his water, when he suddenly felt an intense pain in his lower back. Collapsing to the ground, it felt like he had been hit from behind with a two-by-four. Stunned, he slowly managed to get up and walk into the house, gingerly sitting on the couch and grabbing for pillows to support his back.

Antera came in to say good bye, but took one look and asked, "What happened?"

"I don't know! I didn't do anything, and suddenly my back seized up!" He grimaced with pain.

"Where exactly does it hurt?"

He pointed to a large area on the right side of his lower back. "All over here."

"Okay, too low for kidneys. Could you have pulled a muscle? Or it could be a muscle spasm."

"No, I didn't do anything to pull a muscle! I was just walking! It felt like someone hit me!" The pain was still intense. "I have to go to work, but I can't get up."

"I'll get the phone, you can call them. I'm sure they will understand if you can't start today. Buddhists should know better than most people the importance of right timing and acceptance."

He did call, telling them he would need a day or two before starting the job, and it was fine. On top of his back issue, his dad had been admitted to the hospital just a day before, for a knee replacement, so he called him also. He had just gone into surgery. The other shoes dropped shortly after that.

First, his eldest son's back went out, and he was in major pain like his dad. Then Omaran heard that his younger son had just gone into the hospital for a staph infection on his heart, and may need open heart surgery! He called the Abbey again, to tell them that he would probably need the rest of the week, and explained the serious situation with his younger son. The monk said he would alert everyone at the Abbey and they would begin prayer work that evening.

They both decided to drive down to the Bay Area to the hospital. On the drive down, Antera said, "Do you realize that within a few days' time, all the men in your family went down? I mean, all of you! Three generations! First your dad went into the hospital, then you wrenched your back without doing anything, then both your sons!"

"You're right. That can't be coincidence."

"No. Sounds like a family pattern, maybe karma, or a curse."

"A curse? Are you serious?" Omaran considered it. "Of course you're serious. Oh, I hope not, though it may make sense. What else would explain it?"

"It's possible. Those things really do happen, deliberately like in black magic, or less focused like in feuds between families, or personal grudges and all the negative thoughts those bring."

"I can't imagine anyone cursing my Dad, he is so easy going."

"It could be from further back, like grandparents or great-grandparents," Antera said, thinking out loud. "These things can be passed down, I think. Someone could have cursed one of your ancestors and all male descendants, or something like that."

He thought for a moment, then said, "It does make sense that something is connecting the men in the family, and only the men. But now that we've all been hit, maybe it is too late to do anything about it."

"Maybe it will have played itself out, once all of you are better. How is your back feeling?"

"Still hurts, but I don't want to take painkillers. I just need to move very slowly." He shifted his position in the passenger's seat. He usually did most of the driving, but this time he was grateful she could do it all.

They stayed in the Bay Area until they were sure both sons were all right, doing discreet energy work in the hospital to help speed the healing so heart surgery wasn't necessary, then they headed home. His dad had made it through his knee surgery fine, so everyone was on the mend.

For days, Omaran kept thinking about the pattern and how to heal something that had to do with his dad and probably other ancestors before him. If there was a karmic pattern, he sure didn't want this to happen again. Talking it over with Antera after they got home, they came up with a ceremony to do for the ancestors, involving healing, forgiveness, and a big karma release. Antera held space for him as he did the work. It was very profound and transformative.

Immediately upon finishing the ceremony, Omaran exclaimed, "I feel like a load is lifted from me and all the males in my family, alive and not!" He was beaming. And so it was.

31

Empowering Lightworkers

By now, Antera was once again working as hard as ever on classes and spiritual service pursuits, in addition to their music and her book. When Omaran thought about it, there didn't seem to be any one time in particular when Antera stated that she was rescinding her decision to stop teaching. She had just started working again, and if she made a conscious decision to become engaged once more, she had not mentioned it to Omaran. He thought about it a bit more and decided that the episode had spurred them to create the book and musical, which were just a different form of spiritual service.

Antera had an advice column online, and received many emails from people wanting her help. Many of them, and others they knew personally, were having trouble at this time with manifestation of what they wanted, especially the funds or resources to move into more of their spiritual service work, as they followed their highest purpose. So for their next ceremony, on the Winter Solstice of the year 2000, Antera and Omaran were asked to focus on helping the **lightworkers** of the world.

Lightworkers are people who use Light (spiritual energy) to make changes and heal the planet and its life forms. They are healers, teachers, and artists, as well as people who do more subtle work in the inner planes using Light. Basically, lightworkers are the people who have been making this world a better place using pure energy.

At one point Omaran had wanted to do more than lightwork, and get active in the physical world, because he was upset about all the chemtrails in the sky. But when they had spoken to Isis about it, she had said, "Omaran, you can write letters and go to meetings and become very involved with this, or you can work like the Ascended Masters do, and do energy work around the situation. That is how you change things. Everything starts on the inner planes and is affected to the greatest extent there. By the time you are aware of things in the third dimension it is almost too late. But even then, the greatest results will come from energy work."

He decided then he would rather work with energy, like the Masters.

Mary and others gave them information about this solstice ceremony as they planned it, calling it "Empowering Lightworkers." Antera and Omaran were excited about this, and invited people to send in their projects for energetic charging, whether they would be participating in person or from a distance.

The ceremony would also focus on shifting the power structure around money and resources to make it easier for lightworkers to carry out their service work. There was a power problem in the world, causing many who really wanted to make a difference, or move into a spiritual or healing practice, to be hindered because they lacked the funds or means to do so. The power and money were in the hands of many people who were acting from greed instead of goodness, and those energies needed shifting so more power could be held by lightworkers.

They were asked to do a four-part ceremony, held in three different places with small groups of dedicated people in person. The first one, on the Winter Solstice, would be in Mount Shasta at their home, the second one on the Spring Equinox in Los Angeles, the third on the Summer Solstice again at Mount Shasta, then the last one on the Fall Equinox in Sedona. A triangle would be made between them.

Metatron gave them detailed instructions on how to activate each written project that people sent by email or mail, a step-by-step procedure using the special Atlantean devices that were now situated in their loft above the garage. Composed of quartz crystals and copper,

185

each device had specific uses, and were large enough to sit inside. For this ceremony, they would be used in a bit different way.

St. Germain had also taught them about what he called the *Lightworker's Network of Light*, a vast network of rays around the planet that connects lightworkers. It had taken the Ascended Masters 50 years to complete, and according to St. Germain, had only very recently been finished. It is located about 50 feet above the Earth's surface and covers the majority of the planet, accessible by all lightworkers. It will continue to grow as it was used and re-fed by the lightworkers themselves.

St. Germain's instructions opened this network up for the ceremony, so the energy produced would be projected up and out into it and be a resource for all lightworkers, whether they were aware of this work or not.

Antera and Omaran took some time off from their album to create a new special song for the series of ceremonies. It was truly inspired as it came together quickly, a stirring message of empowerment and action. With Terry's musical additions in the studio, it became even more powerful. It was called "Now! (Lightworkers' Anthem)."

Now, we bear the Light,
A million flames burning bright,
Connecting hearts around the world,
Together we shine like never before,
Together . . . .

In the weeks before the solstice, however, both Antera and Omaran unexpectedly felt quite a lot of resistance, an unsettling energy that started throwing them off balance. Omaran got cranky, his usual response to interference, and Antera accidently burned her hand on the woodstove. It wasn't a bad burn, but it certainly got her attention and started her thinking that there were interfering energies trying to keep them from doing this ceremony.

The next day, when Metatron was giving them more instructions about how to use the devices in the ritual, Omaran also decided to ask the archangel about what was going on with the interference.

Omaran said, "I do have another question about something else. Antera burned her left hand as she slipped near the wood stove, and I've been cranky, which often has been my pattern as we approach ceremonies. We are trying to figure out exactly why that happened, because we feel that when we are in our home something like that shouldn't happen. Did we inadvertently bring in some energy that we don't want here? If so, we would like to know how we can get rid of it and make sure something like this doesn't happen again."

Metatron replied, "There are always gifts in any kind of injury or problem. If you can find the gifts, then you have transformed the energy. The energy will not transform until there is no more frustration or problem.

"I have told you that you are very visible here, in this tower on the mountain. There will be forces ready to block your way. If you are not completely clear within yourselves, you will draw that in. You will allow it in without realizing you have done it.

"I must remind you of the energy you brought back from your last trip. You allowed energy to attach to you rather than transforming it while you were there. Now it has to be cleared from your house. You have not been very diligent in your cleansing efforts. Cleanse your home to make sure the energy stays pure and you do not bring energy in from the outside that is not up to par for the Golden Temple. To maintain a space of the high caliber that you wish to maintain, you will have to be diligent in your efforts and watch whenever anyone comes over. You must consciously change the energy and clean it up right after they leave.

"And if you have gone outside your tower and come back, cleanse your energy field before you enter, or you will always be cleaning up your tower. It is a fine and pure space. But when I say be diligent in your efforts to maintain that purity, this is what I mean. You have gone to a new level, where you maintain your diligence or you will be having problems like this.

"But what's done is done and there are only lessons. Usually humans must learn these things the hard way, unfortunately."

"Yes, we are learning a lot," Omaran commented, "and hopefully not all the hard way."

"Remember," Metatron continued, "You are not like other people. If you could simply keep that in mind, that you need to maintain your clear space at all times, in all groups, and everywhere you go, then this will not happen. Remember that you are always on task, so you must always keep your space clear.

"To other people who do not have their lightbody developed, it is not an issue. They are thrown around depending on where they are and who they are with, and that is their reality. But it is not your reality any more. Now is the time to take conscious control of your environment. And you can do this."

Omaran understood and said, "Thank you." He wasn't at all sure that he could always remember to keep his space clear, but after talking with Metatron, he wanted to make renewed effort. It was so wonderful to have these amazing beings to talk with, and to keep them on track!

After Metatron left, Antera said, "Let's get out the sage!"

And they had plenty of that. Turned out it grew wild all over their property as a ground cover, and during the summer they had cut and bundled enough to last the year. It was now hanging along the walls of their house, drying. She cut a sage bundle down and they did a thorough energy clearing of the house.

With the approaching solstice, energies ramped up daily. They could both feel the power of this one, more so than any previous ceremony they had done. To minimize interfering energies, they put a "mask" over the ceremony, energetically sealing it so it wasn't quite so visible, but at the same time remaining very effective, so that energies could sneak out to the ley lines of the area and the Lightworker's Network.

With the first one of the series in Mount Shasta on the Winter Solstice, a time of plentiful snow, they knew most of the participants would be doing the ceremony remotely. They carried it off with five people in person, a few dozen remote participants, and of course, the hundreds of Masters around them. Whenever the Masters were called for a ceremony, they came in with great force, one at a time, and were felt by all. And everyone felt the power of the activations for the lightworker projects, as they used the devices. The written projects were all left inside the last of the devices for a couple of weeks until the next full moon, maintaining the energy of the ceremony to completion.

A larger group formed for the second ceremony in Los Angeles on the Spring Equinox of 2001, for which they had found a secluded spot on a ridge in Griffith Park, in the heart of the city. The group had dubbed the ridge "Holy Sage Ridge," because of the wild sagebrush that grew along the path. At this site, they buried a metal box containing all the lightworker projects, to stay there and continue to be charged up until the full moon, when one of the participants would go back to dig it up.

The year went by fast, because they were busy with so many projects, plus Antera was still driving to the Bay Area every week. In May, they started preparing for the Summer Solstice, and the third of the series of events, this one again on the mountain. They had not been asked to hike anywhere to help the Wesak energies integrate this year. Instead, they had stayed home and focused on keeping the Light Field strong during the event.

Now they wanted to get an update about the energy around the mountain, to make sure all was ready for the ceremony. Again, they were feeling like the energy wasn't settled. Antera was having trouble sleeping, as she did when the energy wasn't flowing well or there was too much energy to process in her body, causing restlessness. Omaran felt off emotionally. It was time to see if there was anything they needed to know.

Sitting together one evening after dinner, they each prepared by raising their energy to a higher level. It always helped Antera bring through the highest and clearest messages when Omaran helped set the space. He sat with eyes closed and waited to see which of the great Masters would connect with Antera. There was a distinct, uplifting shift, and he knew someone was there.

It was Mary, and she said in her gracious manner, "Greetings my precious ones, this is Mary. Mother Mary, you call me. And since you call me mother I may call you my children. I greet you my dear children.

"I hear your concerns about the energy of the mountain. Since the Wesak, a large mass of energy that was created by the group has been slowly making its way in, and spreading. An opening was created that has allowed in other energies, a bit unexpectedly. You might say a portal was opened into higher dimensional energies that don't normally make their way into the atmosphere and matter of the planet.

"I believe you're both feeling this as a bit of a disturbance, in your physical and emotional makeups. This is why Antera is having trouble sleeping, because these energies tend to affect her physically. And Omaran, you will be feeling it more with your emotional body, as that is where you are generally affected the most.

"Others will react in a similar way . . . anyone who lives here or has contact with someone who lives here. The energies go through you out to others and this is the way it is generally spread. We will all be interested in seeing how it plays out. These are highly evolved energies and they will stimulate growth in many people.

"Does all of that make some sense to you?"

Omaran answered, "Yes it does. We've certainly been feeling them. Is there anything we should do to help?"

"You already did," Mary said, "by deliberately keeping the mountain shielded from that mass of energy. It was slowed down. Because you set yourselves up as shields, you did directly take the energy into your own energy fields to absorb it.

"I do suggest that you continue to monitor your Light Field around the mountain daily, or every other day as you can. And release whatever energies you allowed to attach in your own energy fields, by processing and integrating. That will help everyone. If a few people really integrate these frequencies, then others will be able to also, much more easily."

Omaran asked, "So overall, is this a positive thing?"

"It can be, we don't know yet. It can be very positive if the people on the planet can handle it. It was a stretch to allow this energy in. These large group happenings have a big impact on the planet. With human beings, there is always going to be mixed blessing."

They thanked Mary and she gave them the benefit of more of her wisdom and especially her uplifting energy, before Antera disconnected.

Emissaries of the Order of Melchizedek I

They both always felt so expanded and good after these sessions with the Masters.

Omaran stretched and said, "After what Mary said, I'm thinking that it wouldn't hurt to hike around on the mountain a bit in the next few days, and do some balancing of energies."

"We could take Faith on a couple of afternoon walks. Are you drawn to any place specifically?"

"Yes, I'm feeling that we should first go to that area between Black Butte and the mountain."

"Sure, that sounds good," Antera agreed.

"Yeah, let's do that. It feels right."

After two walks in the next two days, working on integration of higher frequencies as they went, they both felt much better. The energies were quieter and Antera could sleep again.

The third ceremony went as planned, and it seemed each one was more powerful. This one they did in the sequoia grove and medicine wheel, because it was warm outside. The trees had not grown very much the first year, as they developed their root systems, but they certainly had grown in spirit, and they held the energy for the circle very well.

This time, they were guided to include a dance, a circular movement and pattern from an ancient Hopi rain dance. It created a standing columnar wave of energy, which was then used to anchor the lightworkers' projects more fully. This was an experiment, and required some practice with the group, but they pulled it off and had fun with it!

With this ceremony, it seemed that they had gotten the attention of an even greater group of Light beings. They felt very visible from the Light their group had generated. They both felt different, though the difference was hard to put into words.

Asking for input afterwards, they sat as usual in their living room, and opened to receive. Omaran held space while Antera brought though the highest energies she could reach. An energy that was new to them came through.

It said, "This is the Infinite Source of Wisdom. Radiating the pure Light of God from the Divine Source and to the Divine Source.

Bringing forth the Oneness, permeating through your bodies, through your spirits, into the duality, into that which provides illusion . . . the illusion of separateness, the illusion of the splitting apart of the One into the Two. From the Infinite Source comes all Light.

"We are responding to your request for wisdom and knowledge. We have only the all-encompassing knowledge provided for your planet accessible to us at this time. But we wish to transmit through you to the Network of Light, to all the other Light bearers, to all those who vibrate at a higher frequency than the rest, to all those who are the bringers of the higher planet. We send to those who can sense that the planet has many forms and can tune to the form that is its highest expression. These are the beings we address with these energies of purest Light from the Infinite Source, coming through and anchoring into the mountain and out into the network.

"Your ceremonies have drawn attention. We are well aware of the almost-completed third ceremony that began on the solstice and continues until the full moon. But are you aware that during this period of time, every action and thought of those who are involved directly affects the anchoring of these energies? All of you who were involved in the ceremony are still being affected. As the energy peaks, in a couple of days, you will find that your energy also changes. Have you been aware of this?"

This caught Omaran by surprise. "I haven't, and I can only speak for myself. In hindsight, I guess it is something we should have expected. I don't honestly think any of us have a real handle on the scope of this. I'm glad you're telling us now, so we can make sure everyone who is a participant is alerted to this."

The Infinite Source of Wisdom went on, "The fourth ceremony will be the most important. It will be the culmination of the energies. You may have been fooled into thinking those pieces of paper with their written projects are not as important as they are. But the symbols and energy that has been created by the ceremonies and instilled in those pieces of paper is highly magnetic, highly stimulating, highly charged up . . . not to be taken lightly. Were there questions about this?"

Omaran answered, "First, I'd like to say that we are very honored to have your presence with us this evening. There is one thing I want to ask, to make sure that I understood you correctly. Did you mean that all of us who participated have been vulnerable in an energetic way over these past two weeks?"

"Yes, you have been in ceremony, until the ceremony is finished. That requires a certain amount of vigilance, in keeping yourselves attuned and centered. Whenever you are in ceremony, you are vulnerable because your thoughts and actions are put into place very quickly. The lag time is shortened, so you need to be much more careful about what you are thinking, what you are doing, what you are saying."

"Thank you! That helps a lot and we will pass it on to everyone who participated," said Omaran. He couldn't think of any other questions, in fact it was usually hard to think of questions when in a high space, because everything seemed so clear around the Masters.

Afterwards, he said to Antera, "I didn't realize we were supposed to be so aware of the completion of the ceremonies. I need to watch my thoughts more carefully."

"Omaran, you should always be watching your thoughts, you know that! Not only in ceremonies!"

"Yes, yes. Okay, I do know that. What I didn't realize is that the ceremony didn't end until the full moon, which was days after what I thought was the end of our ceremony. And it is a good reminder to be told how important it is."

Antera shook her head. "You'd think after all this time you wouldn't need reminders, Dear. But I'm thankful they give them, and this warning was for the others also, who may be even worse at controlling their thoughts."

"What do you mean, 'even worse'? I've gotten a lot better at it."

"Yes, you have. But even one stray thought can really compromise you, and through you, me. Every thought counts." Antera had learned a lot about protection since she had been with Omaran, because he occasionally still allowed dark energies to come through and target her. He gradually was learning control of his mind and emotions, but it sure seemed like a slow process to her.

At least she was learning some powerful techniques and was much better at maintaining her space around him now than she had been in the beginning of their relationship. Maybe, she thought, it would come together in a class someday. Talking more about it with him she knew to be fruitless, so she got up and went upstairs to the office to do some work on her computer before bed.

Omaran watched her get up and leave the room. He didn't like her criticizing him like that when he was getting better and better at controlling his thoughts. Who did she think she was? Perfect? He grumbled to himself. Then he caught himself from going further down that road. Wait, maybe that wasn't such a positive thought . . . .

Metatron asked them, as the last ceremony on the Fall Equinox approached, to energetically connect the three sites into a triangle, after it was finished. But to also go further, following the lines all the way around the planet until they came back to the beginning. Three great circles, connecting front and back. Antera and Omaran went to the globe to trace them so they would be familiar with the paths in their minds.

"I see where they go, but I wonder why it is significant," Antera mused.

"I guess we will find out later," Omaran said. "Some special geometry? Or maybe it is just an interesting exercise."

32

Nine-Eleven

A couple of days later, on September 11, 2001, disaster struck New York City and Washington D.C. There was an immediate shift in energy around the entire planet, as the shock, outrage, and grief permeated the environment, felt by millions. The magnitude of the disaster, and the reactions to it, brought out both extremes of human behavior: the opening of hearts and selfless helping of others, as well as intense fear and anger at the perpetrators.

Antera was at work in the Bay Area when it happened, and everyone in the office took time to process, stopping work as the news settled in. Omaran, at home, found out when one of his sons called him and all he said was, "Turn on the television." When Antera got home that week, they talked about what it all meant, wondering what the consequences would be. There had never been an attack on U.S. soil before.

A message to check in with St. Germain was impinging on Antera's thoughts a week before leaving on their long drive to Arizona, for the last of the group of ceremonies. There seemed to be some extra need for protection because of what had happened. She told Omaran that St. Germain wanted to have a chat fairly urgently, so despite how busy they were with their normal work, the book, the music, and packing for the trip, they took time to set up a space for this. Omaran sat across from her and they both started raising their energy to a higher vibration to reach the Master.

St. Germain came through quickly, as if he had been waiting. "My greetings. If my tone seems a bit somber it is because, as you can well imagine, we are saddened by the events on the planet of the last week. We are mourning with all of you, spending our time soothing the sadness that has overcome the planet, as well as projecting uplifting energies to help people go beyond the usual reaction. But we are saddened not only because of the disaster, the deaths, and the losses, but also because it was allowed to happen. We had hoped that it would not come to this, even though the energies of this kind of activity have been around for some time, and building. Now that it has manifest, we must set new direction.

"The energies that have manifest in this way have culminated. However, it is not the last of them. We are hopeful because there is always a possibility that the people of the planet will gather together their strength, their compassion, and their ability to rise above the seemingly violent control that is upon the planet, and not give in to what is expected . . . not give in to the 'eye for an eye' type of mentality that has prevailed on the planet for far too long. Whenever there is insanity, insane actions such as these can happen.

"I want you, and all others who are focused on bringing the Light to the planet and uplifting the masses, to know that your work is now starting in earnest. Because of this incident, your services are greatly needed, especially on the inner planes, to put out the energy frequencies of love, caring, and rising above. The more time you can spend putting out energies of peace, the quicker this will be overcome. So your work is far more needed than ever.

"It is not coincidental that your upcoming ceremony comes right after this event. The timing is perfect, because you have the time and focus now to bring even more energy into this ceremony than you could have before. I'm sure you are all feeling that large quantities of energy are needing to be discharged and transformed through each of you. If you feel heavy, this is what is happening as you gather energy to you to be transformed during the ceremony.

"Please take care on your way there. Watch yourselves, noticing how you feel, and keeping your perspective so you do not give in to the kinds of emotions that are stirring on the planet now. You will be carrying these things with you, but you do not have to go into them yourself. And it will be important for you to maintain your higher perspective and recognize what is happening so that you can keep the highest level of focus and create the most Light. I think you will find yourselves lightening up after the ceremony.

"Are there questions about the ceremony?"

Omaran answered, "As far as the ceremony, is there anything we have left out that you would like included?"

The Master said, "The only thing I would suggest is to make sure that you call forth all of the people who are having angry reactions to the incidents so they can be given a special dispensation through your work. For all of them have the capacity to become lightworkers, or they can go the other way and become dark-workers. So if you call them to you, those who can see the Light can be transformed and uplifted into their higher service to the planet."

"Okay, thanks," Omaran nodded. "When you first started talking about what happened in New York City, you said it was allowed to happen. Does that mean that the secret government or our government knew it was going to happen and let it happen because they felt that was the best way to further their own interests—to turn toward violence and military solutions? Or did you mean something else by that?"

"I speak from a higher perspective. The people who were directly responsible are acting out of insanity. But when I say 'allowed to happen,' I speak from the plan that is unfolding and to which all of the humans on the planet are contributing. You all allowed it to happen. Not consciously, but because of the thoughtforms around the planet, the lack of understanding and love. We had thought that it might be transformed before something of this nature would have to occur, because there were many signs of changes happening, but it looks as though they did not happen quickly enough."

"I see," said Omaran. "So I would assume, then, the gift to lightworkers and this planet is that it gives us an opportunity to bring all these things out, to recognize the anger and hate that many of us harbor and transform that, hopefully thereby preventing anything more like this happening, or stopping what seems to be underway already as a retaliatory measure."

"Yes, if indeed everyone could heal their anger. Most people do not have tools available to them to help them through this kind of transformation. And that is where the lightworkers come in! You have more tools than you could ever possibly need, right?"

"Um, yes!" Omaran said, thinking that he had plenty of tools he could be using more.

"If people wake up enough to look for help, then service by lightworkers will be given. Then there is a chance of overcoming this energy so that it does not have to happen again. But sometimes, unfortunately, it takes a lot to make people wake up.

"The other side of the coin is that whenever there is disaster, there is great opportunity. There is always a chance for tremendous and very quick healing and transformation whenever there is a disaster that affects many people. So this may provide a means for some very fast awakening. This is what we are focusing on now."

Omaran said, "Thank you. I don't think I have more questions, but I certainly do feel a bit unsettled."

"And why is that?"

Omaran thought for a moment. "I seem to be fairly susceptible to all these energies that are going on now. And I think many lightworkers, like us, felt optimistic and thought we were all further along. I do feel there is a chance of a gift in all this."

"And this makes you feel unsettled?" St. Germain asked.

"As I think about it now, maybe I'm allowing too much of the outside energies to come in and influence me. They certainly have over the past few days."

"And that is all right, Omaran," Germain said, "if you take the time to transform those energies and heal them. If you choose to take on amounts of grief, fear, and anger and run them through your system as a gift to the world, that is a wonderful gift . . . if you make sure you are actually transforming it and not wallowing in it, as many people are. If you wish to help release these emotions, then you must take the time to do that. Otherwise, it is best, as lightworkers, if you can maintain your perspective. It does not mean you don't feel compassion for all the people who have been hurt. But it does mean that you maintain the higher perspective, because it is only from there that you can actually help people progress through and transform their feelings of hatred and anger into more positive action.

"This is why I have given you the warning for extra protection leading up to the ceremony, because you will be feeling many of these emotions coming at you from all around, more so than you would normally feel before a ceremony. Because you are calling to you all these lightworkers' projects, you are connecting with many people all around the planet. Therefore I tell you to be careful and to maintain your higher perspective, by recognizing what is happening. Does this make sense to you?"

"Yes it does."

"And do you still feel unsettled?"

"Well, not right now I don't," Omaran realized. "I believe you've reminded me what to do if that happens again. So I will deal with it in the appropriate manner."

"Is there anything else this evening?"

"I don't believe so. It is always nice to feel your presence, to be with you again. We both thank you for coming."

"You are my old friends, let us keep in good touch. While you are gone on your trip, you can maintain the sanctity of this area and the protection of the mountain. This mountain is dear to my heart, and I hope to continue the level of protection that it has had."

"We will do our part."

"I will work with your energy for a few moments, and hope to speak with you again soon, perhaps after the ceremony."

They felt a shift as he expanded their energy to an even higher level. They slowly opened their eyes, and looked at each other, grinning. They leaned together and kissed.

33

Triangle of Light

There were seven of them, powerful lightworkers who had traveled to Sedona to do the final ceremony of the series and tie it all together. They stood facing each other around the circle of red rocks they had created, feeling the energy ramping up.

Antera and Omaran had arrived a day early to scope out a secluded place for the ceremony. The drive from home had taken two days, and both their dog and cat had come along. A nice campground along a creek had been reserved, so they had settled there with their tent. Samantha the cat had gotten used to a leash, so she could walk with them.

Driving around to find a place for the group, they had stopped for a bathroom break and to let the pets out for a short walk. As they walked, Antera had a hunch to see what was on the other side of some thick bushes, and found that it opened up to a clearing that was almost flat and round. It was perfect for the ceremony.

Now, as they progressed through the ceremony in the clearing, none of them really noticed how intense the sun was. Mental focus was strong. Wafts of occasional breezes blew the altar cloth in the center of the circle and rustled the bushes along the perimeter. The smell of dust swirled in the air.

With each of the four ceremonies focusing on the empowerment of lightworkers, the group of people joining from a distance had grown. Many hundreds of written requests had poured in for this last ceremony, and they were now all sitting under a power device in the center as the energy was coalesced into a vortex.

The group of Masters and angels was huge and easily sensed by the small group of humans, adding a constant flow of support and love to the work. After powering up the projects for the lightworkers, together they focused on making the connections of the triangle strong, between this site in Sedona, Los Angeles, and Mount Shasta. Then they continued the lines of Light past these points of the triangle and all the way around the Earth in three circles. A tangible click was felt as it was completed.

"And we are done! Yahoo!" Antera hooted.

"Yeah! Woo hoo!" All joined in, joyfully dancing to celebrate.

They met that evening around the campfire to talk about the ceremony and see if there was any feedback from the Masters. Everyone shared the highlights and the energy they felt in the process.

Antera became quiet, noticing that not only St. Germain and the Masters were there, but another group of beings was watching and wanting contact. Everyone settled and became silent while Antera made the connection.

She said, "It is a group calling themselves the Elders of Sedona."

The Elders said, "We are the guardians of this area of Sedona. We are the ones who maintain the flame, the flow of energy from place to place. We have been working with you as you brought the Network of Light into this area.

"We are very grateful for your service. We are grateful that you have done this. You have brought a tremendous amount of Light that was not here before. You have raised the level of vibratory rate in this area.

"The connections that you have established are much deeper than were previously available. And we are now managing and learning how to bring these new energies into and out of the vortexes that exist here, as well as the new one you created today.

"We are excited to have these new connections, we cannot tell you how much, because we have been here so long and have awaited the time when we could get this kind of energy boost here. And we have also established a new contact with the San Francisco Peaks to the north as the spirit of those mountains has been reawakened. We hold the flame of the ancients! We have held it through the millennia, even when humans forgot, even when many who lived here forgot, and ignored us and our work. We kept the flame alive, and we are now in a renewed state, grateful to you for bringing in these new energies.

"As we learn to establish this new flow, it will feel unsettled for a while. But that will not last. We will learn, once again, the ancient ways. Perhaps some of you can feel that the vortex energy has expanded outward. This area has a much different palette—a different range of colors and frequencies and tones than you have where you live. And you will be taking these with you and further engaging the Network of Light."

Omaran waited for more but they were silent, so he said, "Thank you for coming to talk with us."

The Master Germain then took over, saying, "Greetings, this is Germain. I just thought you would like to hear from the resident spirits who have been very much engaged in your efforts today. We give them our thanks for their efforts.

"Soooo, another ceremony has been completed, and this one a great culmination. A peak of energy, and a finishing of what we began so long ago. We have been working on this one for years. I would say that it was successful!

"There was a vortex created where you did the ceremony. Actually, there was a small one there already, and you widened it and made it much more powerful. It's a good thing, too, because there's a lot more energy coming into this area now, and it is needed.

"So we are happy. We are happy to have it finished. We are happy to have grounded in the energies from all of the places involved, and to have circled the globe with some new energy lines. I would encourage you to look at a globe so that you can visualize what you have done.

"Frankly, we are all still reeling from this energetic boost. It was a bit larger flow than we expected. There was more support than was expected. Not only from those who knew about this ceremony, and the intentions behind it, but also others who joined in, in spirit, from all over the planet. We want these energies to integrate and continue on around the planet instead of stopping here and venting.

"You may be interested in the triangle you have created on this side of the planet. You may want to look at the center of this triangle at some point, because that area is of some interest, but I won't tell you why. This is something you will find out for yourselves, and you may even want to visit there.

"So now the Golden Ray has been firmly established and sent out along those energy corridors, and I would estimate a couple of weeks for it to continue all the way around the world and come back. In the strict sense, the ceremony is not complete until it returns here. As you travel your various ways and return to your homes, you may even pass the wave of energy, and you will help it flow more quickly in those directions.

"Because of the world events of late, this ceremony took on more importance, which is one of the reasons it got more support from the Higher Selves of many people on the planet who would not otherwise have even thought to look to their higher service. The Golden Ray energies are about peace and harmony, and they have an intelligence as they travel out, sparking the higher perspective in all those they touch . . . supporting the higher road for all people, including the leaders of all of these countries. This is the image that would be useful for you to meditate on every day until this happens."

Germain then asked if there were any questions, and each participant asked about visions they had seen, or what they had felt during the group work. Answers were given freely, and all were fulfilled.

When they got home, Antera and Omaran did look at a map of the western U.S., and drew in the triangle they had created with the series of ceremonies. St. Germain had said to look at the center point, so they drew lines from each corner of the triangle to the opposite midpoint.

"Oh, wow!" Omaran declared. "Do you see where they intersect?"

"Looks like the Mojave Desert . . . or wait, that is Death Valley, isn't it?"

"Yep. Death Valley."

203

"The deepest and hottest place in North America. That is interesting." Antera was intrigued.

"Well, you know what this means . . . we need to take a trip there."

"In the winter, of course. I wonder if they want us to do a ceremony there in the middle of the triangle," she mused.

"I think there is no question. Germain said it was an important place. We can ask later. I've never been there."

"No? I went there several times on field trips when I was an undergrad studying geology. The rocks are amazing." Antera remembered much of those trips vividly. "It is a very unique place."

"I can't wait! But I don't like the name of it."

"I think it was named after some pioneers who were heading west and didn't make it across."

"Hmmm." He spun the globe around. "Let's see if we can tell where the back side of the triangle is. We know that it should be on the opposite side of the Earth." They traced the circles with pieces of string. "It is this area of the Philippines."

"I wonder what the significance of that is," Antera said.

When they asked, they were told that yes, a ceremony in Death Valley was requested. It would be a different ceremony, with a theme of world peace. Always needed! And the energy from a ceremony in the valley would be connected into the Triangle of Light.

The following day, Omaran realized that he couldn't get Death Valley out of his mind. Something about that place was drawing him. They were rehearsing the songs from their musical, as they did every day, preparing them for recording and performing.

"Why not do the ceremony in Death Valley this Winter Solstice?" Omaran asked when they took a break.

Antera got a big glass of water and drank. Singing made her thirsty. "That wouldn't give us very much time to plan."

"We've done so many ceremonies, we can whip it together in a month, no problem. Maybe just invite the ones who did the Empowering Lightworkers ceremonies with us."

Antera thought about it. "Well, it is a good time of year to go there. But it may be too cold to camp."

"Yeah, we'd have to find a hotel close by where everyone could stay."

And it was decided. They put out a special invitation to a select list of people, knowing that the perfect group would respond. It was only a five-hour drive from the Los Angeles area. They found that the hotel in the valley floor was very expensive, so they found a cheaper one up the west side of the valley and reserved a few rooms.

Before they were all going to meet, Antera and Omaran arrived to scope it out. As they drove down the long descent from the western side, the views were spectacular and vast. Omaran loved it right away. The breadth and expanse, the scope, the colors of the many rock formations. He couldn't get enough into his eyes. Every direction he looked seemed to be more beautiful than the one he had just seen. The areas on the desert floor were mostly open and bare, but on the west and east sides of the valley were high mountains, as high as 12,000 feet above the valley floor.

Distances were vast in the huge valley, and going from place to place took hours. All the valley was a desert with few plants, but they found a patch of bushes on the valley floor, in which there was an area that was mostly hidden from the road. It was a perfect place to do the ceremony, and only a short hike from where they could park. They both felt like they had found the center of the valley, energetically if not physically. They walked around the various sections of the area they had been led to, liking it more and more as they came around the next low sand hill and saw yet another small area where they could be alone.

Satisfied about the location, they headed back to the hotel, as the others would be arriving that evening. The rest of the group arrived shortly after Antera and Omaran returned, and they made plans for the following day. The hotel was not well insulated and very cold at night, probably made more uncomfortable because everyone was fasting prior to the ceremony. Omaran even went to the hotel manager to make sure that the room heaters were turned on, and they were. Clearly the area was more concerned with the intense summer heat than the mild cold of winter.

In the morning, they all put on ceremonial clothes, packed the ceremonial items and lunches, and set out in several vehicles. Antera and

Omaran led the way down into the impressive valley. They parked and walked to the chosen site, over the valley floor, which was covered with a most diverse and magnificent collection of colorful rocks. It was difficult for Antera to walk over the rocks without stopping and collecting some, especially when many called to her, like they wanted her to see them and take them home. But with some effort, she resisted and stayed focused on the energy of the ceremonial space and what they were about to do.

They energetically set up the perimeter to protect the space, defined a ceremonial circle, and set up a large globe on a stand in the center. After everyone was saged to cleanse their energy, they took their places around the circle.

They called in the Masters, then all the people who were participating from a distance, and felt the shift of energy each time, like waves. The nature spirits in the area were promised gifts for their cooperation. The energy grew and grew with each step, and waves of peace and harmony were sent through hands and hearts to the Earth, represented by the globe.

Afterwards, they all looked at each other and smiled, knowing that each person got many private benefits from doing this work, and the large flow of transformational energy was always felt for weeks after a ceremony, if not longer. They all lingered near the ceremonial area for a few minutes, enjoying the magic of the place combined with the power of the solstice and ceremony. Feeling good about both the service work and the personal gain, they broke their fast right there, with their picnic lunch. Because the wind had kicked up, they all had to bundle up to be comfortable. But it was the Winter Solstice of 2001, the shortest day of the year, after all!

Unbeknownst to them, during this ceremony in the deepest valley of North America, they had attracted the attention of a powerful fire deva from deep within the Earth, who would make himself known six years later.

34

Divine Composer

Throughout 2002, Antera and Omaran were still very busy in the studio honing their CD, as well as Antera finishing her book, on top of all their normal work and whatever service work was requested of them from the Order of Melchizedek. Though they were busy, they loved it all, and were excited, especially about the creative projects.

In August, they decided to attend the Pageant of Angels, put on by the I Am Foundation in Mount Shasta. It was their first time attending this annual show. As they sat in the large amphitheater and listened to the 138-person choir sing uplifting songs, Antera was suddenly "touched" by Master Jesus, whom they called Jeshua, his original name. She had communicated with him many times over the years, but this was different. In just a few moments, riding along the waves of sound, Jeshua communicated to her such great love and caring for all of humanity that she started weeping. Then, through this deep love, he let her know that he wanted her to write a song for him. Of course, she said yes.

That very evening and through the next morning, she kept hearing little phrases of his song in her mind, but though it was a Sunday, she had a busy schedule and no free time to spend writing songs. But the Master wouldn't let it go. In late morning, she and Omaran were sitting in the living room working on a project, when the phone rang. It was a friend asking for Omaran's immediate assistance.

And so it was that after Omaran unexpectedly left, she suddenly found herself sitting on the couch in the unusual condition of having unscheduled time on her hands. She briefly wondered what she should do now, before Jeshua's song started pouring through. Picking up a pad of paper, she wrote it down, then went to the piano. By the time Omaran returned two hours later, the song was finished.

They had both written many songs, but never had a complete song manifested so quickly before. Omaran was astounded. He loved it, and cried when he heard her sing it the first time.

Let the Light of forgiveness,
The Light of compassion,
The Light of love
Radiate, propagate and dominate
Before it's too late . . . .

A few days later, Antera could feel Jeshua prompting her again about it, just to make sure she hadn't forgotten that his song needed to be recorded and get out to the world.

He said to her, "I would like Omaran to sing it instead of you. You can do the backup vocals."

Antera wasn't so sure about that. "Are you sure? I wanted to sing it."

"You will see, it will be better with him."

So she agreed, and later, mentioned to Omaran that she wanted to hear how he would sound singing it.

"Yes! I would love to! But I thought you wrote it for you to sing."

"I thought so too, but Jeshua would like you to sing it."

"He said that?" Omaran put his hand on his heart. "Oh, well, of course, I'd be honored!"

He resonated with the idea immediately, for the song had touched him deeply, and it was decided. Jeshua had asked him to sing it! Omaran would not let him down.

They both continued to feel the driving force, an urgency behind the song. It almost constantly played in the back of both of their minds.

So after only a couple of weeks, they were in the studio to record it with Terry.

The first recording session did not go well. Omaran laid a piano track and a scratch vocal, but Terry didn't seem to relate to the song. He said that it sounded like it was for Christians, and suggested making it into a hymn, instrumenting with organs! Antera and Omaran ended the session early, not happy with how it was going.

A week later, they decided to give it another try, and booked studio time for the new song. They went in with some hesitation, but hopeful they could find the sounds they wanted. Immediately, they could see that something had shifted with Terry.

"See what you think of this," Terry said, and played some tracks he had already laid. The instrumentation was inspired, and they liked it a lot.

"So what happened? You like the song now?" Antera asked him.

"Well yes, I really feel it now." He explained. Tears started forming in his eyes. "Last night, I was watching a special on TV and someone played a couple of songs from the musical *Jesus Christ Superstar*, and I was really touched by them. Then I realized that this song has the same feeling, and I got it. I really got what Jesus is saying."

Antera and Omaran exchanged a knowing look. It was clearly the Master at work. The rest of the recording went smoothly, and with only a few more sessions, they had a rough mix. Next, they sent the song to Antera's sister, Janet, for review. She had already helped tremendously with the *Twin Flames* album. After Janet had a chance to listen, they all connected with a phone call for initial feedback.

"Well," Janet began, "I like it, but there is something bothering me about the song."

"What?" Antera asked.

"Are you sure Jesus said that this is his final plea and we'd better heed it before it is too late? I mean, can it really ever be too late? Will the Masters really give up on us if we don't get it together?"

"Well, that is what he said," Antera affirmed.

"Hmmm . . . well that certainly is disturbing."

She went on to make some suggestions about arrangements. When she got the next version two weeks later, and called again, she said that she had listened to it all weekend, when she should have been packing to move! The song had grabbed her and she kept thinking about it, playing it over and over.

"So what made you suddenly like the song?" Omaran asked her.

"I've been feeling Jesus all weekend. I finally got it. Especially the part about it being too late. You know, it took dinner with a Republican to understand that."

Omaran and Antera laughed. "What do you mean?"

"I mean, I had a dinner date with a guy I really liked, and we started talking about politics and it turned out he is a Republican. He was actually talking about his support of a war with Iraq. That was when it hit me that there are people like that in the world, in fact lots of them. I'm a flower child! I don't think war is the answer to anything! So right then I got that it really can be too late."

Once again, they were all impressed with the energy the Master was putting into this project, and how he was reaching the people who were helping to make it happen. The pressure to get it done did not let up, and despite the fact that Antera and Omaran were in the middle of the other CD, and numerous other projects, they continued working on the song until they had a version they liked. It was called "Message from Jesus," later renamed "Light of Forgiveness."

They released it as a two-song disc. These were the days before online music downloads, so pressing CDs was the standard for any music releases. The other song on the CD was the one they had written and recorded for the Empowering Lightworkers ceremonies, "Now! (Lightworkers' Anthem)." Two songs with strong messages.

35

Mystery School

"You know, I'm getting that our next ceremony should be another initiation into the Order of Melchizedek," Antera announced to Omaran.

She had just come down the stairs from the office, rounding the corner to where he was playing the piano in the dining room.

He stopped and thought about that. "Initiate new people?"

"Yes. We were ordained so we could do this as part of the mystery school, and now we have a place to do it here. I think it is time. Maybe the Winter Solstice."

He nodded slowly. "Here? There is usually a lot of snow in December."

"Yes, but we would be indoors. We could do the ceremony in our living room."

He thought about all the furniture moving that would require and frowned. "I don't know . . ."

She knew what he was thinking. "Don't worry, we will have others help with setting it up. After all, we don't get paid, since this is part of our service, so surely others will volunteer as well."

"Maybe. We can think about it." He quickly warmed up to the idea. "If the Masters want it, we will do it."

"I'm putting together the newsletter now, so I'll put the invitation in there." She got some water and started to go back upstairs, then poked her head back around. "Oh, and we need a new song for the ceremony."

Omaran felt the energy of that request, and immediately opened to a creative flow on the keyboard. Over the next few weeks, a song emerged called "The Light," which was mostly his creation, with Antera's input, and they both sang it. It really set the mood they wanted for the ceremony, with very gradual chord progressions and lyrics that developed in a similar way. It was more like a complex chant than a song. With Terry, they recorded only the music so they could sing it live, getting it done just a week before the event.

And as we move into the new,
Light will come and it will lead the way.
And as we move into the Light,
New will come and all will fade away.
And as we fall into the Light,
We will move into the new to stay . . . .

About 20 people signed up for the initiation, which was a good-sized group for their living room. When the Order of Melchizedek put out a call, many people felt it. Their intuition said they needed to be there, to take this step, sometimes without knowing why or what would happen. The mention of this cosmic order often stirred them like a deep remembrance inside, and they simply knew it was something that would feed the soul and help them on a balanced path of spiritual evolution.

By being initiated, these participants would declare their dedication to their spiritual path and highest purpose, thereby calling in a greater level of attention from the Ascended Masters on their journey. It was important to make this declaration out loud in front of others, as this made it intensely profound and brought it fully into consciousness, as well as physically into the many areas of life.

Through their experience, Antera and Omaran had found that most people on a spiritual path were not very grounded. Many could reach very high-level spaces with their consciousness in meditation, but they couldn't always bring those frequencies into the physical world. It was like living in two different worlds. The goal was to bring the spiritual energies into the physical world, rather than trying to escape the world.

Since the order is a cosmic one, concerned with the evolution of consciousness in the entire universe, the initiation they planned was very personal and unique to each person. They were always careful not to encourage followers, or to say that this was the only way, in these times of many ways. The Masters had asked them to do this service without pay, to keep the energy clean. A balanced approach is what they always taught, stressing that all four bodies—physical, emotional, mental and spiritual—needed to evolve at about the same rate to maintain this balance.

The group of participants bravely made the trip to the mountain. The snow was piled high on both sides of the road, challenging some drivers in two-wheel-drive vehicles, but all made it without major problems. The journey they took was a part of the initiation, which for some was enhanced by having challenges or obstacles to overcome to make it there. As each person recounted the challenges they had to make to undertake a journey to snow country, their joy in making it to the event was evident in the passion of their tales. It truly heightened the initiation for each of them and was a deeply moving and permanent part of their evolution.

It was the perfect group to initiate, as Antera and Omaran knew it would be. As they went through the energy preparations and then the final ceremony, all initiates were very dedicated and open to receive the blessings that were just right for them. The song was perfect, and initiations were very powerful. Everyone went home uplifted and ready for the next step on their renewed spiritual path.

Putting on the event was a lot of work and took time off from other projects, but it was very rewarding to the Mount Shasta duo to see how it changed people and helped them speed up their evolution, taking them to a very real new level.

Afterwards, as they sat in the living room to rest, Omaran declared, "I think we should do this once a year!"

"Is this the same person speaking now who was not overjoyed to be doing this in the middle of our snowiest month on the mountain?"

"Well, yes . . . it's just that it was such an uplifting event, not only for the participants, but for us. And the joy in everyone was just inspiring! They all got so much out of it."

"I loved it too, but I'm just not sure that winter is the best time. Think how much easier it is in the summer. Let's think Summer Solstice from now on."

"Sounds good to me."

36

Hitting the Road

In early 2003, with the *Twin Flames* CD and book both almost finished, plans were being made to go on a West Coast tour. Omaran, with his usual exuberance, was sure he could do all the bookings himself—performances, book signings, and workshops. The idea of being on the road was exciting.

"But how will we afford that?" Antera asked. "If we both quit working, we won't be able to pay our mortgage. Are you thinking of a long trip?"

"There are many bookstores along the West Coast. I don't think we'll have a lack of places to go. But we won't be earning any money from this, except for selling a few books and CDs. That certainly won't help with our mortgage." He thought a moment. "I know what we could do! Let's rent our house while we are gone so most of the mortgage can be paid."

"But what about the pets?"

"Hmmm." Omaran thought about that. "Yeah, I hadn't thought that far ahead. Well, we certainly can't leave them anywhere, and our Subaru wagon is too small." They had sold Zippy to get the new car, which was better in snow. "Maybe if we had an RV, they could come with us."

"One of those huge things? No way! I'm not going anywhere in one of those!"

Omaran ignored that, warming up to the idea of an extended trip in an RV. It sounded so adventurous. "I'm sure we will figure it out. Just think of the money we'd save on hotels if we got an RV."

"Well maybe . . . ," Antera conceded, "but you'd better get booking or we will have no place to go."

Omaran planned to find a couple of theaters where they could do the full musical, and many bookstores to perform a few songs or talk about the book. He also looked for places to do workshops about twin flames and spiritual relationships. Yes, they would be on the road for a while!

One day as they were leaving Terry's studio after a successful session in which they further tweaked some of the songs, Terry suddenly got excited. "Oh! Guess what! My good friends Mark and Ellen are coming here to live. I've known them for a long time, and they are actually moving to the mountain now!" He was literally jumping up and down.

"That's great!" Omaran said. "When?"

As it turned out, Mark and Ellen were coming right about when Antera and Omaran wanted to leave on their tour. And they needed a place to rent for a year while they built a house. In fact, they bought a lot practically next door. It was a perfect set up!

As soon as the couple arrived, Antera and Omaran invited them over. Terry had already briefed them on their travel plans and when they all met, they liked each other immediately. They were moving from New Mexico, and planned to start an online business selling solar power systems, so they were very excited, both about moving to the mountain and starting their new business. It was decided that day that Mark and Ellen would be the official renters of their house for one year. Once again, Spirit was orchestrating everything so that all involved had the highest and best outcome.

With a committed date to leave in June, they started looking at used RVs, and scheduled two book and CD release parties, one in Mount Shasta at Terry's house, and a second one in the Bay Area at the Larkspur Theatre, which they had used for several events before. The 28-foot RV manifested very quickly, and to fund the trip they refinanced their home. Off they went with lots of energy and enthusiasm!

They felt like gypsies, without a home, living in their vehicle. It was a comfortable space, and they had converted the bedroom into an office, sleeping in the bed over the cab. They took everything they could possibly need with them, including their books and CDs, office equipment, and sound system so they could perform. Samantha had adjusted to walking on a leash, which was apparently quite unusual for a cat, judging from the stares they got when they were out with her and Faith.

They really enjoyed the shows and talks, going from town to town, and either camping or staying in Walmart parking lots, which they discovered were mostly RV friendly. Sleeping in a vehicle overnight on streets was illegal, so it wasn't quite as easy as they thought it would be to find places to stay. The RV campgrounds were almost as expensive as motels.

They were in Los Angeles, and Omaran was becoming a bit frustrated with the difficulty of finding places to park overnight. He was complaining about it to Antera when all of a sudden they got a flat tire and had to pull off on the closest street, parking overnight in front of an apartment building. They were nervous about sleeping in a strange neighborhood, but no one bothered them, in fact they were quite ignored. Omaran thought that perhaps they should put a sign in their window saying that they had a flat tire and would take care of it the following day, in case any of the neighbors didn't like them parking there, but he was just too tired.

"I get it!" Omaran said the next morning, after a peaceful night during which no one pounded on their door. "Parking in front of an apartment building works! People who live here think we are visiting one of their neighbors, but they don't know who, so they don't pay us any mind."

"I guess so," Antera said hesitantly as they started up to find a tire shop.

"That means if we find apartments, we can park and sleep, no problem. This opens up big possibilities! Wow! Spirit came through again!"

Omaran was very happy about this discovery, because it lightened some of the heavy burden of responsibility he felt he was carrying on this trip. He was the driver, because Antera was not comfortable driving such a big vehicle. She had become the navigator. Driving through towns was stressful because signs along sidewalks were a bit lower than the top of their RV, and he had already hit a few.

They had to find a new place to stay every night, since they rarely stayed more than one night anywhere. He was also the one arranging all the book-signing events and shows, and making sure they got to each one on time. This was done without a cell phone, but they had found a modem that plugged into the computer—their first laptop—so they could get email. It was a new, very expensive service but worth it.

All of this was a lot of responsibility on Omaran's shoulders, and as the months went on, he got more and more stressed. This came out as irritability, and made it very unpleasant for Antera, because they were together all the time. If he got cranky at home and didn't want her help, she could avoid him until he solved whatever his issue was. But in the RV, there was no place to go. He would bury his stress for performances and talks, but as soon as they were off the stage, there it was again.

"Omaran, you need to find a way to be nice. Are you going to be mean the whole trip? I want to enjoy this time on the road!" Antera said as they were driving in southern California.

"I'm not being mean. I just have a lot on my mind."

"It is supposed to be fun, remember? We are on an adventure! If you hate doing this so much, we should cancel everything and go home. You aren't very fun to be with these days."

"I don't hate it! It just isn't as easy as I thought it would be. Anyway, we don't have a home right now."

"Well, I suggest we find a place to stop for a few days. Somewhere in nature, out of cities. We need to recharge and tune in to the Masters. It is so hard to do while we are in cities, and let's face it, we aren't in the flow or it wouldn't be so stressful for you."

He thought for a while as he watched the seemingly unending freeway. They had been on one freeway after another for weeks. He felt good about how he was handling the planning and driving, but he knew that he had neglected his energy work. It was hard to find time or a good space to meditate on the road. It was as if he had completely set aside all he had learned from the Masters, and started operating from his third-dimensional mind. Obviously, something had to change. And this city seemed to be all concrete, everywhere they went . . . except for a few parks, all concrete. Ugh.

Realizing that Antera was right, and they should take a break, Omaran mentally reviewed the itinerary. After a couple of gigs in Los Angeles, they were heading north again.

He turned into a gas station and said, "You know, we are going right by Mount Shasta next week."

"Could we stop on the mountain? I'd love to camp there if we can. How long would we have?"

She didn't wait for an answer, as she got out and walked to the gas station office to prepay for a fill-up. Omaran made travel calculations as he pumped the gas. The RV had a very big tank and gas prices were high, so it was around $100 each time.

When the tank was full, they took off again. He resumed the conversation. "Well, we don't have to be in Seattle for a few days, so I think we could stay somewhere on the mountain for four nights if we left right after the last show in this area."

Excited, Antera exclaimed, "Let's do it!"

"Yes, let's." He nodded as he pulled back onto the freeway.

Just knowing he would have a break soon helped his mood tremendously. Visiting their mountain would be so rejuvenating! But also lurking in the back of his mind was the fact that he knew his behavior had not been good on this trip, and no doubt the Masters would want to talk about that. He hadn't been able to handle all the responsibility very well. Why couldn't he just look at it as an adventure and enjoy it? He got tense again, as old thoughts that said he wasn't good enough started surfacing.

Thus, it was in mid-September that they pointed the RV north to Mount Shasta, camping one night along the West Fork of the Sacramento River. That was nice, but they decided that what they really needed was to be on the mountain itself. They began driving up the main highway that led up the mountain from the town of Mount Shasta, past the road to their home, looking for a place to park for a few days. No place they passed felt right, so they kept following the road all the way to its highest point in elevation, and parked in a parking lot where the road ended. It was perfect. They had never slept at such a high altitude on the mountain.

The spring that fed Panther Meadows was a short walk away, so they had fresh water, plus they had stocked up on food, so they could stay there the whole time. Taking Faith and Samantha out, they all went for a short walk around the area. The late afternoon air was crisp and chilly, but invigorating and clean. The spiritual energy of the mountain was very strong. They both sighed several times, taking it in. It was so wonderful to be back home for a few days!

The plan was to check in with the Masters every evening they were there, and hike every day. There were several buttes to climb from where they were parked. At high elevations, the veils are considerably thinner, so it is always easier to sense other realms. It was such a relief after being at lower elevations where the atmosphere was thicker, and in cities, with dense astral smog and interference.

As they strolled with the pets, taking in the view down to the valley below, Antera said, "Isn't it astounding how much easier it is to think here?"

"I don't know how people live down there for long."

"I guess they get used to it. We did when we lived in the Bay Area."

Omaran wondered to himself why it had all seemed so hard, just a couple of days ago. He said, "It is so much easier to get perspective here."

"I'm just so glad we will be coming back here to our home when the tour is over."

"Yeah." They walked back to the RV.

That evening, St. Germain came to talk. Fortunately, theirs was the only vehicle in the lot after dark, so they didn't need to be concerned about others hearing them. The walls of the RV weren't exactly thick, and whenever Antera brought through St. Germain, her voice got louder, perhaps to accommodate his vast energy flow.

He boomed, "Welcome back to the mountain! It does seem like it's been a long time, and I believe this is the highest elevation at which I have been able to contact you . . . and the highest level of consciousness! I greet you and I give you my blessing, for I am very pleased to talk with you tonight more directly, and to see that you are allowing these wonderful rarified energies into your systems . . . so needed."

"Yes, we are very glad to be here." Omaran said.

"We are all very happy that you heeded the call to come up on the mountain. For these energies can be found nowhere else on the planet! They are very special, as you know, and I come here often, for their nourishing benefits as well, even though I am not in body as you are. This feels like home for many of us, and it is one of our most nourishing spots on the planet.

"Many are gathered here inside the mountain now, it is a congregation of beings and you have been invited. There is a great new vortex being created within the larger one. This vortex is calling all who are aligned with this Earth-school. For we are all in this together and every one of us, myself included, has a part to play in transforming this planet. This has always been our goal, our most important work, my most important work and the work of you who are embodied now, striving to do your part within the greater context.

"Many lightworkers have felt alone in their work. Many have felt as if their work was in vain, as if the planet were not ready for the energies that they bring, and for the transformation that they are willing and able to do.

"We have been trying to encourage all of you so much! And yet, still the connection between all of you hasn't been strong. This connection is what it takes to create the great transformation. It requires this Network of Light, it requires all of you to connect with each other."

Omaran said, "We felt a shift after the Empowering Lightworkers ceremonies, so hopefully that helped."

"Yes, it did, and that is what makes this meeting possible. This is what we are convening about on this mountain now, how to network all of you together, to bring forth a solid front, so to speak . . . a solid Network of Light on the planet bringing you into better communication

221

with each other. So you know you are not separate, and so you can see that you are doing your part because you see the effects on the greater Network of Light.

"If you try to work alone and you do not magnify your efforts by putting it out into the network, then it will seem futile, like nothing is happening. But if you tune into the network, if you consciously call to each other, and magnify and congratulate each other's work, and help all of the other lightworkers be successful in their work, then your own work will become tremendously successful. This is a feedback system that can be used by all of you, but we do not yet see it being used much.

"We do not see many of the lightworkers tuning into this vast network that is available, that is still in bits and pieces because many of you do not use it. This was created over many years, and it is now at a point where it can be fully utilized as a magnificent feedback system to magnify each other's work."

Omaran wondered, "Is there a specific way we should use the network now?"

St. Germain answered, "Yes! You send positive energy to all the other lightworkers, the healers, teachers, people who are doing work of the heart and bringing more Light to the planet. You connect with them and send them the most tremendous burst of love and appreciation, and wish them tremendous success! Wish them to have hundreds and hundreds of clients! Wish them to have many, many people in their workshops. Wish them to have the greatest success they can have! And it comes back to you multiplied.

"Then you send it out again and lo and behold, we have a working Network of Light on the planet! A system of cooperation, a system that works! A system that can transform this planet into the new age so quickly!"

"I get it, and we will put this in our newsletter so others can start to do it too," Omaran assured him.

"Good. This is what we meet about. We invited you two here because we see you are out in the world, you are contacting many other lightworkers. You can add this to your workshops, the importance of connecting, of letting go of the separation, of any kind of competition between you. Let go of all that is not embracing the entire network. It is time to think globally, for all lightworkers!

"We cannot give up! Some of the lightworkers have actually given up because it was a little hard; because there are so many things happening in the world and they feel like their work is not making a dent. But let me tell you it is! Once again we rally all of you. We are simply asking you to tune into each other, so that you can see that you are making a difference. No matter how bad things look in the world, if you concentrate on the Light, if you concentrate on this transformation, then it will happen.

"Remember, as lightworkers it is your job to maintain the Light, and not to be judgmental of those who have not reached a point where they can do the same. They may be younger and need to make mistakes. If you look back in your own history you will know that you likely made similar mistakes. And it didn't do you any good to be judged. It only did you good to be loved and to be helped through.

"So we know it is a challenge, but we hope all lightworkers will withdraw their negative thoughts and feelings from those areas that beg for negative thoughts and feelings. Put that energy into the lightwork grid, where it can do the most good.

"We are all one with the I Am Presence, the God-Force Presence. When you succeed, I succeed. When I succeed, you succeed. And when you raise your Light, I raise my Light. We are all in this together!

"So enough preaching. Please give that message to all lightworkers you encounter. The meeting we are having is about finding new ways for light-bearers to become empowered. And lo and behold, here you are on the mountain at just the right time! Do you have any questions about this?"

Omaran said, "First I would like to say that we both felt drawn back here, and it feels like coming home. It feels so wonderful to be back here, sleeping at this high elevation."

St. Germain said, "And it is true, the higher you go, the closer you are to the Divine. Especially on this mountain."

Omaran felt really good. He was already thinking about where they could include the Network of Light in their workshops on twin flames and soulmates. "I just feel so overjoyed. It feels so good to be here now."

"Very well. And do you have any other questions for me tonight?"

Omaran thought about it. "Is there anything more I can do to help Antera with her hip?"

For about a year, Antera had occasionally had pain in her hip area, for which she had seen a chiropractor, acupuncturist, and massage therapists, all with no help. Because she had been a dancer in her twenties, and had been through several other injuries in gymnastics and horse riding accidents as a teen, she had been seeing chiropractors most of her life and had been able to keep the body going with minimal pain. But this stronger pain was new, if not surprising, given the inherited misalignment of her leg and foot in childhood.

When the pain persisted, she had finally gone to a doctor to have it x-rayed in case there was something wrong with the bones. The x-ray had come back normal, and the diagnosis was tendonitis. She had always worked out and been very active, so resting was difficult. They had joined a chain of gyms so they could work out while touring, and she could still do her workout if she was careful.

St. Germain answered, "As you know, this is a manifestation of the very thing we have been talking about, the hesitancy to move forward. The hesitancy of ALL lightworkers to move forward into their work because they feel it is not effective, and because of the fear of being persecuted. Otherwise, it is simply a physical problem. You can deal with it in many physical ways and some of these you have already done. And you have helped her with the energy work you do. But the larger picture is to transform that energy along the lineage of many lightworkers on this planet, so it is no longer an issue. The karma of the group has to be dissolved."

"So," Omaran said, "I don't mean to be naïve, but does this mean Antera's hip issue is partly from her taking on group karma? And then if we can shift this, will it help others?"

"Yes indeed! Which is why you take on these kinds of things. Whatever pattern you heal in yourself affects everyone else who has that pattern.

"It is all about bringing the greater good into the Network of Light. It is about re-patterning an issue that will help bring about a more powerful network. It is about healing the network. Do you see?"

Omaran replied, "Yes, I do understand on different levels now, levels I wouldn't have seen a few years ago. We take things on because of gifts we have been given, because of our connection with the planet and this mountain."

After the Master left, Omaran said, "I want to work on your leg energetically every day!"

"Sounds good," Antera said, as she changed her position in the chair. "I admit, I used to be hesitant, and feeling less than supported in my outward spiritual work. But that is a pattern I thought I had healed, and I don't really want to shift it for everyone else."

"You and I together are so strong, I think we can shift anything." Omaran was feeling very strong and limitless, as he always did after being with the Masters.

37

Inside the Mountain

The next day, after doing their office work tracking bookings, handling product sales, and other activities, Antera and Omaran went for a good hike up and around Green Butte, taking Faith with them. They both had a sense of anticipation, as if something big was happening or about to happen, and it felt exciting. Knowing there was a meeting going on with many Masters inside the mountain was a part of it, and they thought they could hear some sound that seemed to be coming up from the ground.

Checking in again that evening, they wanted to see if there was more from the Masters about what they were feeling. Settling into their soft chairs in the RV living/dining room, which were actually quite comfortable, they meditated and raised their vibrations to allow the communication.

Antera said, "St. Germain is here, but he is introducing our friend King of the Ancients, who is part of the meeting."

King of the Ancients said, "Thank you for hearing me. Thank you for coming. I want you to know that I and my clan are aware of your presence whenever you come to the mountain. We are watchful of everyone who comes here. We are the guardians of old. We notice the energy of everyone who attends this mountain, for that is our job, to maintain the energy that is here.

"We live inside the mountain, as you know. You have been shown a few of the entry and exit points into the caverns where we dwell. But you cannot go there in your physical body, only in your etheric body. These points are close to the physical and have physical form, but you have to pass through rock. Our bodies are etheric now. Once we had third-dimensional bodies, but we had to let them go so we could maintain this energy field.

"I have called you before, many times. Sometimes you listened, sometimes you didn't. I call you because you have a spiritual lineage that is tied to mine. Your past is connected to mine and to ours, for we have some of the same roots. Perhaps you feel this connection and that is why you are drawn to the mountain, and that is why you work with the Master St. Germain.

"You can come in now, if you can leave your body behind."

Antera described what was going on so Omaran could follow. "He has a staff, and is doing some kind of an energy thing with it . . . we are traveling now. He's opening a door, and we are ushered in, and down some steps. It is a big, big room full of Light Beings, a round room like a big cavern. This is the meeting place. We can sit and watch while we are here. Are you following me?"

Omaran could see it all as she described it. "Yes. I can't hear, but I can see."

"Good. So we're sitting in the back row. It is a circle of beings, several rows, with aisles at the four directions, north, east, south and west. They are chanting, working with sound frequencies, as well as Light. A large vortex of energy is being built with the chant, through the long repetition of the chant for days and days."

Antera tried to hear more clearly what the words of the chant were, then said, "It's in another language, so I can't make out the words. I feel it more than hear it, I feel its effects on me. I feel the sound waves running though my etheric body. The rhythm is so strong . . . ." She mimicked the rhythm by drumming on her legs.

"There is more than one part, like a round." She paused, watching and listening.

"There's something in the center of the circle, an object of power . . . I can't tell what shape it is. It's very bright and it's amplifying the Light and the sound. When they are done this will hold the energy for a very long time, and radiate it."

Omaran said, "I see it too, and I get the feeling that this has come from far away to be charged up here."

"Yes," Antera agreed. "They are working with the rays, concentrating the energy in a balanced spectrum . . . Oh! We have to go now. We're being led out by the King of the Ancients. He's asking us to keep the image of what we saw so we can tune into it.

"Now he's showing me more about how the energy goes out from this mountain along the ley lines, to the rest of this continent, and to the whole world, eventually. And they're doing this work to strengthen this grid, and the Network of Light that St. Germain was telling us more about last night. The King left, and Germain is here to talk again."

St. Germain said, in his usual exuberance, "Well, I hope you enjoyed your little visit! I thought you might like that. We have made progress with the project already. We are all interested in this little experiment to see whether we can effect a major change on this planet using this method."

St. Germain went on, explaining what they had seen in the chamber and more about the project and their part of it, which they were instructed not to share. It was all very new and exciting to Antera and Omaran. When St. Germain was finished, they decided to hike further up the mountain the next day, into what they called the "bowl," so they could get closer to the physical area of the underground meeting place of the Masters.

They started up the hill early in the morning, taking lunch and several water bottles, thinking it would be a long hike. A strong, loud wind blew constantly against them. It was very steep and hard to make progress with the loose rocks under their boots. The higher they climbed, the more intense the energy felt.

Omaran developed a pain in the side of his abdomen. At first, it annoyed him but he tried not to think about it. It didn't go away, making the hike very uncomfortable for more than an hour. Then he decided that was enough, and had the inspiration to try and heal it energetically without stopping. As he plodded upward, he charged up his hands and put them on the area, filling his abdomen with healing Light. Though he had been using his hands this way for many years, in the back of his mind he had always had doubts about his healing abilities. This time, somehow he knew it would work. And it did. The pain went away quickly, without even stopping the steep hike. He was joyful at this validation and test of his faith.

With each foot of increased elevation, as the energy got stronger, it became more and more physically uncomfortable for Antera. Her heart started beating erratically, and she was short of breath. She knew it was more than a reaction to the elevation. They stopped to sit on a large boulder, and reassessed.

After drinking water, they took a few minutes to reinforce the Light Field they had created all the way around the mountain. From here, it looked magnificent! All the smaller Light Fields were working together and continuous, completely surrounding the peak with a pulsing, bright energy.

Then Omaran gazed up the slope. "Are you okay to continue? I'd sure like to get further up. See that ridge with three bumps next to the other ridge? I'm aiming for this side of that."

Antera had no idea which ridge he had in mind, as they all looked pretty much the same to her. She couldn't even think about continuing. "You go ahead. I have to go back down. I feel like I will have a heart attack if I go further—my heart does not like this. The energy here is way too much for my body." She paused. "There is a faint sound. Do you hear it?"

Omaran closed his eyes and listened. His hearing wasn't as good as Antera's, and all he could hear was the wailing wind. "Not really. I feel it though, so maybe it is the chanting of the Masters under here."

"Probably so, but I'm still going down. The energy is way too intense. I guess I could take in the energy much easier when we went inside with our etheric bodies. My physical body isn't as strong as yours."

With some disappointment, Omaran said, "Okay, then. I'm not going on without you. Let's go down. Maybe that was enough, to get this close. The elevation has got to be close to 10,000 feet."

They got up and hiked quickly down the long, steep slope, the wind now blowing on their backs. Once they were back at the RV, Antera felt fine. They needed water so they collected all their bottles and walked to the spring, with both pets, filling the containers and drinking right from the ground. The water was very cold but refreshing. Samantha and Faith drank further down the stream so the spring would remain pure.

For the third day in a row, they tuned in to the Masters that evening, still amazed at how much easier it was to connect at this elevation and on this mountain. St. Germain appeared to Antera's inner sight, looking very bright and glowing in a violet robe.

Germain confirmed that they had gotten very close to the deep chamber. "I thank you for making such a valiant attempt today. We watched your progress and monitored it. If the hike had been easy it would not have had the impact that it had, and you would not have had the energy that came back with you. Though you may not have heard all of the sound physically, the etheric part of your brain registered it very well. There are parts of the DNA of the brain that have not been fully activated and though you may not hear sounds, they still affect you. They affect your ears and brain.

"You have finished what you needed to do, persevering to gather the energies. Whenever you go near the heart of the mountain, you gather particular frequencies to you. And today, you gathered power. Omaran, you had some insight today, didn't you?"

Omaran answered, "Yes, I was thinking that I needed confirmation of my healing ability. But as I walked up, I realized that I didn't need confirmation, because I KNEW. And when I healed my side, I did it because I knew I could, I had faith. I have learned a lot in a short time here."

"Faith has been one of your big lessons, hasn't it? Not just acquiring it, but maintaining it. And this will be your challenge when you go off the mountain. For as you well know, that which is perfectly clear here may become muddy and distorted when you go down into other areas and cities. Away from this pure source, where the veils are so thin, your challenge will be to remind yourself consciously, constantly, so that you do not forget."

"I have had many miracles and shifts in these few days up here," Omaran said reflectively. "I think the knowingness is what was missing before. I feel different."

"And you do look different," St. Germain said. "I will be interested to see how this carries forward with you . . . or whether we will have to pull you up here again for a similar lesson! I hope not. There will always be lessons, but once gotten, you don't need to learn them again. And when you master one, then the next one appears. It will always be that way until you are back with the Source. It is good to remember that always, lest we become big-headed in our knowingness."

38

Initiation

Omaran felt that he had learned some big lessons the last few years, and he wanted to find out what he had to do before taking his next **spiritual initiation**. As taught in mystery schools, initiations are like milestones that mark a soul's progress along the spiritual path. There are tests to pass or lessons that have to be mastered before moving on. They had both been through several major initiations in this lifetime. It seemed that people could evolve faster now than in the past, as long as they kept their mind on the goal and continued learning.

After their last relaxing day on the mountain, Antera said she would help Omaran go before the **Illumined Court**, a group of high Masters who are in charge of the spiritual initiations of humans. Requests have to be submitted ahead of time, and it is quite an honor to have a request accepted. Antera took this very seriously and was appreciative when they said they would see Omaran.

To go before the Illumined Court, an escort is needed. Sometimes Antera was asked to fulfill this role, but generally the escort was the Master or teacher with whom an initiate is affiliated in the inner planes. At some point along the spiritual path, when a person starts initiations, they are "adopted" by one mentor, who watches over the initiate's path. Often this association starts without the person's awareness, but as the person progresses, there is conscious contact. It is then that the more serious teachings begin. This process generally takes many lifetimes.

Omaran had been aware of his mentor for many years in this lifetime, so there was no question who would be his escort. He was a bit nervous to go before the court, knowing that he would be in the hot seat, completely exposed. They knew him from the inside out, and throughout all his lifetimes, far better than he knew himself. They would see all his mistakes and times he screwed up, as well as the good things he had done.

He took some deep breaths as he relaxed and got comfortable across from Antera on the couch in their mobile living space. It was a bit chilly, and Samantha curled up in his lap for warmth.

Antera described aloud what was happening. "So we walk together into the inner sanctuary where the Illumined Court is, your mentor leading the way. We follow this wonderful Light Being into the room where the Illumined Court sits, a group of beings who are sitting in a semi-circle. Your mentor walks up to them and introduces you, saying he is petitioning for you. You have to say exactly what you are petitioning for."

Omaran said without hesitation, "My next initiation."

"He petitions for you, asking for information about where you are in your initiatory progress and what tasks need to be done before you can advance. He bows down, and so do we, in respect for this group of Illumined Masters who can see through your soul past anything that may be in your way, or that you might be projecting outward. There is nothing hidden, they see to the core of your being . . . . You now rise, and your mentor stands behind you, as do I. And they ask for a moment of silence as they assess you."

After a minute, Antera resumed, "One of the beings stands up and says, 'We have made the assessment and we thank you for coming.' . . . They are waiting for you to say something."

"Oh." Omaran felt a rush of energy. "Thank you for seeing me as I am now. I feel quite different than the last time I was here. On one hand I feel I know so little, but I'm very excited at the rediscoveries I'm making, and I am much more ready now and looking forward to more service work."

"They ask, 'What are you requesting of us?'"

"I would like to know what I need to fulfill for my next initiation, so that I may carry even higher energies with me."

The One who spoke for the Illumined Court said, "We see you have progressed far since your last time here. Since your last initiation you have been slowly working through your karma and the thoughtforms surrounding you that were hindering your progress. We see that many of those negative thoughtforms have now dispersed. We see that you are gaining control of your thoughts, which was your biggest task before the last initiation. Since then you have had new challenges and new reasons to put forth your negative thinking. Though you have not been perfect, we see that you are trying and recovering more quickly when you notice that you are creating that which you do not really want to create . . . that which does not further the Light on the planet.

"We see also that you have recently opened up to a new flow of energy throughout the core of your being, widening your core. Your task now is to bridge even more completely the upper and lower centers where you still have a separation, between the conscious and subconscious minds, between the lower chakras and the upper chakras. This needs to be bridged so you can fully embrace all of who you are, and so you can have greater access to the subconscious, reaching deeper into your being to know who you are.

"This can be accomplished through dream work, and becoming more conscious throughout the night and day. Make the effort to bridge this, bringing the dream state into the waking state as much as possible. For whatever is going on in your subconscious will remain there unless you bring it to the forefront. Do you understand?"

Omaran replied, "Yes."

"However, we do have a surprise for you! Though you came here for information about your initiation, you have also come here today to be initiated. Look around you! Notice all the Beings of Light who have come here to do this. You have come through some energy work while you have been on the mountain and this has qualified you completely. Is this something you desire?"

"Oh yes! Yes, thank you!"

"Then step onto the platform, so we can all look up at you."

Antera described the scene as it changed. "Suddenly there's a platform in the middle, and you're in the middle of a circle. They're all looking up at you. I'm out in the circle with the rest of them and you're in this bright Light that is shining on you from above and below, totally surrounding you, expanding your core energy. And they're all around humming and chanting to the I Am Presence."

She chanted out loud with them for a few minutes, then said, "Now the spokesperson of the group comes up to you, and you are lowered back down to their level. He has the special tool that is used for initiation. He holds it up and it is charged up with electric-type energy. Oh, and I see Archangel Michael, he's hovering about and helping to charge it, by touching his sword to it, with the blue-white electricity."

Omaran could feel everything she told him, and he had never felt such power.

"They're telling you that you are a Warrior for the Light, and to be comfortable with this power. They are asking you once again, 'Are you ready to take on this power?'"

"Yes!" Omaran was thrilled.

"So, the initiator has finished charging the initiation tool and hands it to you. Take it in your hands, hold it out in front of you . . . good. Now he tells you exactly where to place it in your energy field. This will help you bridge the upper and lower chakras, and to become more conscious, more intuitive, more aware. It will help you go into the inner planes and receive information easier.

"And he has something else, another symbolic form that he places on you. This is private."

She was silent for a minute while this happened. "You're still in that charge of Light coming down from above, reaming out your systems and charging up the tools. They chant again, 'Be the pure expression of Christ Consciousness on the planet! Be the purest expression of Divine Love! The purest expression of the power of Christ! Be the purest expression of Divine Wisdom!'

"And now everyone raises their arms up and opens their hands and sends you their blessings. 'You are worthy! Let go of all of you that doubts, while you stand in this Light. Let it go permanently, let it go forever, let it go for eternity. You are who you are, there is no room for doubts anymore!' And now the initiator welcomes you to your next level."

There was a joyous celebration as Omaran stepped forward with his mentor, walking around the circle being congratulated by all the beings, each of whom had a special blessing to impart.

After the circle dispersed, and they left the Illumined Court, Antera smiled and said, "I congratulate you, my twin!"

Omaran was radiant.

39

Divine Mother

After their intense, yet fulfilling, time on the mountain, Antera and Omaran pointed the RV to their next engagements. They both felt different and hoped they would be able to maintain their level of consciousness, or at least a percentage of it, at lower altitudes and in lower consciousness areas. They found that it wasn't easy.

The gigs they had were good practice for doing the full musical, so it was worthwhile even for small groups. Apparently some bookstores did not do any promotion at all, and others knew how to draw a crowd. The audiences ranged from 2–45 people. It was tiring to set up their equipment and do a show for a few people, but it was all promotion for them so they continued on.

In November, they were in Washington and took a few days to camp near Mount Rainier, a high volcano in the Cascade Range like their own Mount Shasta. A special star and planet alignment was coming up, including lunar and solar eclipses, which people were calling the Harmonic Convergence. They wanted to be in a special place to experience and anchor the energies coming to the planet.

They took some hikes in the lush green forests in the foothills of the mountain, which were absolutely magical. The abundance of rain here made everything so alive, and the many nature spirits were felt flitting about. So much life!

They sat in meditation during the time of the alignment, inside the RV on their soft armchairs that swiveled and had a small table between them. They could feel the energy ramping up as they closed their eyes and tuned to it. It was the evening, and it had been dark for a few hours. The sound of a gentle rain on their very thin roof was soothing.

Antera said with some awe, "Mother Mary is here, and she says she will bring forth the Great Goddess energy. It is like I am bringing Mary through and she is bringing **Divine Mother** through . . . I can feel the Mother surrounding us . . . nurturing us . . . immense love and power. We are within Her embrace. She really does embrace us. Do you feel that?"

"Yes," Omaran sniffed, almost overwhelmed.

They both started weeping and breathing hard to try and contain the energy of Divine Mother. It was unlike anything they had ever felt. The crying turned into loud sobs, as they both let go of anything in the way of this powerful, loving force.

Antera said between sobs, "She invites us to put our burdens down . . . She sees that we are weary, that we are tired of carrying these burdens. It is time to lay them down. And while She has us in her embrace She says that all is forgiven! All! Everything goes, and we do not need to carry any ill feelings toward anyone or ourselves. Because She is the Divine Mother and She decides to allow grace!

"It is the grace of forgiveness. The nurturing grace that only the Divine Mother can give. Because She sees all and She does not want to see us suffering anymore. She says it is time to purge and cleanse ourselves, and give up all the petty feelings. We are worthy of Her love. And no one can love like Her!

"She is the beginning and the end . . . the Great Creator and the Great Destroyer . . . the one who can fill our deepest needs for love. For that is always the need, the salve that heals the wound. And She wants us to know that She is here in a very big way now. She is with us! She is with the planet! It is time for her to reawaken and be known on the planet!

"It is time for all people to open to the Divine Mother. She is the One who has the Divine Love, the Divine Compassion, the Divine Embrace that is so needed right now for all peoples, who have shut Her out for so long!"

Omaran was overcome with emotion, not so much with the words but with the energy behind them. He stammered, "We love you Divine Mother!"

Divine Mother said, "I am here and I will be known! For no longer can humans work on this planet the way they have. I will not allow it to continue! As I bring forth my Light, everything else will fall away. All of this bickering and suffering, all of the burdens that you have carried for so long will now fall away. There comes a time when the energies must shift, and THAT IS THIS TIME!

"As you open to my energies, the energies of the Goddess, of the Divine Mother, then you know that all your wounds are cleansed and will heal. I will not allow my Light-working children to carry these wounds into the new age. Any and all of you who open to my energies, my nurturing embrace, you will be cleansed, you will be healed! You will become empowered! You will be protected from wrongly applied energies. For once you open to my cleansing and purifying force, you will no longer be affected by any of the other energies that are directed at you.

"Only love will resonate with you. Only love is real. For those of you who have believed for a long time that you are other than love, you will know BEYOND A DOUBT that you are love! Everything else can fall away instantly on my command. And I will command it if you ask!

"It has come to my attention that the time for the Mother Goddess is here! It is the time for the Mother energy to soothe and heal this planet. I have slumbered, I have waited, and now I awaken! If you call me, you will feel my presence in a big way now, for I am here and I am not leaving until every one of my beautiful Light children is cleansed and purified.

"As you feel those old energies, that you have been holding onto for so long, fall away from you, sometimes it may be a little uncomfortable. But this must happen. You must allow this purging of your energy fields in whatever form it takes and know that I am here with you. No other energies on the planet can even begin to affect the energy of the Divine Mother's love! Know you that this is the truth! I am with you all!

"For it is my time. It is time for harmony and balance. As the Great Father gives you His energies, so do I. If you neglect the side of you that is the Great Mother, you will be out of balance, as is the whole planet at this time. So we are bringing it back into balance now, and I will not stop until we are done! I am in this with all of you. I am here! I am here! All you have to do is call forth my energy and know that I am encircling you. Allow all that is not love to simply fall away from you, whether it is comfortable or uncomfortable. This purification needs to take place in every individual, and in the world herself.

"As you shed your burdens very quickly, you will shine brighter and brighter. For, you see, the burdens are not real. They are simply energy that has been pretending for a long time to be heavy, pretending that you are not strong enough, and that you cannot throw it off. But you are and you can. I am here to tell you that now. They can be easily transformed through the love of the Mother.

"I know you can feel my power, and I know you can feel my love! Now feel my breath, the Holy Breath! The Holy Spirit, as I breathe upon you. Let it swirl throughout, reaching every cell of your body, every energetic part of you, out into the infinity of the universe. The Holy Spirit is yours! The Holy Breath transforms instantly! Transforms to the Christ Light!"

Both Antera and Omaran were still sobbing, and felt their hearts opening wider than ever before. It had been such a blast of energy, that it removed everything that didn't resonate with Her love. It was as if the words were pure energy, and actually creating what She said as She spoke. The Holy Breath was real!

It took a few minutes for Antera to recover enough to hear that Mary was finished bringing Divine Mother through, and was ready to speak again.

"This is Mary. The Great Goddess Mother is with us now, and She is very powerful. I brought Her to you to make the initial connection today, but at any time you can call on Her to help you if you need nurturing or love. This period of time between the eclipses is a time of the Goddess. She has awakened, and She is here now.

240

"This will bring up any pain you carry, any burden you carry, as She said, to be healed, to be let go of very quickly if you call on Her help. She is here to help with this kind of purging. She is here to help purge the astral fields around the planet. She is here to help release the burdens that so many carry.

"This is a very important time in history, and we know that how the future will manifest depends on how people react to changes. So we wait and see, but we are all very hopeful. For we know consciousness will be raised, but we don't know how that will manifest into the physical, or how the planet will be purified. If many, many individuals work on their own cleansing and purification, then that will certainly ease the process. If they do not, then the Earth itself will have to purge. And that can take the form of many kinds of physical hazards, shake-ups, weather changes, natural disasters.

"We are hoping that individuals will do their own cleansing. This is a grand opportunity for all of you. Do you have any questions?"

Omaran swallowed hard, finding his voice. "No, I'm just a little overwhelmed right now."

"If you continue to allow the Mother energy to nurture you, your healing will go very fast. And know that I love you deeply. Antera loves you deeply. And you are learning to love yourself deeply. Do you believe that?"

"Yes . . . yes I do."

"Please know that when disturbances come up in your energy field, they are supposed to come up. The Great Mother wants you to purge these, and if you call on Her, She can help you with it. It is a great gift that She is here and it is a great gift to you that She came here today.

"I leave you with my blessing."

When they had recovered, they opened their eyes and looked at each other. Omaran said, "Do you believe what just happened?"

"That was something! I feel like I've been reamed out and renewed with a higher level of love."

"I feel so blessed. My heart is just overflowing." They leaned together and hugged for a long time.

They didn't know it at the time, but their lives had been changed forever. This was the first direct contact with Divine Mother, but it wasn't to be the last. The encounter prompted them to write a new song, "Goddess Is Back."

There's a growing swell spreading over the land,
Insurgent, insistent, making demands.
It started as a whisper, a gentle voice,
Now it shouts for all to hear, we have no choice.
Goddess is back . . .

40

The Bay Area

The tour took them through the rest of 2003 and into 2004, with more engagements, long hours on the road, and a highlight of performing the full musical in a small theater in the Los Angeles area. That was so much fun, it made all the other engagements seem worth the work.

Mark and Ellen were almost finished building their house and would be moving out in August. So the choice Antera and Omaran faced was to either move back home or rent the house for another year. They had spent all their money and accomplished what they had set out to do, but they had no jobs to go back to. Their mortgage had risen considerably as interest rates went up, and they had no income to speak of.

They were parking the RV in the Bay Area, in Marin, and decided to put on the musical at a small theater in Fairfax. That meant they would be in the area for a while, so they asked around for a place to park the RV. Parking in a different place every night had grown tiring. A friend of Byron's named Stacia happened to have a place in her yard designed for an RV, including a sewage dump, which was ideal for the time being. A hose and electric cord were attached, so they could live fairly comfortably and even take showers every day. A small fenced yard allowed Faith and Samantha a place to go outside, and Stacia let them work off most of the rent with yardwork and odd jobs around the house. They picked up their car from where they had left it with a family member, so the RV could stay put. They were back on Mount Tamalpais, and in her energies once again. It was perfect!

Once this was decided, coupled with the fact that they were out of money, renting out their house for another year was the only course of action. This time, however, they kept the loft over the garage for themselves, which had its own entrance, and rented the rest of the house. They would have a place to stay when they visited, about once a month, to gather the mountain energy and do yard work in the growing season. So they found new renters and gave them a year lease, starting in October.

Jobs were needed to pay their way and refill their reserves, and these were much easier to come by in the Bay Area, where they knew plenty of people. Byron invited Antera back to the company almost full time, even though she had been gone a year, so that was easy. Omaran didn't have all his tools with him so couldn't do any building on his own, but he put feelers out to contractors he knew and quickly got a foreman job from a friend he had known since his kids were young. Opportunities quickly rolled in, affirming their choice as the right one.

But Antera grew more and more restless living in the RV. The space had been tolerable for a traveling home, but now that they were parked in one place, it was cramped. After only a few weeks, she could hardly stand it.

"We have to find another place to live! I need more space!" she said to Omaran in exasperation. "We can't go home, and I can't stay here. There has to be another option."

"It is only until next October. We can do this until then."

"Oh no, I can't. I have big energy and I need big space. Or at least bigger."

"Well what do you want to do? We can't afford to rent a house in this area. They are too expensive! And the rent we collect from our home doesn't pay all the mortgage, you know."

She thought a moment. "Even a small apartment would be better than this cramped RV. Maybe that is an option."

"With a cat and dog?"

"Surely some take animals."

"Fine. If you can find one that does, and is not too expensive, and month-to-month, I'll go for it." He thought it would be nearly impossible.

244

"Okay, I'll start looking."

She did. It didn't take long to find a one-bedroom apartment in Larkspur that allowed cats and small dogs. Faith was not a small dog, weighing 80 pounds, but somehow Antera talked them into taking her. They moved in, finding used furniture to furnish it with the bare necessities. The RV was parked on the street, and it had to be moved every three days, the maximum time allowed in one spot. Even this small apartment was much larger and more comfortable than the RV, and Antera was relieved.

41

Silver Horse

Also that fall, a call came from Norma Milanovich, a long-time lightworker and author, asking if they would perform at her conference on twin flames in Phoenix, Arizona. They decided to go, and were excited because it would be the first time they could try out a shorter version of their musical, which they had recently written, in front of about 200 people.

It was also there that they learned about the SCIO machine, a high-tech biofeedback device that could scan to reveal stresses in many levels of the mind-body system, and then give the frequencies to counteract them. It was a highly sophisticated device, reminding Antera of the hand-held medical scanner in *Star Trek*. A participant in the conference had a SCIO running during the event, monitoring the energy of the room, and Antera talked with her about it afterwards. Antera decided she wanted one. The cost was prohibitive, however, over $20,000, but she gave that part up to the Divine, knowing that if it was important to have, the money would be there.

The last day of the conference, everyone went by bus to Sedona, a two-hour drive from Phoenix. After some other stops, they were taken to a beautiful state park that had trails to hike along Oak Creek.

Antera and Omaran walked over rocks and around bushes as they slowly made their way along the creek, looking for a fairly secluded place to sit. The sun was hot and shade was sparse, but they finally settled very near the water in the beautiful canyon. Sitting on some smooth rocks, they watched the creek slowly flow by, with picturesque red-rock bluffs on the other side reflected in a shallow pool. They both took off their shoes to gather the energy of the place through their feet.

Omaran got up and hobbled clumsily over to the water to put his bare feet in, wincing with each step and almost falling over several times.

"Your feet are very tender!" Antera laughed.

"I know. I need to go barefoot more often," he said.

"Even walking around the house without socks helps to toughen them." She had never seen anyone with such thin soles.

"Yeah, yeah. Wow, does this water feel good! Come put your feet in!"

She joined him. The water was cool and refreshing, and opened the foot chakras. They went back to sit on the rocks again, to meditate, with feet buzzing. All along this creek seemed very special, and they both sat reverently in silence absorbing the energies, feeling a slight sense of anticipation.

Soon after she closed her eyes, Antera felt a group of beings wanting to communicate. It was the Elders of Sedona, the group they had talked with after their Sedona ceremony in 2001.

"The Elders of Sedona want to speak to us," she said. "Especially one very shining silvery being, who seems to be the one who will speak. He looks like a Native American from the old days. His says his name is **Silver Horse**. They are in charge of keeping this area stable and balanced, holding the energy of the place."

Silver Horse said, "We honor you for coming here and helping us with our job. We honor you in your mental and spiritual activities. The work you did with the large group this weekend effectively connected this spot much more firmly with the grid work of the planet, and activated this site to a higher level of frequency so that it can be connected to the Christ Consciousness grid. It was connected before, but not to this extent. We want you to know that the ceremony you did here three years ago paved the way for this one. You opened the door so that this activation could take place."

Omaran said, "We are glad to hear about all the positive repercussions of the Empowering Lightworkers ceremonies. So is there another place we can go now, to help heal the land?"

Silver Horse said, "We see that you are making a connection with the Bay Area, which is sorely in need of your help, so we are hoping that your next ceremony will be there."

"Yes," Omaran replied, "we will absolutely do a ceremony there. Why does the Bay Area need help?"

"The area is unstable. We want you to continue the ceremonies that you do for land healing."

Omaran leaned closer to Antera to hear better, as several loud planes flew overhead just then. "Okay, we will. But we really want to be more effective in our land healing work, so whatever you can teach us we appreciate."

Silver Horse went on, "First, we want to make sure that you remember your roots in the Native American heritage, because you both have roots in that culture. The Earth is strong in your field of energy and your thoughts. Some of the practices and abilities that you used to have long ago, during those times, you are reawakening now. But there are more abilities, more skills that you can both awaken. These are skills that you used not only in the Native American culture but in other previous cultures, when these skills were acknowledged.

"We know that you will continue to develop them through your songs, through movement, through your energetic work and mental focus, through your connections with the nature spirits, plants, animals, and rocks, and through the natural elements . . . and through your deep, deep and abiding love, for that is the force that drives all of your activities."

Omaran said, "Thank you for your kind words. Yes, we feel that connection to the old Native American spiritual teachings."

"To fully implement the old abilities, there are certain things that you should have with you, whenever you travel, or have a ceremony. You need what used to be called a medicine bag, a bag with special objects that help you hold your power. My suggestion is that you meditate on what these objects are. I want to give you one suggestion for this bag, and that is a special feather that you find or buy that will represent your wings, your ability to rise up above and see far, from the perspective of birds. It represents wisdom. I'm sure you will also have stones and other objects in there that have special meaning. Every medicine person has a bag of these power objects they carry with them always. That is my suggestion. It is the Indian way."

"Thank you, we will do that. It helps a lot."

The Elders left, and as they opened their eyes, Omaran was already planning when to do a ceremony in the Bay Area, and what to put in his medicine bag. They knew they had both had a number of lives as Native Americans, and they related to some of the spiritual and ceremonial aspects that culture had before the Europeans came to this land.

"A medicine bag, what a great idea!" Antera said. "But how do we do this particular kind of land healing he's talking about? I hope he gives us more information about how to do it."

"Yes, we need more training. Maybe if we talk to the **Angel of Mount Tam**, she will help. I assume that is where we would do a Bay Area ceremony."

The Angel of Mount Tam was what they called the deva in charge of Mount Tamalpais, the small mountain north of San Francisco. She was a highly evolved being of the nature world, in charge of the mountain and surrounding areas. Over the years they had lived in that area, they had hiked all over the mountain and done several solstice and equinox ceremonies up there, and the deva had spoken to them a few times.

"Good idea," Antera said. "Let's contact her when we get back there and ask what she would like us to do."

"To be honest, I'm a bit concerned about Silver Horse saying that the land is unstable and needs our help."

"We know it is unstable tectonically."

"But this means something could happen soon. We definitely need more instruction in how to balance that. I mean honestly, all we've really done is clear areas and ley lines using our land healing crystals, and create Light forms. This will be a whole new level."

They had started doing land healing in earnest ten years earlier, in 1994, when they had given a series of land healing seminars around the Bay Area called "Anchoring Love and Light." Even though they considered this an exciting topic, over the years they had come to the conclusion that most people were far more concerned about themselves and their own healing, than they were about healing the planet. Generally these kinds of classes had not been well attended.

But they had continued, just the two of them, doing all the work around Mount Shasta as directed by the Order of Melchizedek, because healing the planet was one of their missions, and obviously much needed. They had also continued their experimentation with various techniques that were suggested to them by Ascended Masters, as well as remembering the ancient ways from long ago. Now Silver Horse had become a new source of information as a native ancestor. He would be involved for many years to come.

The seismologist part of Antera thought that the request to do land healing in the Bay Area could very well be related to imminent earthquakes. The Bay Area was very active tectonically, with earthquakes as a major hazard, and she was aware of these risks. For years, she had wondered what could be done energetically to help these forces expend themselves without too much destruction for humans. The physical hazard reductions weren't enough, and clearly there were many variables affecting the level of damage, including the timing of earthquakes and the frequency content of the seismic waves. She wondered if the land healing could help with these risks.

When they got home, they started planning a ceremony for the Spring Equinox of 2005 on Mount Tam, taking advantage of the enhanced power available on every equinox and solstice. They hoped this would give them time to get more information about what they would be doing before they started inviting people to join them.

42

Christmas with Jeshua

During the week between Winter Solstice and the New Year, Antera and Omaran decided to take off from work so they could replenish themselves and spend more time in meditation and healing. They were both a bit run down, especially Omaran, whose physically demanding work was hard on his body. He really was looking forward to the week off.

Meditating for hours every day and taking hikes on Mount Tam was just the ticket to nurture them. When they hiked, they always stopped wherever and whenever they were drawn, to sit and take in the energies of the many beautiful places on the small mountain. Streams flowed abundantly, and the forests were green, the plants happy. Omaran had spent more time on this mountain than Antera, but she also dearly loved everything about Mount Tam, especially the energy, which felt cleansing and healing to her.

It was during this time that Jeshua decided to give them some teachings. While sitting in meditation in their living room one morning, he made his presence known to Antera. She told Omaran, who helped to hold the space for this great Master to speak.

Jeshua said, "I greet you both at this very special time of year. There is much attention on the life I led as Jesus at this time, from those who are religious and those who simply appreciate the energies I was destined to bring to the planet. I thank you both for tuning in and listening at this time and focusing on the most high and lofty thoughts that bring good things to all people, including yourselves. This is what this time of year is about. This is what the best energies of this holiday season give to the planet."

"Yes, this is a special time, and we are very glad you are here," Omaran said.

"I had hoped that the message you put forth in your song would reach more people, especially those who need to hear it the most. But it is always in Divine Will how these things work and so we release it and we move on to new things."

"We hoped to get it out to more people as well," Omaran said, "but we know that the people who got it and listened were no doubt touched." They had sent 1000 free copies of the CD to influential people in government, hoping some of these people would listen, but had heard back from only a few.

Jeshua went on, "I do still hope that the energies of good will and peace will manifest on the planet, and it is on the verge of doing so. But of course you know that whenever thoughts centered on love and Light come up, it will also bring up that which is not aligned. The chaos, the seeming evil, and people on the planet who are doing things to disturb the planet will be brought to the forefront, as the energies from the Most High and Christ Consciousness, that you and those like you carry, fully manifest and filter into the consciousness of everyone. All thoughts that are not of that energy will come up for healing, as we have told you many times, and as has always been evident in the history of this planet.

"In times before, when the opposing forces were fully exposed to the consciousness of the biosphere of this planet, they were able to overcome the consciousness and disrupt the implementation of the consciousness grid. This time, however, we feel that the grid is very well in place. Even though it is not apparent if you listen to your news, it is fully in place within the hearts of every person on this planet.

"The Christ Consciousness is firmly and deeply rooted among the population everywhere. Which means that no matter what comes up and what energies are exposed, the grid and the Christ Consciousness that you have all been waiting for will survive and flourish. I have no doubts about this!

"Even though I express concern from time to time about what is happening and those who oppose, yet I hold firm in my belief that all will come to pass as we hope. Of course we are concerned with what will happen during the chaotic period that will ensue. And there may be some Earth changes and powerful purging with the nature spirits and those of the fourth dimension, who are constantly fighting.

"This can manifest into natural disasters and harm to humans. But it is all a part of the process and it has always been our hope that we do not need to have such a calamity that everything shuts down as it has in the past, and as many people have prophesied."

Omaran said, "We are very happy to hear that."

"There is a belief that to bring forth the new, many people must die, and there must be a shutdown of systems so great that people are forced to overcome their selfishness and grow very quickly, starting anew. This is deeply rooted in everyone's subconscious minds. But we are hoping that it will not have to happen again because of the work that all the lightworkers have done to engage the higher consciousness much deeper than ever before.

"It has taken many, many thousands of years to come to this point in the Earth's history. So it is your task as lightworkers to hold the Light as firmly as you can! Know deep within your being that the Light will shine; that all the disturbances you see and hear about now will pass. As long as you are all holding the Light firmly in place and anchoring it where you have chosen to anchor it, amid the chaos, this transition will go smoothly.

"Do not get distracted by what you see and hear around you. There is so much that is not worth your attention. Keep your attention fully focused on what you want in the world, and on the activities and thoughts that bring forth a greater world Light. The more strongly the Light is held, the smoother the transition will be, and the less painful. The less strongly the Light is held, the more destruction."

"Thank you for giving us that hope," Omaran commented. "We try to hold the Light strong, but we don't always succeed, at least I don't."

"I watch as you go about your daily activities and sometimes struggle, and I know how difficult it is to be human. I have been through it many times myself. Even in my lifetime as Jesus, when people deified me or put me on a pedestal as if I were special, I had serious doubts at times. I had struggles in my mind and heart, which I continually worked to purify, so that I could hold the tremendous energies that were given to me to project on the planet, and so I could bring forth and ground into the human sphere the highest and most pure energies that were possible to bring through at that time.

"I had to continually work to achieve this, battling with my own **demons**, my own doubts, my own fears. This is all part of the process of becoming the most perfect vessel of Light that you can become.

"You may let go of self-judgment or doubt, of anything that gets in the way of transmitting the most perfect Light. And you will notice that you, yourself, are blocking the Light because you are holding onto energy that is not helping—unnecessary energy, unnecessary judgment and thoughts that aren't even true. As you discover these things, simply let them go. That is how it is achieved. That is what I did.

"I always went off by myself whenever I had a chance, whenever something arose in me that doubted my ability to be the voice of God. Can you imagine, that I was asked to be that voice? I had tremendous doubts about my abilities, times when I even thought I was a fake.

"It is human to doubt! And while you are human, you will have doubts. It does not matter how clearly you can see into the other realms, it does not matter what you know intellectually; there will be doubts occasionally. The trick is in acknowledging the doubt as part of your human self and a normal process, and letting it go . . . loving it and letting it go.

"Speak to me Omaran, my dear one."

Omaran said, "It's nice to hear you say these things, because I have those doubts. What I want most is to be the purest vessel that I can be, and I know my doubts get in the way. I know that's where my anger comes from, not living up to what I feel I should be living up to, and letting my fears rule me. My faith isn't always strong. I want to be what you see in me."

Jeshua said, "And I want you to see what I see in you. Then you can be it. You are a pillar of strength. If you consider how many lifetimes you have been here, all the suffering you have endured, and how you kept on fighting, holding your energy to be a Light on the planet despite all of it . . . this is true strength!

"It is not perfection that you need to aim for. It is only perfection in the moment. Realize that you are perfect in the Light of the God-Goddess. You are perfect in my eyes just as you are. You are right where you need to be right now. If you can realize that, you can let go of the judgments and the 'shoulds' that you continually come up with.

"These are the very thoughts that limit you. These are the thoughts of self-judgment. You hold a standard so high, that you always feel you are coming up short. You are perfect! If you can just let go of your thoughts of judgment about yourself, you will shine ever brighter. Do you understand what I mean, my brother?"

Omaran answered, "Yes I do. Yes, just to be perfect in the moment."

"That is right! You have a choice in every moment about how you act and what you think. That is your only choice, and that is all that matters. The past is gone, you have punished yourself many times for past deeds, the future is yet to form, and it is based on the present."

"Yes, that all seems so simple now."

Jeshua came to them two other times before the New Year, primarily working with Omaran on his doubts and fears. The transformation he had during those few days was huge. Having that level of personal attention from the Master put Omaran in a state of deep gratitude and awe.

43

Angel of Mount Tam

On a relatively warm day in January, with no rain in sight, they bundled up for a hike on the mountain to see if the Angel of Mount Tam would give them some more specific ideas about what was needed in the area energetically, and maybe help them plan the land healing ceremony on the equinox in March.

They drove up the windy road and parked at the trailhead of their special spot. The wind was cold, but they knew they would soon be in the shelter of bay and madrone trees. Not wanting anyone to know about this place, they took off on the trail when no cars were going by, walking fast so they would be over the hill and out of sight quickly.

Even in January, many wild herbs were growing along the path, and they knew that when they came back on the equinox many would be in bloom. They arrived at their destination and sat on some rocks, with their backs to the sun for warmth.

"I love this place. We should come here more often," Omaran said.

"I wonder if part of the reason we needed to come back to the Bay Area is to do this land healing."

"Could be. Of course we both want to get back to Mount Shasta. But we will make the most of our time here. And as you know, I am thrilled to be here and working with this mountain!"

They both sighed and absorbed the energy of the place. Antera focused her attention on the deva of the mountain, wondering if she would appear. Sure enough, the Angel of Mount Tam was there immediately, as if she had been waiting for the couple to arrive, and was ready to talk.

The deva said, "Perhaps you can think of me as a local representative of Mother Earth, for I work with her continuously. My domain is all of the mountain and the surrounding areas that are of the same rock forms. I am the holder of harmony and balance here and the bringer of new energies as they emerge from within the planet and from the cosmos.

"I come to you because you are the emissaries who come here and help me with my job. As you walk along my folds and my rocks and my valleys, and as you pay attention to and give blessings to the trees, mosses, animals, and waters, you are helping to balance and maintain the energy that is so important to this area. I come to thank you for this."

Omaran said, "It is our pleasure, of course. We love this mountain so much."

"I know you are aware that I have been calling you to me, nearer to my heart. I call you because I need you. The Earth Mother has pushed you in my direction so that you can help with the balancing of this land, and so you can rise above to my peaks and look down on the land as I do, feeling the strength and wisdom that is here on my mountain. Wisdom permeates every rock, every tree, every animal, and all flowing water. It oozes from my pores and flows freely to anyone who comes here and enjoys the surroundings. And there is great strength here, in the form of the mountain and the depth of her roots, deep into the Mother, holding together the land.

"But know that it will not be held together in this form forever. The form is constantly changing and change is upon us. The landform changes that are upon us are inevitable, but energy changes form everywhere in this Universe and it is not to be mourned.

"So as we see the changes upon the landscape you must know that it is all in perfection and a perfect representation and mirror of all that is present. All of the thoughtforms and other energies that are present here must be mirrored in the physical world. Everything that has been created by humans, who are the dominant creative forces at this time on the planet, must eventually manifest in the physical world. Therefore, any changes that occur, whether they be destructive or constructive, are perfect and will alleviate stress.

"When the astral world is too different from the physical world, there is stress. This stress can only be relieved by the physical world changing to meet that which is in the world of thought and energy forms. Right now they are too different, and therefore forms will change in the physical. Do you understand?"

Omaran answered, "Yes, I think so. Please continue."

"I want you to especially understand that this is how it should be. This is beneficial, because when the forms change, they release stress, and things come back into harmony . . . the inner with the outer. So even though when forms change quickly it can cause problems with people's lives, still it is important to realize that there are no accidents and all that happens is a part of how these systems work."

Omaran interjected, "So I think you are saying that there is too much buildup of negative thoughts and emotions in the astral realm here, and that will cause earthquakes or other changes of form, to balance it out. Is that right?"

"Yes."

"So what can we do to help with our land healing?"

"The work you have been called to do here with me, and with other nature spirits who hold the energy of forms and places, is to help release and calm the thoughtforms that are creating the stress, so that the form changes in the physical world will not be as dramatic . . . so there will not have to be very large changes to alleviate the stress between the worlds.

"You can help to alleviate the stress within the world of thought and feeling, or what you might call the fourth dimension. By doing this at particular spots and alleviating the stress, creating more balance and harmony, you then make it less necessary to change the physical to bring the two into balance with each other. This is the process that you are asked to do. When you go walking on my mountain I feel you doing some of this, subconsciously and sometimes overtly. You are blessing the areas that you walk through, by bringing forth the Light to the life forms and by giving your gratitude for the beauty and cherishing it. These are all wonderful feelings and thoughts that go out and cancel out some of the more negative thoughts.

"I ask you to go a step further in this with your ceremonies, and that is to open yourselves as stress releasers, as conduits of transformation in the larger area. The fourth dimension is entirely too busy, too full. As long as it is in the condition of overflow, of chaos, of entities at odds with each other, the disruption and influence on the land will be great. And the potential for disastrous changes remains. So in your places of ceremony, you can open up a conduit of transformative Light that can dispel these energies, to harmonize and balance these areas."

The Angel of Mount Tam went on to describe a process they could use to do exactly this, clearing an area within a column of Light, and creating areas of stability using the energy of ceremony. It sounded very exciting.

She said, "Dig back into your memories of how you used to do this, working with Mother Earth and the devas of particular areas, to harmonize and balance the land, and to heal people. You had it down to a science then, and you could sense that if there were a lot of unhappy people in one area, that was where to focus. Now, of course, there are many unhappy people, making this a huge job.

"But you must remember, whatever happens is part of the Higher Plan. You do your part to create whatever harmony you can, and then you let it go. You do not hold onto the thought that it will go according to the plan that you think is best, but you allow whatever changes need to happen, so that the third and fourth dimensions can come back into harmony with each other. You can alleviate some of the stress but you cannot alleviate all of it at this time.

"So I ask you to do what you can and do not feel that you have failed if there are still Earth changes, because this happened to you before. There could be a re-stimulation of the sorrow that you felt before when you could not change things fast enough. Do you remember?"

"Yes, we have some memories of Lemuria, and Atlantis too, and the sorrow of not being able to prevent disasters there. Is that what you mean?"

"Yes. That is why I tell you this. I thank you for every time you come up on my slopes and you enjoy my mountain paths. And I find your dog joyful, and wonderful to have on my paths. She is a delight. So thank you."

The deva left, and Mary then came to Antera and wanted to say a few words. Antera switched to her frequencies.

Mary said, "Hello dear ones, I thought you might enjoy a little encounter with the Mistress of the mountain. She has enjoyed your presence here so, and wanted to formerly welcome and thank you for the land healing work you have done and will do. I'm so happy to see that unfolding, because I know the two of you are very talented along those lines, and can do so much. I believe it is joyful work for you as well.

"Perhaps I can answer some questions, if you have any."

Omaran said, "I would like to ask a couple of questions about the land healing. Are there any areas that we should go to first because they need the most help, or is it just anywhere in the Bay Area?"

"It is not just the Bay Area, it is the entire state, and north of the state, in need of balance. Two important spots to hit first are: one centrally located in the Bay Area such as Mount Tam, and another one centrally located in Los Angeles. You have done ceremonies in both of these places before and this would be a good place to start. Then you can build around these in the more outlying areas.

"It is not that this area is in danger of falling into the ocean or anything like that, but as the Angel of Mount Tam explained, there is quite a discrepancy between the two dimensions, and it will alleviate itself in some form. We do not know what form that will be yet, we just know that the discrepancy will have to be accommodated, and the activity in the fourth dimension must manifest into the physical. So whatever you can do to eliminate some of that energy, by working with the nature spirits and those of that dimension, can really help."

Omaran said, "I'm not sure I understand one thing. When we do the ceremonies we'll be bringing in Light from the highest source possible, through us as conduits into the third dimension and the Earth. How do we get it to the fourth dimension?"

"The fourth dimension is between the physical world and Source, so if you are bringing energy in from the Source and into the physical world, creating that bridge, you are going through all of those dimensions."

"Well thank you, Mary," Omaran said, "this has really helped."

After Mary withdrew her energy, they sat for a while talking about the process they had learned. So now they had enough information to plan the ceremony in March.

Omaran climbed off the boulder and lay down on his back in some oak leaves, and Faith came over beside him. He petted her as he looked up at the intermittent clouds, then said, "You know, this seems like a bigger project than I thought it would be when Silver Horse asked us to do this."

"Yes," Antera agreed. "Mary said the whole state needs balancing!"

"Hmmm . . . ." He closed his eyes and thought about the size of California. "Well, two of these ceremonies we can do. I'm excited."

"One here and one in Los Angeles, yes. But I have the same feeling that this is a bigger mission we are embarking on."

Indeed, if they had known then how large this land-healing project would become in the years ahead, they may have been too overwhelmed to start. But as with all lightworkers who are led by the Ascended Masters, they were given only one manageable step at a time.

In preparation for the equinox event on Mount Tam, Antera recorded a land healing meditation to guide the group through the visualization that the Angel of Mount Tam had given them. It would be a very powerful process to go through, they could tell, and having it recorded meant Antera could also participate, rather than doing it live and focusing on leading the group.

They also wrote a new song as a prayer to the planet, inspired by their love of Earth, to be played in the ceremony. It was called "Dear Mother Earth," and when they recorded it in the studio, it brought Terry to tears, which was a good sign that the essence of the song came through.

> *Thanks for the land we live on, the waters too,*
> *And all the beings who call you home.*
> *Thanks for the beauty here, the sweet air we breathe,*
> *Accept our love, you're not alone . . . .*

Antera and Omaran also put together their medicine bags, as suggested by Silver Horse, using some special objects they had gathered through the years, as well as one object that represented each of the four elements: earth, fire, water, and air. It was a fun project and the power in having the objects all in one place was palpable. When they needed some extra energy they found they could gather it from their pouch. This would be the first time the medicine bags would be used in a ceremony, to amplify the effectiveness of the work.

The fog was thick and the air was cool, but the small group of dedicated people huddled on Mount Tamalpais and prepared for ceremony. There were ten of them, including Michael and Jeen, Antera's sister, and Byron, bundled up in coats over their ceremony clothes of white and green. Aligned in the purpose of purifying the area of unbalanced energies, they knew that even though their numbers were small, they were a powerful group and very focused.

Several of them huddled together to block the wind as they lit the incense, and they got a small fire blazing in a metal container. The altar was set up in the middle of the circle, including some power objects and gifts for the nature spirits.

When they were ready, they all lined up for purification, and each participant was cleared with sage and a rattle before entering the sacred space, marked by a circle of stones. As they joined together to link their intent for the work and call in the help of Masters, angels, and nature spirits, the energy of the place and all the unseen participants was easily felt. All was charged up and ready to be focused. Through song, chants, visualizations, and movement, they built it up even more, then ended by releasing the built-up energy in a powerful gesture into the surrounding area and down into the ground.

"We did it! Success!" Omaran cheered.

The others chimed in, feeling the elation from the energy of the ceremony. They packed up and went back to the apartment in Larkspur where Antera and Omaran were staying, for a warm meal. After everyone left, the couple talked about events that led up to this ceremony.

"That felt very powerful. I think we cleared a lot of energy and balanced a large area," Antera commented as they relaxed. These ceremonies were fun but also required much planning and intense mental focus, which generally left them tired.

Omaran said, "Yes, very strong, I feel really good about it. And even though it was windy and cold and foggy, I thought everyone really did an excellent job!"

"They are definitely real troopers," echoed Antera. "So in a few days we go south to L.A. to do it again, while we are still in the equinox energies. It will be a larger group down there, with some more experienced people, so I'm sure we will be able to stabilize a larger area."

Omaran's smile was big. "I love this work!"

"I'd like to see if I can reach the Angel of Mount Tam and see if she has any initial feedback for us."

"Aren't you too tired?"

"Yes, I'm tired but I want to try, because otherwise it will be after we get back from L.A. before I'll have time."

"Great! It would be nice to hear from her." Omaran arranged chairs and got ready.

The Angel of Mount Tam said, "Thank you for the work you did on my mountain! Dispelling the darkness as you did, you have created a wonderful beam of Light throughout my peak, and some of the surrounding areas. I can see the influence of this as it spreads throughout the area and I thank you for this. I thoroughly enjoyed your ceremony here.

"And so did all of the nature spirits! Not only from the area where you did the ceremony. They came from far and wide—many others, except for those who were bound to particular places or plants or trees.

"They are anxious to know whether you could sense or see them, because there were times when they thought someone looked their way and could see them. They were standing around the circle with all of you and some of the more mischievous ones were in the center, dancing around the middle and having a jolly good time with it all.

"But they were very cognizant of the seriousness of the work, paying close attention when you did your meditation and created the column of Light."

Omaran said, "I can only speak for myself. I didn't see anyone directly, but I certainly knew they were there, I felt them. I appreciate and send my love to all of them."

"They are happy beings now, and even if you can't see them, they know they were sensed by some of you and they like this. It is such a different experience to be called in and acknowledged by you, because for the most part humans completely ignore them, and do not even acknowledge their presence. People walk right past special, magical places without even a sense that there are beings there who cherish and maintain these forms and patterns of energy.

"So to be acknowledged and brought into the ceremony was a first for them. This particular ceremony involved them completely, and they felt they definitely had a part in the land healing, which is their specialty. Some of the nature spirits are assigned to that area now and they will stay there and keep it magical so that you can do future ceremonies there if you wish."

The deva added, "And they loved your wonderful gifts to them after the ceremony—the herbs, cornmeal, rice, stones, feather and other things."

"We are glad they liked the gifts, and we are grateful for their help. It is fascinating to learn more about them."

"Gifts are how you make them happy, and cooperative. They do not have the moral sense of right or wrong as you do in the physical world, so they can be coerced into many different kinds of things. They do not have that kind of sense because their world is not as polarized as yours. So you might think they are doing bad or mischievous things, but they are not really bad.

"You can, of course, talk with them and exchange your gifts for their gifts and what they can do. And you may also do this in your own home. For there are nature spirits who maintain the energy in your home. They reside in little places you make that are special for them such as in plants, or crystals. You might become aware of the particular elementals and spirits that reside in these places, and maintain the form for you and keep the energy flowing in your house. They have very special functions.

"But enough about that! I do hope that you will be creating more columns of Light in this area, not just right on the mountain, but all around. I feel that these will also anchor in new ideas and thoughtforms that will help bring positive change on the planet as well as negate some of the pollution."

44

Stabilizing

The ceremony in Los Angeles was held on Holy Sage Ridge in Griffith Park, the same place they had done the Empowering Lightworkers ceremony a few years before. Carrying all the equipment and ceremony items, the group of fifteen hiked up the steep, slippery path to the ridge. The second official land-healing ceremony went even smoother than the first, and the purge of dense energies created a large shift they could all feel.

It was a quick trip, and when Antera and Omaran got back home they were anxious to hear from the Masters about how effective the ceremonies had been. They took time after work the next day to connect in and ask. Antera contacted St. Germain, who told them that the two ceremonies were very successful and had cleared out some dense energies.

The Master told them, "We do very much appreciate this work and we want you to fully realize that this work is instrumental and essential in the transformation of energies on this planet. The more people you can have doing this in their own homes or areas, the faster we can transform this planet into one that is harmonious and peaceful. So I want to see these columns of Light springing up all over the land!"

He also told them that, though they were powerful and very successful at purifying and transforming energies, the columns of Light formed would not last. There was a way to make a different kind of point that was permanent. It would require burying identical sacred objects

266

at each site, which he described, hoping they would be able to make them. These permanent sites would be called "**pinning sites**" because they would be more stable and support the other sites, which from now on would be called "**clearing sites**."

After hearing the information from St. Germain, Antera said to Omaran, "I guess we need to do pinning sites around this area to prevent damage from earthquakes. Do you think you can make those forms he was talking about out of wood?"

"Oh, sure . . . I can do that after work. I can probably get the wood out of scraps we would normally just recycle. And for some reason I have a feeling you'll want them sanded smooth as well, is that right?"

"Yes, they have to be smooth. I'll paint them if you will make them."

"It's a deal," Omaran said. "I'm excited about doing this new kind of ceremony and making them permanent sites!"

"It is pretty cool. How many do you think we could do around this area?" Antera wondered.

"I think four would be good, at least that's the number I'm getting. Maybe as far west as we can go fairly easily, out to Point Reyes. We could do that after work, because the days are getting longer, and we could take dinner or something. Then one in the east . . . ."

"I think one should be out in the Central Valley, so it will be supportive for the ones around Mount Tam. St. Germain said they could all be connected together energetically, so they will help each other."

"Yeah, and then maybe something down in the South Bay. We could do that on a weekend."

"I'll get our California map!"

The enthusiasm of the Masters was catching, and it all happened quickly. Omaran stayed after work the next day, and cut out four wooden objects with the work table saw, then sanded them smooth, and by the next day Antera was giving them their base coat of paint. She knew there were supposed to be important symbols painted on them, but she didn't know exactly what they would be. Tuning into the ceremonies they had done, the nature spirits, and the higher purpose of the project, the images slowly appeared to her over the next few days, so she added them to the objects.

She was also shown a symbol to be painted on a rock and buried with the rest, symbolizing the land healing project in general and the love for their Earth. So upon telling Omaran, he went to Muir Beach, their favorite ocean site, to collect a few rocks that were smooth enough for her to paint. Considering that Muir Beach was on the Pacific Ocean and next to Mount Tamalpais, where this project began, it seemed fitting that the Earth Healing Rocks, as they began calling them, should come from there.

As she sat painting at their dining room table, without looking up, Antera casually proclaimed, "We're going to need a chant or song to completely anchor in the energy after the meditation, Dear. Do you want to write it?"

"Sure," he replied.

"It can just be a chant if you don't get a melody. I'm seeing us doing a clockwise movement during the anchoring."

"No problem, I'll see what comes in." They would be going to Mount Shasta that weekend, so he hoped he could book some recording studio time.

She went on, "We already have our opening song, "Dear Mother Earth." I just know we need a lot of music in this ceremony because the nature spirits love music and singing, and we really need their help for this . . . so we need a closing song also. Remember that song I heard at the Three Wells in Mill Valley? The one the nature spirits sang to me when we lived there?" She had often walked to the special series of waterfalls, a sacred area where she loved to meditate.

We sing our praise to the Earth,
We sing our praise to Spirit,
For we are truly blessed, yes we are truly blessed.

"You mean 'The Praise Song?'" Omaran asked.

"Yes. That would be good for the closing of the ceremony, don't you think?"

"Yes, it would be perfect, and we could do the part that is a round. I'll call Terry after my walk."

Omaran took Faith for a walk down to the Bay and as he was sitting on a bench, looking out at the ferries and a few light water craft, the chant, along with a tune, came to him. When he and Faith got back he announced, "I've got it, I'll just write it down so I don't forget it. It's got a tune, too."

He went straight to the piano, pulled out a clean music sheet and got to work writing it down. It took less than an hour, and he then shared it with Antera, who loved it.

Spirit comes spiraling into the Earth,
Healing Mother Earth.

They practiced both songs the rest of the week before going to the studio in Mount Shasta for recording that weekend. Fortunately, Terry was available, and loved the project, even adding his bass voice on the chant, which ended with a long OM. They came away with working versions. By having everything recorded, each ceremony could be exactly the same, and, though they didn't know why at the time, they knew this exact duplication was important for these ceremonies.

It was this project that kept them going during this period of time they were living in the Bay Area but wanting to be home. It kept them busy after their work hours, planning and preparing for two trips to do the four pinning ceremonies that were next.

During dinner on a Monday Omaran said, "How about Wednesday for Point Reyes? We could do it after work. It isn't very far and the days are getting longer. Then we could take off Friday, go out to Stockton, do one there, and then head back toward the ocean over the weekend and get in a couple more."

"Sounds like a lot of driving," she said as she swallowed a mouthful of steamed vegetables.

"Parks, the ocean, a Friday off, who could ask for anything more?" Omaran was always excited about trips.

"Alright, let me see if I can get everything ready in time."

She did. He knew she would, she always did. He had never known Antera to miss a deadline, and he was constantly amazed at how focused she worked. Wednesday, after work, they headed out to Point Reyes, an area as far west of Mount Tam as possible, for their first land pinning site.

Upon arrival, they stood looking at the turbulent ocean, watching the waves crash onto the land. Strong onshore winds blew at them, chilling them right through their jackets.

"Wow, this isn't comfortable." Antera stated as she held onto her sun hat.

"It's a very cold wind. But we don't want to be right next to the ocean anyway, as we don't want our ceremonial site to get washed away. Let's find a more sheltered area." They both turned around and looked.

"Yes. We have to get away from the people, too. How about walking into that area past the parking lot and into the grove of pines?"

They hiked a short distance, carrying all their ceremony items, including two small folding stools for sitting, and a CD player for the songs and meditation. Secluded among the trees, they found a white sandy area they both liked and began setting up. Without discussing it, they started calling in the nature spirits first. Antera began by playing her flute, a beautiful wooden instrument made by a Native American, which Omaran had given her for her birthday before they left on the tour. It had pure, sweet tones that the local nature spirits liked. While she played, Omaran walked around the circle they had created, also putting out the call, letting them know a ceremony was starting.

They played the CD and sang along with their opening song, then listened to the meditation. They could feel their own excitement as well as that of all the beings present. The highly effective visualization, with the help of the Masters and nature spirits, created the column of Light, which was then purified and solidified to be permanent.

As the meditation came to an end, they stayed sitting on their stools and reveled in the power and beauty of what they had helped create. They were both quite expanded and in their higher bodies, and it took them a few minutes to come back totally into the physical.

Antera said, "We need to anchor it into the ground right now."

"Okay . . . I think I'm ready."

They walked around the circle and sang along with the recording of their new chant/song as they brought Divine Spirit into the column and then chanted OM as they lowered it into the ground. After that they talked to the nature spirits who had volunteered to help maintain the column and explained a little to them about the purpose of the project and how the sacred objects would hold the energy for a long time.

The last song was a celebration and thanks, to finish it all off. After burying the objects, they sat a bit longer, just feeling the energy of what had been created and once again thanking everyone involved before they left. Agreeing that it was far too windy to eat their dinner outside, they hopped in their car and dined while they looked at the mighty Pacific as the sun went down, splashing beautiful golden light on the water.

Before leaving, they took off their shoes and moseyed along the shore, and a rock called out to Antera. She walked over and picked it up. It was a palm-sized grey stone, perfectly smooth and oval shaped, with an inclusion in it of darker stone. When she looked closer, she saw that the inclusion had the shape of a bird on one side, and a wing on the other. She had never seen anything like it, and immediately knew it was a gift for the land healing, from the nature spirits. It was to become her cherished Bird Rock, and from then on it sat on her altar or she carried it with her.

A couple of days later they hit the road to do three more pinning sites, in three days. The idea was to surround the Bay Area to help stabilize it, as Silver Horse had originally asked, and as further encouraged by the Angel of Mount Tam, who was also concerned about the area. They piled in the RV, which had been parked on the street and moved from place to place for many months. Samantha and Faith came with them, back in what had been their home for a year. Faith was happy to be going anywhere as long as she was with her people, but Samantha wasn't all that happy about being in the RV again. She settled down after a few hours.

The first stop was in Stockton, in the central valley of California, still fairly close to the Bay Area but well east of the major earthquake faults. They had found some parks on the map where they hoped to find a secluded place to do the ceremony, so they started by going to each of these. Several of them were sports fields and not at all suitable. They finally settled on parking the RV fairly close to the San Joaquin River. To hide, they had to climb into some very thick bushes, and settle on quite a slant. It was not the ideal flat area they were used to, but it had to do. Using the compass to determine magnetic north, they adjusted it for true north to align the altar properly.

"So . . . you will be on the uphill side, will that work?" Omaran asked. He knew it was much easier for him to be comfortable than Antera, but he wanted to sit in the north, and she on the south side, so there wasn't much choice at this site. He dug out an area with the small trowel he had brought to bury the sacred items, and tried to make a more level place for her stool.

"I can handle it long enough to do the work."

Many nature spirits came in when they called, some keeping their distance and others jumping right in to see what was going on. Antera could sense some sitting on her arms, and they were especially interested in the Bird Rock in her hand. She giggled. Omaran sensed the flurry of activity also, a response greater than the other site, as if the nature spirits knew they were coming.

It was their second time through the new pinning ceremony, so it went smoothly. They sat on their teetering stools for the meditation. They thought they were far enough away from others that no one could hear the music and chants, and if anyone were curious, they would have to climb into the bushes, which seemed an effective deterrent. Happy and relieved to get away with it, at the end they explained to the nature spirits the purpose of the form that was created, and connected the site energetically to Mount Tamalpais and the other land pinning site at Point Reyes. Second point done!

"It almost feels like the next two sites are already anticipating our arrival," voiced Omaran as he drove the giant vehicle out of the parking lot and headed for the coast, south of San Francisco.

"Yes. When we connect all four, it will encircle the mountain. Very powerful! This is going to be perfect!"

They found a place to park and sleep, and the next day arrived at the ocean, turning south toward Monterrey. Stopping along the ocean between Big Sur and Carmel, they hiked up the bluff away from the sea as far up as they could get before it got too steep. Still visible from the road, they hoped they were far enough away that they would not attract attention. During the ceremony a couple of people did stop to stare for a minute before moving on.

The third point was completed by late afternoon. They packed up and walked back down to the RV.

"I don't believe that will be the only time someone sees us as we do this," mused Omaran. "At least they were far away."

"I think we better start cloaking ourselves if we want to stay hidden. Let's do that from now on, before we start walking to the ceremony site," said Antera.

"Good idea."

The next day, they drove to the general area they wanted for the last point, along the coast near Half Moon Bay. Though they had been given the general area by the Masters, they knew it was up to them to find the exact location of a working site, so flexibility was needed. A site in this area was not as easy to find. They drove the coast highway for several miles, a road Omaran knew well from earlier in life when he lived in San Jose, but though there was beach access in a few places, the other side on the bluff didn't look accessible. They didn't want to do the ceremony on the beach so they continued on.

Omaran finally said, "This area doesn't look as promising as the others so far, but we could always come around a corner, and there it will be!"

"I think we should stop for a moment and send our energy ahead to find the perfect place."

"Alright, I'll pull over as soon as I get a chance. That may be a little while."

"That's fine," said Antera.

As soon as he could, Omaran pulled over and together they sent their energy ahead to find the perfect spot for the fourth land pinning. In a few minutes they both felt very good about it, and off they went again. After only a few minutes of driving, they came to a place where they had a good parking place large enough for the RV, and it looked like they could go right across the road, climb a little bit, and get to some flat land for their ceremony.

"Let's go check it out, I think we can get up there without too much difficulty," Omaran said after looking it over. He was a good judge of distance and steepness.

"Can you carry the stools and most of the ceremonial stuff?" asked Antera. "I think I'll need both my arms to scramble up there."

"Yeah, almost everything will fit in the backpack, and I can carry the small stools in one hand."

She knew it would be awkward for him, but he was such a good sport he would never let on how hard it was to climb with only one hand free. Off they went, Faith leading the way, and while it was steep, it didn't prove to be too difficult. The shelf they aimed for was about 30 feet wide, and they scouted around. There was a small grove of cypress trees, which at first glance seemed best, but they soon discovered a lot of trash there. Apparently many others had made the short climb up to this bench of land that faced directly west and had a fantastic view of the ocean! So they chose a place a little removed from the trees, checked to make sure they were indeed alone and cloaked the area as they had been instructed to do several years ago by the Masters, asking not to be disturbed while they were doing the ceremony.

It went smoothly, and when it was over Antera said, "Maybe because this was the fourth ceremony in . . . how many days?"

"Five," Omaran replied.

"Well, this one was certainly the best attended as far as nature spirits. It makes me think word has gotten around and when we stopped and took time to send our energy ahead to the perfect place, it gave them a chance to get here before us. They were waiting for us."

"Yeah, I believe it. I couldn't see any, but it sure felt like this one was almost crowded. I'm glad you mentioned that, I thought I was feeling all the people who have been here before."

"That might have been a part of it, but this one was like a full house. They loved the singing and music, in fact they're still dancing around. Let's play the last song again while I clean up and you bury the sacred objects."

"Good idea. This was a fun project, and we are finished! Yay!"

They felt a bit tired as they started driving back to their apartment to get ready for the work week. But they talked and laughed on their way home, thoroughly enjoying their experience. This work felt so familiar, and fulfilling, and they were grateful to have done their part to heal the land, and helping one of their favorite mountains.

It was the next weekend before they could check in with the Masters to get feedback on the land-healing work, after a busy week. When they finished dinner, they sat in their living room, getting comfortable. The Angel of Mount Tam was the first to speak, saying she was very pleased and grateful for the land healing. She told them how to connect the points energetically, making a feedback loop between them that was very strong. She also said that not only do the points purify the area, but they add positive energy to the Network of Light.

The Angel said, "The more points the better! You may be able to fully stabilize the West Coast, and create a lot more harmony here."

Afterwards, Antera said, "Wow, I thought we were done, but now it seems we need to stabilize the whole West Coast. That would be a lot of pinning points."

"Yes . . . ." Omaran was already thinking about more trips to take.

"The Angel was showing me a zigzag pattern like a stitch on a sewing machine all along the coast, on each side of the San Andreas Fault! That would certainly help stabilize it."

Omaran had learned a little about faults and earthquakes since living with Antera. "But doesn't the fault have to slip sometime? Isn't that a natural process?"

"Yes, you're right." She was surprised he knew that. "There are stresses in the crust that need to be relieved. We don't want to stop the tectonic movement. Only ease the human components, the astral pollution that humans have contributed to that stress. Then when the fault does slip, it may not cause so much damage to humans."

"That makes sense. So, we need to do a zigzag, huh? A zigzag!" Omaran went to a bookshelf and pulled down their large California road map, spreading it out on the floor.

45

Return of the Demon

Omaran came home in a bad mood, fuming but not wanting to think about why. Feeling tired and dirty, and disappointed in his body for being tired and not having the strength and stamina he used to have, he showered and changed clothes for the evening.

Saying very little during dinner, what he did say contradicted just about everything Antera said, until she stopped trying to make conversation. She didn't want to make a big deal about his moodiness, and hoped he was just tired, though she knew his tiredness was almost always based on emotional upsets. As soon as she was finished eating, she simply got up and took her dishes to the kitchen.

"Can't you even stay here until I'm done eating?" He growled.

"You didn't seem to want to talk with me, so there was no reason."

"That is just rude."

"Omaran, why are you being so irritable?" Antera asked. "You are arguing with everything I say. Are you just tired?"

"I'm fine. You're the one with the problem. I'm fine at work, then I come home and I don't feel good, so it must be you!" He glared at her and sent an unexpected blast of energy.

She felt like she was hit in the stomach. Why was he attacking her? "If you were fine you wouldn't be mad. There's no reason to attack me just because you aren't feeling balanced."

"I'm not attacking you! You are attacking me! You are the problem! What's wrong with you?"

Another energy blast was thrown, hitting Antera squarely on the chest this time. She knew the warning signs of incipient rage looking for an outlet, and decided to retreat. No reasoning would calm him now. He was escalating out of control. This was obviously a demon and she had to get away. She hadn't seen this intense demon for years, but there he was again. She warily walked quickly away and went into the bathroom, locking the door.

"I'll talk with you later, when you can be nice," she said through the door.

He yelled, "We will talk now! Don't go away when I'm talking to you! You have to listen!" He banged on the bathroom door, shouting for a while, and she thought he may break it. But then she heard him walk away, and there was a loud crash like something had broken, silence for a minute, then the front door slammed. Perhaps he had gone, but she waited a few minutes to make sure it was safe before coming out.

She found quite a mess. He had flung the salad dressing jar from the dining table to the floor, and there was broken glass along with salad dressing on the tile and carpet. She found the pets, who had hidden in the bedroom, and soothed them, then picked up the glass so they wouldn't get cut. But he would have to clean up the rest of the mess himself.

He had been on edge for a few days, but she never suspected the demon would come back. The first few years of their relationship, this demon, or one like it, had appeared many times, taking over her husband with outrageous, threatening behavior for no apparent reason. At first, she had been shocked that he could change personalities so quickly, being loving and nice one moment then attacking her the next. With repeated encounters, she had learned how to deal with him better, but it had never gotten easy.

The demon she knew from earlier times had often appeared psychically as a giant gorilla beating its chest. This current one she hadn't seen until it was too late, perhaps because her guard was down. But they were intelligent and devious enough to hide well before suddenly appearing, with a surprise attack.

Taking a deep breath, she released some of the pain he had thrown at her. No matter how good she was at protection, it was difficult when the energy was coming through her spouse. She had never wanted to keep a wall between them, as she had done earlier, out of desperation. Tears streamed down her cheeks. She had thought this was a thing of the past. He had healed so much, how could he let this happen again? Where did this energy come from?

Generally, Omaran didn't remember much afterwards of what he said and did when he was taken over, so it was fruitless to discuss it with him, and in the past he had never really understood how damaging it was to her. It was literally a takeover, and this demon's desire was to hurt her in any way possible. Fortunately, Omaran had enough control not to do anything to physically hurt her, but the impact of the attack energy was sometimes extreme, especially to her sensitive psychic senses, and required much healing afterwards. So she had long ago learned not to engage at all, but to get away until Omaran came back.

Continuing to breathe deeply, she got out a sage stick to smudge the apartment. Her energy field had taken a blow, and she would need to heal herself. It could have been worse, but this was simply not acceptable. Not at all.

Omaran didn't come home until later that evening, after Antera was in bed. She heard him cleaning the floor, which meant he was back to himself, but she did not get up. He slept on the couch.

"I thought about it, and I guess I am just so frustrated by having to work so hard physically, and I really want to go home, but we can't yet," Omaran began, when approached by Antera the next day.

"But do you understand what happened? If that demon is going to be with you again, and you are going to allow him to attack me, I will leave. Period. My health isn't all that great since we've been here, and I simply can't take that now."

They had both been feeling drained, first from being on the road for a year, then with the stresses of living near a city. It was hard to believe they had lived in this area before and gotten used to the psychic and physical pollution. She knew Omaran was physically exhausted from his day job, and the only thing keeping him going in spirit was their land healing. But even knowing that, there was no excuse for this.

"I'm really sorry," he said miserably. "I can't explain why I got so crummy. I just wasn't able to stop it."

"You will control your words and behavior, you have to. It threatens not only me but all the work we are doing together!" She walked away and sat at her computer to get some work done.

He knew he wasn't right. There was a cloud over him and he couldn't seem to shake it off. Calling Faith, he took her outside for a walk in the hills behind their apartment. During the walk, he decided he would ask Antera for help, maybe calling in the Masters to see if there was something they could do or tell him. In his rational mind, he knew there was a good reason for this happening, and that if he just figured out the lessons, he could heal. He didn't want to hurt Antera!

Faith saw a squirrel and strained at the leash. Omaran unhooked it and let her run, as it seemed to be a safe area. The demon kept coming back to his mind. Was it really one? How could he get compromised so easily and quickly? He knew that some part of him had to be resonating with this or he wouldn't have responded like he did. He had learned that from their hike on Black Butte a few years earlier. As St. Germain had told him then, he wouldn't have had to go through the major release he did on that hike if there was nothing inside him that resonated with the negative energies.

So what was this negative resonance? Was it because of his work? It was true that he came home tired after work, because being a foreman involved a lot more physical effort than being a contractor, as he had been for the previous 30 years. Construction was hard work, but he didn't mind that. Plus, he really liked the contractor he was working for. He thought about the time years ago when someone had asked him, "What's the easiest part of construction?" He had pondered it for a few minutes, running many phases of construction through his mind and finally had replied, "The ride home at the end of the day."

He didn't believe that he was resonating with anything negative at work, because there really wasn't anything bad or depressing there. All the guys on the crew were wonderful people. And the rest of his life was good, too. He could not figure out where this was coming from and it was extremely distressing.

That evening, Antera agreed to connect with the Masters. Mother Mary came through her to talk with Omaran.

In her loving and understanding way, Mary explained, "I don't know if you're aware, but there is a large cloud of negativity just over the hill from you because of the prison. There are a lot of unhappy people there. That is one of the reasons you are living where you are, to maintain the energy. But it creeps over the hill and you have to be careful.

"That is some of the rage that you have had problems with, Omaran. It creeps over and around the hill, this very large cloud of unhappiness, rage, and sadness. You can imagine what it would be like, being locked up. It is not a happy time for those people and therefore it spreads out from there."

"Thank you, Mary. I guess that explains why it came on me so suddenly and without apparent reason."

They had known that there was a prison nearby, but they rarely went by it, so it hadn't occurred to them that the suffering energy of that place could be impinging on them. No doubt there were plenty of demons there!

Omaran was reminded, by Mary, of the need to be diligent in his protection, and to recognize immediately if he wasn't feeling good emotionally, so he could catch it sooner before entities could attach. He knew that intellectually, but it had always been one of his biggest challenges. Overall, though, he thought he was doing much better, besides this one slip up.

She went on, "Omaran, you have come through some hard lessons lately."

He said, "Yes, I feel like I'm finally beginning to turn to all of you, if not right away, very quickly . . . and to open my heart. I'm trying, I'm trying."

"You are making headway, and becoming more aware of your pain, so you can take yourself out of the emotion. That's really what you are doing, you're noticing the emotion and as you notice it you're taking yourself out of it."

He considered that. "I never looked at it that way."

"Once you can take yourself out of it and realize that you are not the emotion, then you can control it. Then you can stop thinking whatever thoughts caused the emotion, and control your thoughts more. Just realizing you are not the emotion is the big step for you. After that it is a piece of cake. Controlling your thoughts will not be difficult once you can separate them out. For you, it is the separating them out that is the biggest step, and noticing what is happening."

"Thank you for pointing that out."

Mary continued, "This helps you keep your perspective. I have been seeing your little wins along the way, the times when you catch yourself before you let it get too far. This is good, and you can congratulate yourself for every little time, because that makes you do it more."

Omaran agreed, "It does. I do feel better about it, for as long as I can keep it in mind."

"And now we see that there needed to be a big blowup before you would take this seriously."

"Thank you, Mary. You aways know what to say. I will do better."

Mary said, "About the land healing. You know, it brings up your skills from long ago when you did this kind of work as a job . . . when it was your responsibility to maintain the harmony of the land, to mitigate the negativity that was created. But you know, back then it was a much easier job, because there were fewer people and that was before the astral realm got so very crowded.

"Since then, much of the emotional body of the planet has gotten dense, almost concrete, and solid. Because of this situation right now it is a much bigger job, and this is why you can only do a small area at a time. Whereas before you used to do whole continents, now you can only focus on a small area because there is so much to clear. But with a lot of small areas, if you keep doing this, soon you will have large areas.

"This is why the Angel of Mount Tam says to do as many as you can, and after a while they will overlap, and you will have a much clearer area. As long as they are in place, the negativity will not grow again, because they will continue to transform all the negativity that comes in."

"I wish I could remember more about the land healing we did on Lemuria."

"I believe some will come back to you as you do this work. But because it was different back then, you used different techniques. There was not the huge charge that you are dealing with now. Whereas it might be useful to gather some of your skills from previous times, now you have different methods. What you are doing now is very, very effective."

Mary also suggested that they do the clearing ceremony in their home. This would purify the energy better than sage or any other tool. They thought it was a great idea, and did it right afterwards, the first time inside a building. The difference was huge. They both felt much better, and a weight was lifted.

"Why didn't we think to do this in our home before?" Antera wondered.

"Never even occurred to me. We have only done these outside."

Antera said, "You know, I guess we have the demon to thank for giving us the need for a purging and clearing in our house. We may not have done this so soon otherwise." She smiled at Omaran, and he knew he was completely forgiven.

He thought about the process they had just done. "Now that we see how effective it is, wouldn't it be good to share this method with others?"

"Yes . . . maybe we could record a CD of the songs and meditation to make it available and easy for others to do in their homes or offices."

"We already have a rough mix of the new songs, so we just need to do some tweaking to make them good enough for a CD. I'll talk to Terry, and let's listen to them to make a list of what we need to do on each song."

"How about now?" Antera asked.

They got right on it while they were inspired, listening to the songs carefully to make them professional quality. The next two trips to the studio produced the finished product. Now it could be shared!

46

Sewing Up the Coast

Omaran was busy getting ready for their next land healing trip, a longer one to central and southern California. As usual, he had a plan of how to best get to the places they wanted to visit for ceremonies, both inland and near the coast, to create the zigzag pattern. He had found parks and public land that looked promising, but they wouldn't know whether these green areas on the map would provide seclusion or not until they went there.

They had both arranged for a week off work, and he was getting the RV ready, which hadn't been used for weeks . . . only moved from parking place to parking place.

Antera carried out a box of food to the RV. "How is it coming? Will we be ready to leave tomorrow morning?"

"I think so. Still a lot to pack. Did you finish all the painting?"

"Yes, all the sacred objects are done, but some will need to dry on the way," she answered.

Antera sat in one of the chairs and looked around. They had spent over a year living and traveling in this vehicle.

"I hope this is the last trip in the RV," she said. "Neither pet really likes traveling, especially Samantha. Also, after this trip I'd like to sell it. Right now it seems more like a burden, and maybe we could use the money to get that SCIO machine. I'm getting very strong guidance that we should have one."

284

Omaran thought about that. "Maybe. But I'm happy to have this now so we can take the pets with us, and go off on an adventure. You know how I love to travel."

She smiled at him. "That you do. And what better excuse than doing work for the Masters, making this planet a better place."

Sitting down next to her, he said, "Yes. I keep thinking about this project and how it expanded. Isn't it just exactly how the Masters work, asking us to do a few points, seeing how successful they were, then asking us to do the entire West Coast."

"I wonder if they had that in mind all along and just didn't tell us."

"It would have seemed like a big project to us then, maybe overwhelming, but now that we have some experience, it seems doable. Wow! It's still the whole West Coast, and we've only got four columns in so far."

"I think," said Antera, "the Masters knew what they were doing in starting us off small, giving us a chance to experience these clearing and pinning points ourselves, before expanding the project."

"Of course. And I love what the Angel of Mount Tam said about how these columns pull in negative energy from outside and transform it. I don't know of anything else that works like that."

Antera nodded. "And think about the potential that these points have . . . I thought they were just for helping out the two main areas that we had our ceremonies on, which they are doing. But this can do a lot more . . . a lot more!"

They headed out the next morning, first to Fresno in the Central Valley south of Stockton. There they found a wonderful park, where they were able to hide in the trees for the ceremony. They had done significant energy work together before leaving home, including sending out a call for nature spirits, so it was no surprise to find dozens already expecting them and very excited to help. Success!

Continuing south, they headed to the southern end of the Central Valley, to Bakersfield. Omaran had a brother, David, who lived there and offered a shower and a bed. They took him up on the shower, but slept in the RV parked outside the house, to be with the pets.

The next day they headed to the outskirts of Bakersfield, and found a fairly good park that only had a few people in it, so they were once again able to find a secluded place and pull off another successful ceremony. They explained to the nature spirits how the column was connected to the other points, and that there would be new points connecting in the future as they were created.

With the two inland points done, they headed west toward the coast. David had advised them on the best roads to take, and that night they drove into the coastal mountains. Looking for a place to park and sleep, they finally found a road going off the highway, and Omaran planted the RV next to it.

"This may be private land," Antera cautioned.

"I didn't see any signs saying 'Don't park here or we'll come get you,' so it must be fine. Anyway, I'm tired. Let's heat up some of that leftover soup."

They made it through the night without anyone threatening them with a shotgun, and the following morning they continued west toward the ocean.

"Now, this is the kind of work that I could get used to doing," said Omaran as they cruised through the mountains.

"Well, you'll have to get used to it without the RV in the future."

"I think the RV is going to miss us."

"Don't worry, we'll find it a good home."

For the third column on this trip they found a high bluff they could hike up to, overlooking the ocean south of Santa Barbara. The hardest part of the ceremony was burying the sacred objects in the ground, as the soil was hard-packed clay. Fortunately, they had both a small shovel and a small pick, so Omaran was finally able to dig a hole deep enough.

That night, they found a place to sleep right on the beach. After dinner, they took a walk with the animals on the shore. Samantha didn't know what to make of the water and waves, and tugged on her leash away from the water. They carried her part of the way. Faith, of course, loved it, playing and wading as dogs do.

Antera sighed wistfully and said, "I guess I could get used to this. Reminds me of living at the ocean when my kids were young. I love the sound of the waves."

"Me too. Very relaxing. Many years ago I stayed with a friend right on the beach in Malibu for three months. It was nice, falling asleep to the sound of waves crashing every few seconds."

"Oh yeah, like you need to relax, Mr. Fall-Asleep-Anytime. How many waves did you hear, two before you were asleep?"

"Very funny."

Antera breathed deeply of the moist air. "You know, it seems like I can already feel some of the tectonic stress being relieved. Maybe it is my imagination, but there is a shift from these few points we've done."

"I believe it! This is powerful work."

The next day's goal was finding a place that would be directly west of the Fresno point, so they traveled north along the beach. They had picked out a place called Avila Beach for the fourth point. Before they came within sight of the town, a road appeared that went off to a large bluff that overlooked the town and ocean, so they took that.

"Well, this looks perfect!" said Omaran as they parked in a touristy parking lot. "Looks like a lot of cars here, though. Popular spot."

"Hikers, I guess. Look at all the trailheads," replied Antera. "I'm sure we can find a trail that's less traveled." They both laughed at that.

They chose one and hiked about half a mile. There were trails everywhere, crisscrossing every which way, so it took some effort to find a small grove between them where they could pretty much hide. The ceremony was completed without interruptions, thanks to their cloaking efforts, and they now had a good start on sewing up the coast of California!

A few days after returning home, they were sitting together for dinner and, after sharing their days, Antera told Omaran, "St. Germain came to me today and said that we need to help maintain the columns that we have created by checking in with them a couple of times a week to see how they are doing. We can move energy around in case any need help. Would you like to be in charge of that?"

"Oh." He thought about it. "Well, yeah, actually I would like to do it. I'm not exactly sure if I know what to do really, but I guess I'll just start. That will certainly help keep it fresh in my mind . . . I can picture all the places we've been—of course, it's only eight so far. Yeah, I'll be happy to do that."

So, Omaran made a list of all points created, and gave each of them names. He started checking in twice a week to look with inner eyes at the sites, say hello to all the beings there, and perceive as best he could how each point was doing.

47

Energy

Though they knew this lifestyle was temporary, living in an apartment near the city and working at jobs started to take a toll on their health. Their energy levels were decreasing, and at times they felt drained. The job Omaran was doing was physically very demanding, and much different from when he had his own company. Then he had been able to take a break whenever he wanted, to pick up supplies or do paperwork. But working for another contractor meant he worked eight hours a day, five days a week, using his 62-year-old body very physically.

He came home every night very tired, and his lower back ached. Antera gave him massages, which helped temporarily, but each day he would again strain the muscles. He used his will to keep going, which had always worked for him, but it was a stretch.

Antera was also feeling less energetic, and noticed that many spots of sun damage on her skin had started growing like never before. As a redhead who grew up in southern California, at a time when being tan was thought to be healthy, she had tried to tan as a child, but it was impossible for her skin, which only made freckles and burned. So by the time she was 20 she'd had thousands of these sun-damaged areas. Fortunately, none had gone cancerous, much to the surprise of dermatologists she had seen over the years. Now, since returning to the Bay Area, many were growing and looking very irritated, perhaps moving toward being cancerous. But she didn't want to go to a doctor again because she had so many spots, and she didn't want the alarmed energy she would get from a dermatologist.

One day, when walking Faith, she climbed the ridge just behind their apartment and took a slightly different route. She was listening to a cassette tape with a headset as she walked. Suddenly there was loud interference and static, so she hit the stop button and looked around. A huge tower loomed above her, right there, very close to their apartment but not visible until she had walked over the hill in this direction. Cell phones were becoming more common, though not something she or Omaran wanted, so she thought it was probably a cell tower.

It got her thinking about radiation, and its harmful effects. Obviously the skin growths were created because of too much radiation from the sun, and some research told her that human-made electromagnetic energy, the silent pollution, could also contribute to her skin and many other health issues.

She also knew that their desire to go home and the discontent they both felt while living here had to be another factor underlying her skin issues and Omaran's back pain. They were both working in their meditations on being more content with where they were and what they were doing. But it also at times felt like they were trapped, because they couldn't go home until their renters left in October, and they needed the money they were making before then anyway.

That evening, Mary helped them out of the pattern of discontent with a wonderful pep talk.

Omaran told her, "The tour wasn't easy, and now I have to work in construction again because we need money, and it is hard on my body. We know we need to be here now, but we are really looking forward to getting home to our other mountain."

Mary told him, "We know that this is a difficult time for you. This is also a wonderful time for you. You can look at it that way, you know. Whenever you have a challenge it is a wonderful time because you can make the biggest leaps. Leaps in faith. Leaps in your abilities. Calling forth your abilities from other lifetimes, or earlier in this lifetime, so that you can REALLY do anything you want to. You have had glimpses of this power. You have had glimpses when you really felt that you could do anything, you knew nothing could get in your way; when you could create as much money as you wanted and do the work that you so love to do.

"You are not trapped, you are not slaves! You are free thinkers. You are powerful beings able to do whatever you want with your lives! The only limitations are put there by yourselves, within, of course, the society. But even within such a restrictive society there are always opportunities. It does not matter what limitations other people have. You can be limitless, if you can remove the restrictions of your own minds and not buy into what other people think.

"You are living in a place where there are many restrictions in people's minds, so to break through those is a challenge. But it can be done! And surely if anyone can do it I think you two can.

"Remember when I talked about looking at every opportunity of your life as expanding or contracting? Every thought you have expands or contracts you. Contracting thoughts are usually based on fears, or habits. Sometimes thoughts are simply habitual. So you think them because you have always thought them or you have heard them many times. Habitual thoughts that contract you can be changed by recognizing them and deciding not to go there again. Build other habitual thoughts to take their place.

"This is why chanting and forms of prayer that are repetitious tend to work their way in through the unconscious and replace those other thoughts. They become habitual, and they give you more expansion in your life without even thinking about it."

"Yes," Omaran said. "I remember you talking about paying attention to thoughts and noticing if they expand or contract us. I love that concept. But I'm afraid I have not always done it, and I haven't been feeling expanded lately."

Mary continued, "Everything is energy around you. Everything. And energy can be transformed from one thing to another. So look at your life as expansive and it will become expansive. Look at the blessing in every moment, give thanks for everything you have that is working, and more and more of your life will be working to your benefit. Counting your blessings is a good practice before you go to sleep at night or every morning, and also during your day to day experience. Look at the wonderful life you have and the wonderful things in your life . . . the people and pets, the sky, mountain, air and water, the food that you have in such plentiful quantities, clothing, and so many wonderful things. Giving thanks for everything in your vicinity charges them up and gives you an atmosphere of expansion. This helps everything work more fluidly and more efficiently.

"Bringing this expansion back into your lives is what you need to do whenever you start to feel frustrated or closed in or you can't find a solution to a problem. Simply give thanks for what is working, or for any opportunity that you have, to serve in the way that you find joyful. This will bring the blessings into your life so quickly you will be astounded.

"This is what I want to see for you, my brother and sister. I want to see the life you want, growing stronger, with expanding opportunities. I give thanks to you for all of the work you have done and will be doing to help balance this planet, to bring joy to others, and to teach others.

"Many eyes are on you. I don't tell you that to make you feel bad or self-conscious, but I believe you should know this. Many eyes are on you, many beings watch you. You do attract attention. Do you know that?"

Omaran said, "Probably not to the extent that you know."

"You are in the spotlight. Remember, every thought is known to the universe, every one! It's completely transparent where I am. Just so you know that. Perhaps it will help you to curb some of those thoughts that do not help you expand."

They thanked Mary for such an uplifting talk, after which both of them felt much better and grateful. She knew just how to inspire them. When Omaran was talking with Mary or any of the Masters, the teachings seemed very simple and sometimes even obvious, but afterwards, in daily life, he realized how profound these teachings were.

They had listed the RV for sale upon their return from the last land-healing trip, and after reinstalling the bed and returning it to its standard layout on one of their weekend trips to Shasta. But after a few weeks there were still no offers. Antera had the idea that the elemental in charge of the vehicle may have some resistance, so she decided to check in with him. Sitting inside the RV, she asked for contact with the spirit, and what was going on. He told her that he missed them and felt abandoned when they didn't go on any trips. He was lonely and not fulfilling his perceived mission, which was to carry them and the pets to many places, as he had done on the tour.

She then explained that it was time for a new purpose, a new owner who would go to different places and appreciate him more. Maybe even a family with kids! Making this sound much more exciting than staying with them, she did her best to convince him that it was a good thing to get new owners.

Three days later a couple with two young girls called, visited, and loved it immediately. They made an offer, it was accepted and off it went on new adventures with a very excited family who were probably unaware of the also-excited spirit of the RV.

The money from the sale was immediately used to buy a SCIO like they had seen in Phoenix. Antera took several week-long training courses in Los Angeles to learn how to use it, and was fascinated by its capabilities. She used herself and Omaran as test cases, trying out many of the over 200 therapies, for every kind of stress.

As she suspected, radiation did register on the machine as a big stress on her health, affecting her immunity and overall health numbers. She worked on her skin and immunity, clearing out stress from radiation, and boosted everything that needed boosting. It was fun to gradually see her health numbers increase as her energy came back. After working on herself almost daily for a couple of months, her skin looked fine and she had her energy back. She was impressed!

She worked on Omaran almost daily as well, even when he wasn't home. The machine seemed to work as well from a distance as it did when strapped in electronically. One day, she put him on an oxygen program in the afternoon, and let it run for an hour.

That evening he said, "Suddenly this afternoon, I found myself almost running up some stairs. I had energy at a time when I'm usually dragging. I don't know why, but I was glad!"

She told him she had sent oxygen at that time, and his response was, "Well, do it every day!"

The machine also worked on non-physical issues, such as clearing entities, soothing emotions, and removing resistance. Antera cleared both of their brain waves every day for a while, which showed stress and interference from the outside, and that also gradually cleared. Now they really got what the Masters had been telling them for years, that everything was energy, everything! The SCIO was confirmation of this over and over, working solely on energy, with energy. There could be no doubt now!

This was very exciting to both of them, and they were so grateful that this tool had come into their lives. The possibilities were endless! They both got better and better, physically, emotionally, mentally and spiritually.

Antera knew that this machine had probably saved her life, and made it possible to continue living under the cell tower and in the city and still be healthy. There was another factor that had been affecting them, also made clear by using the SCIO. They were under psychic attack. The Masters had warned them to be very diligent in their protection, because of the kind of lightwork they did, but this level of attack really took them by surprise.

Ever since they had gotten together, as twin flames, there had been interfering energies trying to separate them. It was something they had accepted, and learned to deal with. But this new energy was more than that, and required new techniques. The SCIO really helped in making them more aware of the energies being aimed at them, and was instrumental in clearing them off and increasing their energetic immunity.

St. Germain confirmed that they needed protection, and taught them some other techniques to help, and their education expanded. One evening, Omaran asked the Master, through Antera, about what they were going through, hoping for more clarity.

Omaran said, "I know I've been very naïve. But lately, I've noticed that I'm coming under some kind of attack every Thursday. Last Thursday I thought I was well prepared, I brought in all kinds of energy, but it still got to me Thursday morning. Fortunately I realized what was going on fairly quickly, but is the energy that is being directed towards us more machine-made than in the past? I tried to shield myself and I don't think I was effective. What can I do to be more effective?"

St. Germain said, "Well now, this is a big subject. There are many different kinds of energy being directed at both of you. Don't think you're invisible. The Light that you and Antera create together is very visible. It gives people hope, something to look toward in their own relationships, something to look toward in their faith and spiritual journey. I don't want to hear you say again, 'Why me? I'm not important.' Give that up! You are in the sights, both of you.

"So, that said, you have different kinds of energy being directed at you two in particular, and others that are directed at groups that you are part of, and some energies that are simply around you.

"Okay, so let's talk about the first part, the energy that is directed at you. This energy is purposeful and directed at you and others like you. Its purpose is to bring you doubts. It will influence your emotional body, giving you a sense of failure, of being a nobody, of depression. It is that kind of energy.

"And this is being sent to many people whose Light is visible. This kind of energy being directed at lightworkers is very damaging because they don't know what is happening, for the most part. They don't know why they are having those thoughts, they don't know why they are feeling depressed, discouraged, angry, or sad. They think it's theirs and it's not, they are being impinged upon. It is being directed at them.

"Then there is the electronic energy. This is another form and there are many different kinds of energy that are being directed at whole groups of people. This energy can be in many different frequencies and wave forms, and there has been much research done to figure exactly what kinds of wave forms can be projected at a person to keep them from being effective in different ways, physically, mentally, or otherwise. This is definitely made by machines and projected electronically.

"Then there is the energy that is just around you in the astral world, all of the harmful creations that will come in an instant if you have thoughts that attract it. So, for example, you could have an attack come at you from these entities that are making you feel a little upset, and then suddenly all the energy around you that is upset, comes in and magnifies it.

"Being fully aware of this is so important now—to know how you are feeling at all times. And IMMEDIATELY, if you feel yourself getting upset, go within and think, 'I do not need to go there, this is not my upset.' Recognize it as something coming to you with foreign energy and dispel it immediately before it builds up. Because if you allow it to build up, oh, guess what will happen. You've seen it. It's going to get worse. More and more people are going to find themselves going crazy, with rage and depression.

"Look at all the depressed people! This is not normal. People are normally happy. So then you get the drugs and other damaging contributors, and it's a downward spiral. This is one reason you are here, to look at it and help to educate people about it. And sometimes you need to experience the worst of it to really get it. We hope you have seen the worst of it and will not have to go there again."

Omaran said, "Me too! Thank you for explaining all that. It will help me so much. I must admit that while I appreciate on a certain level that many of the experiences I go through will help others so they won't have to make the same mistakes, still, I'm looking forward to the day when I won't be an example of what NOT to do!"

When Antera had disconnected from Germain and opened her eyes, Omaran asked her, "Do you remember all that?"

Antera tended to remember most of what came through her right afterwards, but with time it tended to fade like dreams. Omaran always transcribed the recordings and then she read them later. She said, "Yes, I think so."

"We have many kinds of energy to shield out. I guess I can't stick my head in the sand anymore."

"Talk about learning the hard way! I guess we will really get these lessons."

48

Zig-Zagging

With the RV gone, their next road trip required finding care for their dog and cat. They wanted to finish with southern California, which would require a few more sites, ending with a visit to Antera's parents in the San Diego area.

"I was thinking," Omaran began out of nowhere, "Maybe we could leave Faith and Samantha with Michael and Jeen for a week while we head south."

Antera looked up from her computer, shifting Samantha to a more comfortable position on her lap. "We could ask," she said, and turned back to her work.

"We don't have any points in northern California," said Omaran, thinking out loud. "Maybe after we leave the pets in Redding, we could get a couple sites in the northern part of the central valley, then drive south to do more in southern California. Then we'll only need a couple more along the north coast to be finished with the state."

"Are you thinking of doing all that on this trip?" asked an incredulous Antera.

"Not the northern points along the coast, but we should be able to get the rest without too much trouble. We're getting pretty good at this, and we move fast. All we're doing out there is working, it's not like we're sightseeing, but I love going to all these places."

"It really is fun doing this together, and we're seeing some places I've never been to, plus we're helping to heal the land. Sounds like a pretty good job description to me."

They took another week off from work, grateful for the flexibility of their jobs. Though they needed the money, it was worth it to complete the project they had been given by the Masters. Jeen and Michael graciously agreed to host the pets, so from Redding they started their work by traveling south to Chico, staying the night with Omaran's other brother, Bob.

Bob gave them directions to a lovely site in Bidwell Park, a beautiful large park with many hiking trails. They found a perfect place for their ceremony next to a very old oak tree, with branches that spread out over a large area like it was embracing the ground. It felt very cozy and nurturing, and no one came by until they were finished. They were getting better at the cloaking. The spirit of the oak tree made himself known during the ceremony, and they both felt very blessed.

From there, they drove further south on Hwy 5 to Sacramento, for another inland point in the zigzag pattern, which would connect nicely to the Point Reyes site. They exited the freeway going east, and took a road along a dry creek bed that looked promising. No people were around.

"I don't want to bury anything in a creek bed that could be washed away," Antera said.

"Looks very dry, but in future years I guess it could flood. What about that small hill? It would be an island in the river when it flows."

Antera looked at the small rise. "Yes, that is high enough. Let's do it!"

They parked the car and loaded up their packs and arms with their ceremony items, and walked over the rocky ground to the site. As they walked, they put out a call to the local population of nature spirits, who came from all around, some of them just curious and others anticipating their arrival with joy. The ceremony went well, and the elementals were rewarded with gifts as always.

From there, they went to spend the night with Omaran's sister Lynn and her husband Chris, who lived fairly close by. The next day, after a delicious breakfast, they got back on Hwy 5 to make the six-hour drive south to Los Angeles.

To support the place they had done the astral clearing ceremony in Griffith Park, their plan was to do a site nearby, on the ocean. Aiming for Malibu, they were lead to a perfect place on a road that was off Hwy 1, between large estates. At least they hoped it was between, and not on private land. It was fairly high so there wouldn't be any danger of the column sliding into the ocean or getting washed away. They found a wonderful spot where they were completely hidden but they could see the Pacific. No one bothered them, and they finished as the sun was going down in the ocean. They sat for a few minutes, enjoying the colors in the sky and sea.

They spent the night in Los Angeles with Janet, and in the early morning drove to the next area they had in mind, a desert far enough inland to be on the other side of the San Andreas Fault. Pulling off on a dirt road into the desert, they followed it not knowing where it would head, and hoping the car would not get stuck in sand, which seemed a distinct possibility. Omaran avoided the obvious areas where the sand was deep, and drove until the highway was far enough away to prevent attention from people driving by. Getting out of sight was not possible in this dry landscape of very few trees or large rocks.

"I like that spot over there," Antera said, pointing to a couple of fifteen-foot Joshua Trees.

Another dirt road, in even worse shape, went in that direction, so Omaran drove toward the trees. As soon as they arrived and opened the car doors, two large owls took flight in their silent way, from one of the trees.

"Oh, wow," exclaimed Antera. "That was special!"

"I guess there's no question where this column is supposed to be."

"And what it will be named. How about Two Owls?"

"Perfect!"

They set up quickly and did the ceremony, glad it wasn't too hot yet. While they were singing the first song, a huge noise made them look up to see a group of fighter jets flying low overhead. Another group flew over a few minutes later, and they hoped they hadn't attracted the attention of some kind of military operation. When finished, they packed up quickly and left, job well done.

Back on the highway heading south, they could see a giant military base on the other side, which they hadn't noticed when driving in. They knew that some of the negative energy from the base would be transformed by the pinning site they had just created. The next stop would be Joshua Tree National Park, about a three hour drive, and they hoped to get there in time to finish the second inland point before dark, thankful for the long summer days.

"No wonder they made this a park! It is gorgeous!" Antera said as they drove in.

The scenic rock formations and unique plants and trees formed a beautiful landscape. The road meandered around magnificent outcrops as they slowly drove to take it all in. The late afternoon shadows made the boulders look very dramatic. Several trails looked inviting.

"Let's drive this loop to see it all before deciding where to stop," Omaran suggested.

"Okay. I'm really enjoying seeing this. But I'd like to go out and sit on some of those rocks to collect the energy."

"We will, there's plenty of light left."

After driving for a while, they were drawn toward one trailhead. There weren't many people around, probably because of the time of year, and they were grateful for that. The sun beat down and the heat was intense even this late in the day, and as they parked and got out they immediately donned hats.

"It's just magical here, and the nature spirits are really collecting. They are all around us, like they have been waiting," Antera said as they hiked along the trail.

"I feel them! They are excited."

"This may be the largest group we've had yet at a ceremony."

Omaran chuckled. The joy was catching. "Follow us!" He gestured with his arm, beckoning the group of small beings. "I feel like the Pied Piper!"

They laughed as they hiked about half a mile, then took off from the trail to a large rock formation, where they could be hidden. It was an ideal site, and they nestled in a fairly flat area among the tall, round rocks that was big enough to set up their altar, chairs and ceremony items. Some shade was offered by the boulders. Their voices echoed delightfully off the rock walls during the singing in the ceremony, and the large contingent of nature spirits danced around. They stayed to soak up more desert energy until there was barely any light in the sky and they had to leave to see their way back to the car.

Though it was dark, they drove for a couple of hours to get closer to their last site on this trip, which would be the southernmost point on the ocean. Stopping at a motel along the way, they arrived at the target area just north of San Diego the next morning, and found a place high on a hill overlooking the Pacific. This point, when completed, finished the zigzag pattern in California, except for the northern coast. They could feel the power of all the points working together as they connected them, and it was amazingly fulfilling to see it all come together.

49

Home for Real

Back home in Larkspur, they resumed their normal work schedules at their jobs. But even after being restored to better health, thanks to the SCIO, they still wanted to get back to their mountain home as soon as they could. Driving there once a month had kept them going, and in late summer they approached the end of their apartment lease.

"I sure am looking forward to going home for good," Antera said wistfully one evening after dinner. "I miss Mount Shasta and the home we built." She sat on the couch reading, with Samantha snuggled next to her, despite the weather being warm.

"You sure?" replied Omaran from the kitchen where he was washing dishes. They had an agreement that if one of them cooked, the other one did the cleanup. "We could always move to a small house for one more year, then go back."

"Omaran!"

"Alright, you're right, it's just that we'll be starting all over again just like we did when we first moved there."

"And how did that work out?"

"Yeah . . . I get your point. We'll be fine, of course." He knew it was just his doubts coming up again, about being able to make a living in the small town, and he had to overcome those!

"I just wish we could get back there earlier. I know our renters are not out of our home until the end of September, but I don't want to wait until then. We've waited so long!"

"It will be here sooner than you think." Omaran started the dishwasher.

"I know!" Antera brightened up. "What if we go home a month early and camp on the mountain until we can move in? We can sleep in the loft a few nights and get showers. I'm sure they won't mind."

"No way, it is too late to camp."

"Oh, come on, are you being a wimp? We have lots of warm stuff."

"I don't think so."

"Just think about it." She knew the way he worked. He resisted new ideas at first, but if she left him alone, he thought about them and changed his mind in a day or so.

And that's what he did. The next day he decided it was a good plan after all. Within two weeks' time, they quit their jobs, left most of their things in the apartment, and went back to the mountain to camp for the last month.

However, after about a week of camping at a chilly 6000-foot elevation, one morning Antera shivered as she got out of the tent and said, "It is too cold at this elevation! I don't think I can do this anymore. And Samantha is always on me for warmth."

"Yeah," said Omaran as he blew mist from his mouth. "I think it's time we move indoors. Let's break down our camp and talk to the renters tonight. Maybe we can stay in the loft of our home the rest of the time. It's only three weeks."

So they spent the last few weeks living in the loft over the garage while the renters packed up to move out. Finally, at the beginning of October they moved back into their home after being away for over two years. If they were joyous, Faith and Samantha were ecstatic.

"Wow, I missed this place so much! I never want to be gone so long again." Antera sighed as they sat curled up on the living room couch together, three weeks later. The move-in was almost finished.

"It sure is nice to be home," Omaran agreed. "I think I'd forgotten what we have here. This is so fantastic. I still want to do trips in the future. After all, we haven't even really finished California yet, and we still have Oregon and Washington to do. But we'll never rent out our house again. Shorter trips, that's all."

"We may need to do more than the one clearing ceremony to get the energy of the renters out of here. But we will have our energy back in place soon."

"It does feel different. But what can we expect after two years?"

"Now that we are here, obviously we have to figure out how we will pay the mortgage again, and get some work. Byron even toyed with the idea of renting a small office up here for some of the operations, when I told him I was moving back home. Not sure I want to do that, but I'll think about it."

"An office up here? So then he could come up and sleep in the office like you did when you were driving down there!"

"Something like that. But we'll see."

"Hmm. I guess I'll look for some small remodels as soon as we are settled. That will seem super easy after working full time down in the Bay Area."

"I bet."

"I'm thinking about our next trip to finish sewing up the coast," Omaran said. "We could do a couple of points on the northern California coast in one short trip. With a point here on our property, at least we'd be done with this state."

"All right, but let me get used to being home first before we go off again!"

"Of course, Darling. We can get in a few hikes on our mountain before it gets too cold."

"That would be heavenly." Antera sighed, thinking about all the fabulous places they had found on hikes. "Plus, we may have some more lightwork to do here, to make sure the energy is flowing properly around the mountain. We've been gone a while. The energy does feel different."

"You're probably right. I haven't been checking in with the Light Field nearly as often while we've been away."

"Now that I am sensing it, there is probably quite a bit of lightwork to do on this mountain. But we will still finish the work the Masters asked us to do on the West Coast. That is a great project!"

"I can't think of a more fun project. We are so blessed to be given this land healing as part of our spiritual service. Wow, I am so grateful!"

"Me too! And we are so lucky to have each other." Antera turned her head to his and they kissed, giving thanks for all their blessings.

The Story Continues…

The adventures of Antera and Omaran continue in the second book of the series, *Emissaries of the Order of Melchizedek: Book II*. Follow their story as they continue their land-healing work, finishing the West Coast only to be asked by the Masters to anchor it further east in the Rocky Mountains. There they meet the Ancient Crystal Beings, who are awakened by White Buffalo Calf Woman, a Native American prophet. They also meet and help free hundreds of trapped souls, with the cooperation of ancestral Native Americans. A powerful inner-Earth deva, the Guardian of the Deep, surfaces for the first time in Death Valley and expresses interest in their land healing.

Closer to home, they learn how to vent pent-up energies from Mount Shasta, and how to work more closely with nature spirits. They are drawn to a special place on the mountain, which was prepared for many years to bring in a higher form of the Divine Feminine energies, and this leads to their discovery and initiation into Divine Mother's Order of the Blue Snake. Their mystery school also develops and grows as they initiate more spiritual seekers in the Order of Melchizedek.

More Information . . .

For more information about products, events, webinars, the Mount Shasta Pyramid, and the Center for Soul Evolution Mystery School, join the email list and visit the websites:

www.twinsong.us

www.soulevolution.org

Facebook: facebook.com/antera.antera, facebook.com/omaran.omaran

Twitter: @anterashasta

Glossary

All definitions are those of the authors, and they are appropriate for the usage in this book and for the spiritual path. Throughout the text, the first occurrence of each glossary word appears in boldface.

Angel of Mount Tam: A highly evolved deva in charge of the area around Mount Tamalpais, north of San Francisco in California.

Ascended Masters or Masters: Souls who lived many lives on Earth and progressed on the spiritual path, first to enlightenment and then to ascension. We capitalize these terms out of respect for these great beings.

ascension: The last part of spiritual evolution on Earth, during which all lessons have been learned and a person's mission has been accomplished. In the *ascension* process the person becomes pure Light, usually by raising the physical body to a higher dimension so it disappears to the physical world. After this process, the person is called an Ascended Master.

astral: The fourth dimension, which is one dimension higher than the physical-etheric. This is where harmful thoughts and damaging emotions hang out, such as anger, revenge, jealousy, fear and sadness. Called astral pollution, this energy has built up over thousands of years and influences many people without their knowing it. The land-healing work, specifically, transmutes this energy into Light, thereby helping all of humanity.

Atlantis: An ancient civilization that was located in the Atlantic Ocean. The Atlanteans were highly technological, using crystal energy for power. The land was destroyed in about 10,000 B.C.E., largely because of their misuse of energy and power. Many people alive today in Western Civilization had significant lives during the time of Atlantis and want to make sure humanity does not make the same mistakes this time around.

body elemental: The earth elemental who takes care of the human body, coordinating all the processes and body systems. They can be talked to like a friend.

chakras: Energy centers in the human body that span many dimensions and help transform energy from higher levels down to the physical-etheric level. The chakras can be seen or felt by the psychic senses. Humans tend to store much of their karmic pain and trauma in their chakras, and this pain blocks or inhibits spiritual energies from flowing. One of the most important tasks in one's spiritual evolution is clearing the chakras.

Christ Consciousness: A type of awareness that humans strive for, which is all-knowing and consciously aware of the energetic connections that exist between humans and All That Is.

Christed Being: One who has achieved Christ Consciousness and is a Master of the Christ Light. Jeshua and other great Masters have demonstrated this process for humanity.

Christ Light or Christ energy: A specific type of powerful energy that can be called by humans on a spiritual path, to stimulate spiritual growth. The energy stimulates Divine Love and compassion for all beings and things.

clearing site: A place where a land-healing ceremony was done, and huge amounts of astral pollution were cleared, using the process taught in Antera and Omaran's beginning land-healing class.

demon: An especially powerful type of entity that is very intelligent and can sometimes invade people and cause them to have harmful thoughts and emotions and to act destructively.

deva: A nature spirit that is more evolved than the elementals and does more of the design work in nature, like an architect. Devas are in charge of larger groups or areas. For example, plant and animal devas oversee specific species and landscape devas oversee specific areas of land.

Divine Love: The highest form of love, which is unconditional and far beyond human or romantic love. Humans aspire to have only Divine Love in their hearts toward everyone and everything. This naturally results from healing the pain people carry from their past.

Divine Mother: The feminine aspect of Divine Presence, the creative force of our universe. Divine Presence does not actually have gender. However, thinking of it in terms of "Divine Mother and Divine Father" makes it easier for the human mind to comprehend and embrace.

Divine Plan: Also called the Higher Plan, this is the overall plan that is always in place, designed by Divine Presence for the greatest evolution of humanity and consciousness. A big lesson for humans is to accept that there *is* a plan, and even though they can't always understand why things happen. At the higher perspective of the soul there are no accidents. The greatest good is the ultimate outcome of all events.

Divine Presence: The energetic source of creation for everything in our universe. Though it is also called Source, Creator, God-Goddess, Universal Creative Force, and other names, the term *Divine Presence* is used in this book to transcend religious teachings and to emphasize the fact that Divine Presence is an energetic force and not a being.

Divine Will: The Will of Divine Presence, which is constantly creating the Divine Plan. One great lesson for humans on a spiritual path is to surrender to Divine Will and eventually align their personal will with it, instead of aligning with their pain or lower ego.

Djwal Kuhl: A spiritual teacher who lived high in the mountains of Tibet in the 1800s with a group of advanced Masters. Now ascended, he continues to teach esoteric topics to students on a spiritual path who have the ability to connect with him.

elements: The four aspects or raw materials that make up our physical world and all the forms in it: earth, air, fire and water.

elementals: Nature spirits who create the forms of nature. They are called this because each uses only one of the four elements. Therefore, there are water elementals, fire elementals, earth elementals and air elementals.

etheric: An energy level that vibrates slightly faster than the physical level, so it can sometimes be electronically measured or sensed with physical senses. Humans have an etheric body that contains the blueprint of all physical organs and systems, as well as many energy flows such as meridians. The etheric body is slightly larger than the physical body and can be seen by many people as a blue-grey layer next to the skin.

entity: In this book, the term *entity* describes non-physical beings—specifically those who are drawn to harmful thoughts and emotions and can invade the auras of humans, making them feel worse. Most entities are simple energy parasites, while others are much more intelligent and powerful.

four bodies or four-body system: Physical, emotional, mental, and spiritual bodies are considered to be the four bodies of human beings. All four need to be purified, preferably at close to the same rate, to progress on the spiritual path in a balanced way.

Golden Ray: An energy that is gold in color and highly tuned to spiritual evolution and higher consciousness. It stimulates these qualities in humans. The Golden Ray is used by lightworkers to help create the Golden Age, a time of harmony and peace on Earth.

Great White Brotherhood: A subset of the Order of Melchizedek that is focused on the spiritual evolution of humanity on our planet. Known in current times as the *Great White Brother-Sisterhood*, it is a group of Ascended Masters who lived many lives and ascended on Earth. *White* in the name refers to white Light.

grounding cord: A cord of Light that starts at the base of the spine and ideally goes straight down, deep into the Earth. It can be seen psychically. Essential to a healthy human system, it gives stability and energy when functioning properly.

higher dimensions or higher realms: The energetic realms that are not perceived by human physical senses. They are called higher because they vibrate at faster rates and higher frequencies than the physical realm.

Higher Plan: See *Divine Plan*.

Higher Presence: See *I Am Presence*.

Higher Self: See *I Am Presence*.

Holy Spirit: In this book, the term *Holy Spirit* refers to the breath of Divine Mother. This is a very nurturing, healing energy.

I Am Presence: Another name for the Higher Self, Higher Presence, or monad. It can be thought of as the soul's soul. As we spiritually evolve, our focus in life progresses from the ego and personality, to the soul, to the Higher Self as we make our way back to the Creator.

Illumined Court: A place in the higher dimensions where spiritual initiations are often held. Many powerful Ascended Masters and angels preside over the courtroom, and initiates are consciously called there when it is time to move into the next level of initiation, escorted by an Ascended Master.

Isis: An Ascended Master who originally came from the star system Sirius and lived on Earth in Ancient Egypt, where she helped create the mystery schools. A great teacher, she then left our planet for thousands of years, only coming back within the last century to once again teach humanity the ancient wisdom.

Jeshua: Later called Jesus by the Romans, Jeshua lived on Earth in his most famous lifetime 2000 years ago. His mission in that lifetime was to bring compassion, Divine Love, and forgiveness to Earth in order to assist humanity in its spiritual evolution. Jeshua continues this work now as an Ascended Master.

land healing, land healers: A phrase used by Antera and Omaran when they first began using energy and Light to heal areas of land, and which continues to be used now in a broader context. Here *land* includes water, air, humans, and even human-made buildings.

Lemuria: An ancient land consisting of islands in the Pacific Ocean, which had the earliest human civilization and was destroyed around 50,000 B.C.E. This is where Antera and Omaran were originally trained to do land healing together.

ley lines: Channels of energy that exist just beneath the Earth's surface. Likened to meridians in the human body, ley lines carry flows of energy from one place to another. Each ley line has a dominant set of frequencies—some beneficial to humans and some detrimental—and they have been used for thousands of years, especially in assessing optimal locations for buildings.

Light: In this book, the capital *L* in *Light* is used to indicate non-physical energy, which is sensed by psychic senses, rather than light seen with our physical eyes.

lightbody: The body that is formed in higher dimensions as a person progresses in his or her spiritual evolution. It is created through meditation and focused lightwork. The lightbody is seen by the Ascended Masters as an indicator of how far a person has progressed.

Light Field: A permanent form of sacred geometry, created out of Light, which has the purpose of uplifting consciousness and purifying an area with a field of energy. As directed by the Ascended Masters, Antera and Omaran created the Light Field around Mount Shasta that is described in this book.

lightwork: Work that uses non-physical energy, or Light, for specific purposes that heal or transform the physical world and people.

lightworker: A person who regularly does lightwork.

Mary: Also called Mother Mary because she was the mother of Jeshua (Jesus), she is an Ascended Master who is now very available for guidance to people on a spiritual path, as they open to receive her words of wisdom and her loving energy.

medicine wheel: A sacred form used by Native Americans for ceremony and to balance and harmonize the land. Usually constructed of rocks, it includes a circle with a cross inside (the symbol for Earth), and it is aligned with the four directions.

Melchizedek Order: See *Order of Melchizedek*.

Metatron: An archangel in charge of all other archangels who sometimes teaches humans, especially about the workings of the universe, sacred geometry, and the history of humans from the perspective of Divine Presence.

mountain spirit: An evolved nature spirit, also called a deva, who is charge of a mountain and its surrounding area.

mystery school: A school that teaches metaphysical concepts and ancient wisdom passed down for thousands of years to help people move forward on their spiritual paths quickly and smoothly. It is called a mystery school because the most advanced lessons are kept hidden, or secret, until students have learned basic lessons and progressed far enough in their spiritual evolution to show their readiness.

nature spirits: Beings who inhabit our planet but whose bodies vibrate mostly in the etheric or astral realms, so they can't be seen by most humans. They create the forms in nature. See *elementals* and *devas*.

Order of Melchizedek: A vast group of Light Beings who oversee the evolution of consciousness in our universe. All Ascended Masters and angels are members. It is important for humans to establish their connections with the order in each lifetime as they embark on a spiritual path, and this is most effectively done in front of a physical group of witnesses.

Overlighting Deva of Healing: An evolved nature spirit whose specialty is to oversee healing processes in humans.

pinning site: A place where a land-healing ceremony was done, and sacred items were buried to make it a permanent grid point. The beginning of this project is described in this book.

portal: A non-physical doorway, usually allowing passage from one realm to another.

power spots: Places in the land where spiritual energy is concentrated, generally where ley lines meet or cross. Throughout history, power spots have been felt by energy-sensitive people and have been utilized as sacred or religious places.

psychic attack: Energy directed from one person to another with harmful intent. This can be emotional energy such as anger, negative thoughts or criticism; or it can be stronger thoughtforms that are deliberately created to cause harm.

psychic energy: Energy that is seen or felt with the psychic senses, rather than the physical senses.

realms: Used interchangeably with the term *dimensions* in this book. In general use, a realm is a broader range of vibrations than a dimension, and less precise.

Silver Horse: A Native American ancestral spirit who lives in Sedona, Arizona. He used to be a medicine man and has much wisdom to share. He helped develop the land-healing work described in this book.

Spirit: When capitalized, a general term indicating higher guidance, such as from Higher Self or spirit guides or Source.

spiritual initiations: Ceremonies that advance humans along their spiritual path, from one level to the next. As people progress in their spiritual evolution by purification, healing and training, they do so in steps, culminating in initiations. These ceremonies take place in the higher dimensions after people have learned to expand their consciousness to perceive in these dimensions, through meditation. Usually each initiation takes many lifetimes to complete.

spiritual path: The path every human takes, starting when they first awaken and realize that there is more to life than the physical world. Progression on the path continues from lifetime to lifetime, in each life making it a bit further with spiritual initiations, until enlightenment is reached and there is no longer any need to reincarnate.

St. Germain: An Ascended Master, known for being a powerful alchemist, who has been helping humanity evolve for thousands of years. St. Germain introduced to humanity the Violet Flame, a tool for transmuting dense energies into Light, among many other teachings and gifts.

third dimension: A name for the physical world, which is sensed with the five physical senses. Also called third-dimensional reality or 3D, this is the world most people think is real until they have direct spiritual/psychic experiences or study quantum physics, which scientifically supports what has been taught in metaphysics for thousands of years.

thoughtform: An energy form, often a picture or symbol, that is created by the human mind. Generally the more the thought is repeated or charged up with emotions, the stronger the form. Thoughtforms can be seen or felt with the psychic senses.

twin flames, twin souls, or twin rays: When first differentiated from Source, souls are generally created in pairs. The two then incarnate separately to gather experience and make their way back to the Divine. Twin souls don't incarnate together physically very often, but they are always in contact in higher dimensions. Ideally they reunite in their last lifetime, each as a whole and complete soul.

Twin Flame Archetype: A planetary thoughtform that is anchored and held by one twin flame couple, to represent the pure pattern of twin flame union. This was passed to Antera and Omaran in 1998 from the previous holders, facilitated by St. Germain, as described in Antera's book, *Twin Flames*. This archetype has helped to bring the concept more fully into the consciousness of humanity.

Universal Mind or Higher Mind: The highest level of awareness our human minds can reach, in the later stages of evolution, where everything is known and all is Truth. All humans are connected to this Higher Mind but can only access it in rare instances, until the human mind and emotions are purified.

veil: An energetic curtain that separates human awareness from the Higher Mind, causing people to forget who they are in each new lifetime and reducing the ability to sense energies of higher dimensions. Thinning of the veil is common at power spots and high elevations. As people spiritually evolve, psychic senses develop and the veil naturally thins.

vortex: A place of energy movement near the surface of the land, where flows of energy meet to form a spiraling motion. Looking down from above, they spin either clockwise, which takes energy down into the Earth, or counter-clockwise, which draws energy up out of the Earth. People who are sensitive to energy can often feel the spiraling motion of a vortex.

Wesak: A Buddhist festival to celebrate the birth and life of Gautama Buddha. It is usually scheduled by Buddhists on the full moon in May. For a number of years, a group held annual gatherings at this time of year in Mount Shasta, which drew spiritual seekers in the thousands.

Y2K: Short for Year 2000 and the problems anticipated when the year changed from 1999 to 2000. Computers were only using two digits for the year instead of four, so turning to a year ending in *00* was potentially disastrous. It was thought that there was too much software to fix in time, including much that runs the infrastructure of Western Civilization.

Printed in the United States
By Bookmasters